T0391984

How Low Interest Rates Change the World

# How Low Interest Rates Change the World

*Global Trends Caused by Low Rates and Emerging Factors Shaping the Future of Rates*

Jesper Rangvid

# OXFORD
## UNIVERSITY PRESS

Great Clarendon Street, Oxford, OX2 6DP,
United Kingdom

Oxford University Press is a department of the University of Oxford.
It furthers the University's objective of excellence in research, scholarship,
and education by publishing worldwide. Oxford is a registered trade mark of
Oxford University Press in the UK and in certain other countries

© Jesper Rangvid 2025

The moral rights of the author have been asserted.

All rights reserved. No part of this publication may be reproduced, stored in a retrieval system,
transmitted, used for text and data mining, or used for training artificial intelligence, in any form or
by any means, without the prior permission in writing of Oxford University Press, or as expressly
permitted by law, by licence or under terms agreed with the appropriate reprographics rights
organization. Enquiries concerning reproduction outside the scope of the above should be sent
to the Rights Department, Oxford University Press, at the address above.

You must not circulate this work in any other form
and you must impose this same condition on any acquirer.

Published in the United States of America by Oxford University Press
198 Madison Avenue, New York, NY 10016, United States of America

British Library Cataloguing in Publication Data

Data available

Library of Congress Control Number: 2024948795

ISBN 9780198946380

DOI: 10.1093/9780198946410.001.0001

Pod

Links to third party websites are provided by Oxford in good faith and
for information only. Oxford disclaims any responsibility for the materials
contained in any third party website referenced in this work.

# Acknowledgements

This book explores the intersection of finance and economics—more specifically, how interest rates affect the economy—a subject that I find endlessly fascinating and intellectually stimulating. I have been fortunate to have had the opportunity to discuss this topic with many exceptional colleagues from both academia and industry throughout the years. These individuals have not only listened to my sometimes unconventional ideas but have also challenged and refined them, ultimately helping me to develop concepts that, in the end, hopefully make some sense.

During my academic career, I have had the opportunity to collaborate with numerous diligent coauthors. I would like to particularly acknowledge Andreas Schrimpf, Carsten Sørensen, Claus Munk, Henrik Ramlau-Hansen, Linda Sandris Larsen, Maik Schmeling, Malene Kallestrup-Lamb, Ofer Setty, Oliver-Alexander Press, Pedro Santa-Clara, Rikke Sejer Nielsen, Stig Vinther Møller, and Ulf Nielsson, but also my other coauthors. Our dialogues and discussions have been instrumental in shaping my thoughts on economics and finance, and, consequently, the ideas presented in this book.

In my industry experience, I have had the privilege of applying my academic knowledge to real-world challenges. I am particularly grateful to Kirstine Damkjær, Niels Elmo Jensen, Peter Engberg Jensen, Peter Kjærgaard, Peter Schütze, Ralf Magnussen, and others, all of whom have significantly influenced my approach to bridging the gap between academia and industry.

I am also deeply indebted to several individuals for their contributions during the writing of this book. I extend a particular thank you to Henrik Ramlau-Hansen, who meticulously reviewed the entire manuscript and provided invaluable insights. I am also grateful to Lasse H. Pedersen and Lars Calmfors for their thoughtful feedback on specific sections of the book. Additionally, I appreciate the constructive input from two anonymous reviewers at Oxford University Press, whose early comments significantly improved the manuscript.

I would also like to thank the staff at Oxford University Press for their support and guidance throughout the process of turning this manuscript into a published book.

Finally, a heartfelt hug and a huge thank you to those who mean the world to me—my wife and our two children.

# About the Author

**Jesper Rangvid** is a distinguished academic with extensive industry experience.

As a Professor of Finance at Copenhagen Business School (CBS), Jesper has made contributions to a wide range of topics, including asset pricing, financial crises, international finance, financial institutions, and household finance. His research has been published in leading international scholarly journals such as the *Journal of Financial Economics*, *Journal of Financial and Quantitative Analysis*, *Review of Finance*, and *Management Science*. Jesper has been recognized for his research and its impact, receiving honours such as the silver medal from the University of Copenhagen, the Tietgen Award, the Best Teacher Award at the CBS Executive MBA, and other awards.

He is the author of *From Main Street to Wall Street: How the Economy Influences Stock Markets and What Investors Should Know*, published by Oxford University Press in 2021, a book that explores the relationship between the macroeconomy and financial markets. He also authors *Rangvid's Blog*, where he shares insights on finance and economics.

In addition to his academic achievements, Jesper Rangvid has extensive experience serving on commissions and boards of non-executive directors of both private and public organizations. Currently, he chairs the Council for Return Expectations and sits on the boards of Advantage Investment Partners, Finansiel Stabilitet (the Danish Financial Resolution Authority), and Formuepleje. Previously, he has held board positions at CBS, the Doctors' Pension Bank, the Doctors' Pension Fund, Grandhood, and SKAGEN Funds. At CBS, Jesper serves as Associate Dean, overseeing the CBS Executive MBA programme, and codirects the Pension Research Center (PeRCent).

In 2012–2013, Jesper chaired the government-appointed committee that examined the causes and consequences of the financial crisis in Denmark, producing what is commonly known as the 'Rangvid Report'.

His expertise is frequently sought by Danish and international media on economic and financial matters, and he is a popular speaker within the financial community.

Outside of his professional life, Jesper is married, has two grown-up children, and enjoys running, favouring distances between 15 and 25 kilometres. He lives outside Copenhagen but spends as much time as possible in Spain, just south of Barcelona.

# Contents

| | |
|---|---|
| *List of Figures* | xii |
| **Introduction** | 1 |

### PART I.   FALLING RATES

| | |
|---|---|
| **1. The Level of Interest Rates: Today and Historically** | **13** |
| 1.1 Interest Rates during 1980–2020 | 14 |
| 1.2 Long-Term Developments in Global Interest Rates | 16 |
| 1.2.1   Dispersion in Yields across Countries | 17 |
| 1.2.2   Long and Short Yields | 19 |
| 1.3 Yields on Corporate Bonds | 21 |
| 1.4 Very Long-Term Interest Rates for the UK | 22 |
| 1.5 Seven Centuries of Interest Rates | 23 |
| 1.6 Checklist | 26 |
| **2. Inflation and Real Interest Rates** | **27** |
| 2.1 Global Inflation during the Past Four Decades | 29 |
| 2.2 Long-Term Trends in Inflation | 31 |
| 2.3 The Historical Behaviour of Real Interest Rates | 35 |
| 2.4 Seven Centuries of Inflation and Real Rates | 38 |
| 2.4.1   Real Rates | 39 |
| 2.5 Checklist | 40 |

### PART II.   CONSEQUENCES OF FALLING AND LOW INTEREST RATES

| | |
|---|---|
| **3. Debt and Low Interest Rates** | **45** |
| 3.1 Sovereign Indebtedness in Advanced Economies | 46 |
| 3.2 Historical Debt Developments: Two Case Studies—The US and the UK | 48 |
| 3.2.1   The US | 48 |
| 3.2.2   The UK | 52 |
| 3.3 Pros and Cons Regarding Public Debt | 54 |
| 3.3.1   Pros of Public Debt | 54 |
| 3.3.2   Cons | 55 |
| 3.4 When Is a Lot Too Much? | 60 |
| 3.5 Private Debt | 61 |

viii Contents

| | |
|---|---|
| 3.5.1 Pros and Cons of Other Private Debt | 63 |
| 3.6 Total Debt | 64 |
| 3.7 Checklist | 65 |

**4. House Prices and Low Interest Rates** — 67

| | |
|---|---|
| 4.1 Developments in House Prices | 68 |
| 4.1.1 Different Countries | 70 |
| 4.2 Interest Rates and House Prices | 70 |
| 4.2.1 Why Should Falling Interest Rates Push Up House Prices? | 71 |
| 4.2.2 Do Interest Rates Affect House Prices? | 72 |
| 4.3 Economic Growth and Credit Growth | 74 |
| 4.3.1 Economic Growth | 75 |
| 4.3.2 Mortgage Debt | 76 |
| 4.4 Checklist | 78 |

**5. Stock Markets and Low Interest Rates** — 79

| | |
|---|---|
| 5.1 How Interest Rates Affect Stock Markets | 80 |
| 5.1.1 Interest Rate and Earnings | 80 |
| 5.1.2 Interest Rate and Discount Rate | 81 |
| 5.1.3 Interest Rate and Aggregate Risk Premium | 82 |
| 5.2 Long-Term Evidence on the Global Relation between the Interest Rate and the Stock Market | 82 |
| 5.3 Evidence from the US | 85 |
| 5.3.1 Interest Rates and Tax Expenses of US Corporations | 88 |
| 5.4 Interest Rates and Expected Stock Market Returns | 90 |
| 5.5 Bond Returns | 92 |
| 5.6 Checklist | 95 |

**6. Inequality and Low Interest Rates** — 96

| | |
|---|---|
| 6.1 Is a Perfectly Equal Society Desirable? Or, When Is Inequality Too High? | 97 |
| 6.2 Trends in Inequality | 97 |
| 6.2.1 Inequality Has Increased during the Past Four Decades | 100 |
| 6.2.2 Inequality Fell Prior to 1980 | 101 |
| 6.3 Inequality and the Interest Rate | 104 |
| 6.4 Why Do Interest Rates Affect Inequality? | 106 |
| 6.4.1 Monetary Policy, Interest Rates, and Inequality | 107 |
| 6.5 Do Low Interest Rates Cause Rising Inequality or Does Rising Inequality Cause Low Interest Rates? | 109 |
| 6.6 Other Factors Contributing to Inequality | 110 |
| 6.7 Has Inequality in Fact Increased? Debates about the Data | 112 |
| 6.8 A Final Word about Wealth Inequality | 113 |
| 6.8.1 An Example Where Inequality Matters | 114 |
| 6.9 Checklist | 115 |

Contents    ix

**7. Financial Risk-Taking and Low Interest Rates**    **117**

7.1 Understanding How Low Rates Can Increase Financial Risk-Taking    118

7.1.1 Low Interest Rates Might Lure People into Investing in
Financial Assets Using Borrowed Money    118

7.1.2 Low Interest Rates Might Incentivize People to Invest
More Riskily    119

7.1.3 Low Interest Rates Increase the Risk of Overvalued
Financial Assets and Financial Bubbles    119

7.1.4 Low Interest Rates and Risk-Taking in Banks    120

7.2 Do Low Interest Rates Lead to More Risk-Taking?    120

7.2.1 Retail Investors    121

7.2.2 Pension Funds    121

7.2.3 Mutual Funds    123

7.2.4 Banks    124

7.3 'Mispricing' and the Level of Yields    126

7.4 Low Interest Rates and the Global Financial Crisis of 2008    129

7.5 Low Interest Rates and the UK 2022 LDI Crisis    132

7.6 Checklist    134

## PART III.  WHAT CAUSED A FOUR-DECADE FALL IN INTEREST RATES?

**8. What Caused a Four-Decade Fall in Inflation?**    **139**

8.1 What Determines Inflation?    139

8.1.1 Monetary View on Inflation    140

8.1.2 Inflation Caused by Demand and Supply    141

8.2 Can Money Growth Explain the Fall in Inflation since 1980?    142

8.3 Demand-Pull and Cost-Push Effects    145

8.3.1 Monetary Policy and Central Banks    145

8.3.1.1 Monetary Policy in the 1970s    145

8.3.1.2 The Change in Views on Monetary Policy    147

8.3.2 Globalization    149

8.3.3 Oil Prices    151

8.3.4 Demographics and Labour Supply    153

8.4 Checklist    153

**9. What Caused a Four-Decade Fall in Real Interest Rates?**    **155**

9.1 Theory: Determination of the Real Interest Rate    156

9.1.2 Economic Growth and the Real Interest Rate    158

9.2 Real Economic Growth and the Real Interest Rate    161

9.3 Demographics    164

9.3.1 Life Expectancy    164

9.3.2 Population Growth    167

9.4 Fewer Safe Assets    168

9.5 Central Bank Purchases of Safe Assets    169

**x  Contents**

| | |
|---|---|
| 9.6 Changes to the Income and Wealth Distribution | 171 |
| 9.7 Secular Stagnation | 171 |
| 9.8 Decomposing the Fall in Real Rates into Underlying Factors | 172 |
| 9.8.1  Evidence from the US | 174 |
| 9.9 Checklist | 175 |

**10. What Caused the Rise in Inflation and Interest Rates after the Covid-19 Pandemic?**  **177**

| | |
|---|---|
| 10.1 Putting the Post-Pandemic Rise in Inflation and Interest Rates into Perspective | 178 |
| 10.2 Why Did Inflation Increase So Dramatically after the Pandemic? | 181 |
| 10.2.1 The 2020 Recession and the Bounce-Back | 181 |
| 10.2.1.1 Demand Soared after the Pandemic | 183 |
| 10.2.2 Expansionary Policies | 186 |
| 10.2.2.1 Monetary Policy | 188 |
| 10.2.3 Goods/Services Demand Shifts and Supply-Chain Challenges | 192 |
| 10.2.4 Rising Commodity Prices | 195 |
| 10.3 Nominal Interest Rates Rose in Response to the Inflation Surge | 196 |
| 10.4 Checklist | 198 |

## PART IV.   WHAT DOES THE FUTURE HOLD?

**11. Trends That Could Keep Rates Low**  **203**

| | |
|---|---|
| 11.1 Trend 1. Interest Rates Have Been on a Downward Trajectory for the Past 700 Years. Why Should This Change? | 204 |
| 11.2 Trend 2. Population Growth Falls | 205 |
| 11.3 Trend 3. We Will Live Longer | 208 |
| 11.4 Trend 4. Lower Economic Growth Rates Reduce Real Rates | 211 |
| 11.5 Uncertainty: Climate Risk and Geopolitical Risk | 212 |
| 11.5.1 Higher Geopolitical Risk | 214 |
| 11.6 Deglobalization | 215 |
| 11.7 Nominal versus Real Interest Rates | 216 |
| 11.8 Checklist | 217 |

**12. Trends That Could Elevate Rates**  **218**

| | |
|---|---|
| 12.1 Trend 5. More Retired People Relative to the Number of Working People | 219 |
| 12.2 Trend 6. Rising Debt Levels | 221 |
| 12.2.1 Scenarios for UK Public Finances | 222 |
| 12.2.2 Scenarios for US Public Finances | 224 |
| 12.2.3 Other Countries | 225 |
| 12.2.4 Public Debt Also Rose between 1980 and 2020 | 226 |
| 12.3 Transition to a More Sustainable Economy | 227 |
| 12.4 Investments in Defence | 228 |

Contents    xi

| | | |
|---|---|---|
| 12.5 | Central Bank Asset Purchases | 229 |
| 12.6 | AI, Productivity, and Interest Rates | 229 |
| 12.7 | Weak Link between Economic Growth/Population Growth and Interest Rates over the Very Long Run | 230 |
| 12.8 | Checklist | 231 |

## 13. Putting It All Together: What Is the Outlook for Rates?    233

| | | |
|---|---|---|
| 13.1 | Summarizing the Main Channels Affecting Future Interest Rates | 234 |
| 13.2 | Evidence from Statistical Analyses in the Literature on Future Real Interest Rates | 235 |
| 13.3 | The Future of $r^*$ | 238 |
| | 13.3.1 Evidence from the US | 238 |
| | 13.3.2 Global Evidence | 239 |
| 13.4 | Market Expectations | 240 |
| | 13.4.1 Expected Real Rates | 242 |
| | 13.4.2 Expected Inflation | 243 |
| | 13.4.3 Are Market-Based Measures of Expectations Good Measures of Future Outcomes? | 245 |
| 13.5 | Concluding on the Outlook for Interest Rates | 246 |
| 13.6 | Checklist | 246 |

## 14. Debt, Inequality, and House and Stock Prices Considering Interest Rate Scenarios    247

| | | |
|---|---|---|
| 14.1 | What Happens If Interest Rates Fall? | 247 |
| 14.2 | What Happens If Interest Rates Rise? | 248 |
| 14.3 | What Happens If Interest Rates Stay Where They Are? | 249 |
| 14.4 | Checklist | 250 |

| | |
|---|---|
| *References* | 252 |
| *Index* | 258 |

# List of Figures

1.1. Yields on long-term government bonds, 1980–2023. Average across 17 advanced economies    14

1.2. Yields on long-term government bonds, 1870–2023. Average across 17 advanced economies    17

1.3. Yields on long-term government bonds in 17 countries, 1870–2023    18

1.4. Yields on long-term and short-term government bonds in 17 countries, 1870–2023. Averages across 17 countries    20

1.5. Yields on US corporate debt, 1919–2023. AAA-rated firms and BAA-rated firms    21

1.6. The monetary policy rate, the Bank Rate, of the Bank of England, 1694–2023    23

1.7. Global yields, 1310–2023. Seven-year rolling average    24

1.8. Changes in nominal global yields over subsequent 40-year periods, 1310–2023    25

2.1. Inflation rates and yields on long-term government bonds, 1980–2023. Average across 17 advanced economies    30

2.2. Global inflation rates and yields on long-term government bonds, 1870–2023. Medians across 17 advanced economies    31

2.3. Median price-level developments across 17 advanced economies, 1870–2023. Logarithmic scale    32

2.4. German annual inflation, 1870–2023. Logarithmic scale    34

2.5. Real yields on long-term government bonds, 1984–2023. Difference between median nominal yields and median inflation across 17 advanced economies    36

2.6. Real yields on long-term government bonds, 1870–2023. Difference between median nominal yields and median inflation across 17 advanced economies    37

2.7. Global inflation, 1310–2023. Seven-year rolling average    39

2.8. Global real yields, 1310–2023. Seven-year rolling average    40

3.1. Public debt in relation to GDP together with the nominal yield on long-term government bonds, 1946–2022. Average across 17 advanced economies    46

3.2. US public debt relative to US GDP, 1800–2022    48

3.3. Deficit/surplus on US government primary budget balance, 1800–2023    50

List of Figures  xiii

3.4. US public debt relative to US GDP, 1800–2022    51

3.5. UK government budget balance relative to GDP    53

3.6. UK government public debt relative to GDP    53

3.7. Greek public debt relative to Greek GDP, 2000–2016    57

3.8. Yield on Greek sovereign debt    57

3.9. Yields on 10-year US Treasuries together with AAA-rated corporate bonds and BAA-rated corporate bonds, 1953–2023    59

3.10. Yields on 10-year US Treasuries together with yields on 30-year mortgage bonds, 1971–2023    59

3.11. Economic growth and debt-to-GDP ratios. Averages across many countries    61

3.12. Household debt relative to GDP, together with the nominal yield on long-term government bonds, 1950–2022. Averages across 17 advanced economies    62

3.13. Corporate debt relative to GDP, together with the nominal yield on long-term government bonds, 1950–2022. Averages across 17 advanced economies    62

3.14. Total debt (i.e. the sum of public and private debt, with private debt split into household and corporate debt), as a fraction of GDP, together with the nominal yield on long-term government bonds, 1950–2022. Average across 17 advanced economies    65

4.1. Average of real house prices across 17 advanced economies, 1870–2022. Real house prices are normalized to '1' in 1870    69

4.2. Cumulative increases in real house prices, 1980–2022    70

4.3. Real house prices and interest rate rates during 1870–1945    72

4.4. Real house prices and interest rate rates during 1946–1979    73

4.5. Real house prices and interest rate rates during 1980–2022    73

4.6. Annual growth in global (average across 17 advanced economies) real per capita GDP and average growth across subperiods    75

4.7. Real house prices and mortgage debt as a fraction of GDP, 1870–2020. Averages across 16 countries    77

5.1. Average of real stock prices across 16 advanced economies, normalized to "1" in 1900, together with the average of nominal long-term interest rates in advanced economies, 1900–2023    83

5.2. Real house prices and real stock prices across advanced economies, normalized to "1" in 1900, 1900–2022    84

5.3. CAPE and US long-term interest rate, 1881–2023    86

5.4. Market value of US corporate equity relative to US GDP and US long-term Treasury yields, 1953–2024    88

## xiv    List of Figures

5.5. Aggregate interest and tax expenses as a share of aggregate EBIT (Earnings Before Interest and Taxes) for S&P 500 non-financial firms. Annual data, 1962–2022                                                                89

5.6. CAPE-yield and US long-term interest rate, 1881–1960                     91

5.7. CAPE-yield and US long-term interest rate, 1960–2023                     91

5.8. Moving average of bond returns over past five years and yields on long-term government bonds, annual cross-country averages, 1875–2023                                                                        94

6.1. Wealth distribution in different countries. Share of total wealth in a country accruing to the bottom 50 per cent and the top 10 per cent of the population, 2021                                                        99

6.2. Income distribution in different countries. Share of total income in a country accruing to the bottom 50 per cent and the top 10 per cent of the population, 2021                                                       100

6.3. Share of aggregate national income accruing to top 10 per cent income earnings in 1980 and 2021                                                   101

6.4. Share of aggregate national income accruing to top 10 per cent income earners every year between 1980 and 2021                                  102

6.5. Share of aggregate national income accruing to top 10 per cent income earners and bottom 50 per cent income earners, 1913 through 2021. Average across 17 advanced economies                                     103

6.6. Developments in US real family incomes. Real incomes for families in the bottom 20 per cent and the top 5 per cent of the income distribution, 1966–2018                                                                104

6.7. Share of aggregate national pre-tax income accruing to top 10 per cent income earners and long-term interest rate. Averages across 17 advanced economies, 1980–2021                                             105

6.8. Share of aggregate national pre-tax income accruing to top 10 per cent income earners and long-term interest rate. Averages across 17 advanced economies, 1913–2021                                             106

6.9. Share of aggregate national pre-tax income accruing to top 10 per cent income earners and long-term interest rate in the US, 1915–2021          111

6.10. Share of aggregate national pre-tax income accruing to top 10 per cent income earners and long-term interest rate in France, 1915–2021        112

7.1. Long-term interest rates and pension liabilities in pension funds (The Netherlands, the UK, and the US)                                            122

7.2. The lending spread in UK banks, calculated as the difference between the corporate borrowing rate and the deposit rate together with the Bank of England Bank Rate, 1955–2023                                      125

List of Figures   xv

7.3. Actual value of the S&P 500 together with its theoretical fundamental value, where the latter is based on future dividends discounted by a constant discount factor   128

7.4. Difference between the actual and the fundamental stock price, relative to the actual stock price. The figure also includes the 10-year US Treasury rate, 1871–2023   129

7.5. Federal Funds Rate in the years leading up to the global financial crisis in 2008   130

7.6. Real house prices in the US, normalized to one in 1970   131

7.7. UK–German yield spread (10-year bonds) during 2022   134

8.1. Inflation rates and annual growth rates in the narrow money supply, 1870–2023. Medians across 17 advanced economies   142

8.2. Average rate of money growth versus average rate of inflation, 1990–2023, country by country   144

8.3. Federal Funds Rate and US inflation   146

8.4. US real monetary policy rate, calculated as the Federal Funds Rate minus inflation, including averages over 1974–1981 and 1981–1985   147

8.5. The highest rate and the lowest rate of inflation among 17 advanced economies, year by year   149

8.6. (Export + imports)/GDP, 1870–2020. Medians across 17 advanced economies   150

8.7. Annual percentage changes in oil prices   152

9.1. Determination of the equilibrium interest rate   156

9.2. SS curve moves to the right   157

9.3. II curve moves to the left   158

9.4. Growth in real GDP per capita, 1984–2022. Annual global growth, rolling average of past 10 years' global growth, and a linear trend line. Annual global growth is the average across 17 advanced economies   162

9.5. $r^*$ and trend growth in the US, 1961–2024   163

9.6. Life expectancy at birth in low-, middle-, and high-income countries, as well as worldwide, 1965–2021   165

9.7. Fraction of the global population aged 25–65, aged 65 and above, and the difference between the two, 1950–2023   166

9.8. Annual growth rate of total population in 17 advanced economies   167

9.9. Central bank balance sheets relative to GDP, normalized to one in 2003. Eurozone and the US, 2003–2020   170

9.10. Decomposition of fall in US $r^*$ between 1975 and 2015. IMF estimates   174

10.1. Inflation in the euro area, the US, and across OECD countries, January 1990 to March 2024   178

**xvi List of Figures**

10.2. Inflation in the euro area, the US, and across OECD countries, January 2021 to November 2022 — 180

10.3. Nominal yields on 10-year government bonds in the US, Germany, France, and the UK, January 1990 to April 2024 — 180

10.4. Initial jobless claims in the US per week, January 1967 to April 2024 — 182

10.5. Quarterly growth in US real GDP, 1947–2024 — 183

10.6. Annual percentage growth in real GDP in the US and the euro area, 2000–2023 — 184

10.7. Total personal disposable income and personal outlays in the US, monthly data, billions of USD — 185

10.8. Stock of excess savings in different countries, percentage of GDP — 186

10.9. Accumulated excess savings in the US (billions of USD) and US core CPI inflation with a one-year lag (annual percentage change) in the US. Monthly data — 187

10.10. Annual growth in real disposable income and real GDP in the US, 2006–2021 — 188

10.11. Combined values of Fed and ECB balance sheets in billions of US dollars and the S&P 500. Weekly data, January 2016 to October 2022 — 189

10.12. Annual percentage growth in US aggregate money supply (M2) forwarded 15 months and US inflation, 2017–2024 — 190

10.13. Annual percentage growth in US aggregate money supply (M2) forwarded 15 months and US inflation, 1960–2024 — 191

10.14. Ratio of US personal consumption expenditures, goods, to US total consumption expenditures, 2012–2024 — 192

10.15. Global supply-chain pressure index — 194

10.16. Supply- and demand-driven inflation in the US, January 2020 to February 2024 — 194

10.17. Commodities for Index: All, excluding Gold, 2015=1.0, January 2015 to March 2024 — 195

10.18. One-year yields (government bonds) in the US, the UK, France, and Germany — 197

10.19. Real interest rates in selected countries, calculated as the yield on 10-year government bonds minus the current inflation rates — 198

11.1. Global nominal yield, 1310–2023. Seven-year rolling average — 204

11.2. Projected population growth rates in different regions of the world — 207

11.3. Global life expectancy at birth — 209

11.4. Expected developments in life expectancy for a newborn in low-, middle-, and high-income countries — 210

## List of Figures   xvii

11.5. Expected economic growth, 2025–2060, measured in USD at constant prices and purchasing power parities (PPPs) of 2010 — 212

11.6. Geopolitical risk index since 2010 — 215

11.7. Geopolitical risk index since 1900 — 216

12.1. Proportion of the global population aged 25–65, above 65 years old, and the difference between the two groups — 220

12.2. Ratio of people in age group 25–65 to people in age group 65+, globally — 221

12.3. Scenarios for UK public deficits relative to expected UK GDP, 2023–2073 — 222

12.4. Scenarios for UK public debt to expected UK GDP, 2023–2073 — 224

12.5. Historical developments in US federal debt held by the public and scenarios, both relative to US GDP, 1900–2051 — 225

13.1. Historic trend growth and $r^*$, as estimated by the New York Fed, and potential real economic growth, as projected by the Congressional Budget Office — 239

13.2. Projections of $r^*$ in large economies, 2022–2050 — 240

13.3. Yield on 10-year Treasuries, 10-year forward rates in 10 years (10y10y) and 10-year forward rates in 20 years (20y10y), 1953–2024 — 242

13.4. Yield on 10-year inflation-indexed Treasuries, 10-year forward real interest rates in 10 years (10y10y), and 10-year forward real interest rates in 20 years (20y10y), 2005–2024, though 20y10y for 2010–2024 — 243

13.5. Expected inflation over the next 10 years (10y), expected inflation over the next 10 years, 10 years from now (10y10y), and expected inflation over the next 10 years, 20 years from now (20y10y), 2005–2024, though 20y10y for 2010–2024 — 244

# Introduction

This book explores the societal impact of changing interest rates. Taking its starting point in the remarkable four-decade decline in global interest rates from 1980 to 2020, the book explores five global trends it caused, the underlying factors that drove interest rates lower, and six emerging trends likely to shape the future path of interest rates.

## Interest Rate Changes

Interest rates fluctuate constantly—every day, hour, and minute. However, when examined over extended periods, they exhibit slower, more persistent movements. Interest rates tend to remain relatively stable for years, gradually increase over an extended period, and then experience a prolonged decline. While temporary fluctuations occur, these overarching long-term trends are quite distinct. This book concentrates on such persistent changes in interest rates and their consequences.

The impetus for this book is the dramatic decline in interest rates in advanced economies from the early 1980s through 2020. Around 1980, interest rates peaked in many countries following a rise throughout the 1960s and 1970s. Rates reached double digits—often 10 per cent, 12 per cent, 14 per cent, and sometimes even higher. Then, a remarkable shift occurred. Over the following four decades, interest rates steadily declined. By 2020, just before the Covid-19 pandemic, interest rates had reached historically low levels. In some countries, rates even dipped into negative territory, an unprecedented phenomenon in economic history. It turned out to be the largest fall in interest rates over a four-decade span in the past 700 years.

The book will demonstrate that this substantial decrease in interest rates had profound societal consequences. But why are interest rates so important for economic developments?

*How Low Interest Rates Change the World.* Jesper Rangvid, Oxford University Press. © Jesper Rangvid (2025).
DOI: 10.1093/9780198946410.003.0001

## Borrowing and Saving

The interest rate is the cost of borrowing money, expressed as a percentage of the amount borrowed. When borrowers pay interest rates, lenders receive them; that is, the interest rate is also the payments received when lending money. Changes in interest rates thus affect the cost of debt and the returns on investments.

People borrow to finance significant expenses such as buying a home, purchasing a car, funding an education, and so on. Corporations borrow to invest in new machinery, equipment, and other expenditures critical to their growth prospects. Governments borrow to support people in need and to stimulate economic recovery during downturns when government expenditures are large and their revenues small. Governments also borrow to finance large public investments, like building infrastructure and funding education and healthcare institutions.

The money borrowed by households, businesses, or governments must come from somewhere—it comes from savers. For example, people save money during their working years to fund their retirement. They also save to make a downpayment on a home, financing the remainder through borrowing. Some firms save funds temporarily, awaiting more favourable investment opportunities. Governments also sometimes generate more income than needed for current investments, making them net savers.

On a global macroeconomic scale, savings are channelled into investments, such that the total amount invested equals the total amount saved. The interest rate plays a vital role in balancing the demand for investments and borrowing with the supply of savings.

## The Impact of Interest Rates on Borrowing and Saving

When interest rates fall, borrowing becomes less expensive, making loans more affordable. Hence, low interest rates increase the likelihood of people taking out loans. Similarly, firms and governments are influenced by interest rates in their borrowing decisions.

At the same time, when interest rates are low, investing in financial securities with returns linked to interest rates becomes less appealing, making saving less attractive. Overall, changes in interest rates impact investments funded through borrowing and our motivation to save. And when interest rates fall as persistently and significantly as they did during 1980–2020, the consequences are significant.

## Consequences of Falling Interest Rates

This book contends that the persistent decline in interest rates from 1980 to 2020 fundamentally altered the world we live in.[1] It argues that ever-lower interest rates were instrumental in driving five global trends during the 1980–2020 period.

## Trend 1: A More Indebted World

The four-decade decline in interest rates coincided with a dramatic surge in indebtedness across households, firms, and governments in advanced economies. For example, during the period of falling interest rates, total debt—the combined debt of households, firms, and governments—more than doubled relative to economic activity, rising from 135 per cent of GDP in advanced economies in 1980 to around 300 per cent in 2020. The persistent rise in indebtedness over the 1980–2020 period is the first trend significantly influenced by falling interest rates to be discussed in the book.

## Trend 2: Elevated House Prices

Lower interest rates make it cheaper to borrow to buy a home, often the most significant investment individuals make in their lifetime. The book shows that global house prices showed no strong and consistent pattern before 1980. However, following 1980, they embarked on a steady upward trajectory, paralleling—with opposite sign—the fall in interest rates. Persistently rising house prices is the second global trend fuelled by falling interest rates that the book discusses. In many countries, house prices (adjusted for inflation) more than doubled; in some countries they almost tripled. In 2020, before interest rates started rising after the pandemic, house prices had become historically elevated.

## Trend 3: High Stock Market Valuations

Owning stock means owning part of a company. The value of stocks is based on companies' future cash flows (earnings and dividends), or more precisely

---

[1] As both nominal and real interest rates declined during the 1980–2020 period, the book often refers broadly to 'falling interest rates', mainly distinguishing between the two when it is necessary for clarity.

the discounted value of these cash flows. Lower interest rates reduce the discount rate, thereby increasing the present value of future cash flows. Lower interest rates also boost earnings by lowering firms' interest expenses. Consequently, the four-decade decline in interest rates led to a corresponding surge in global stock markets, a third megatrend during 1980–2020. As an example, in 1980, when interest rates were high, the total value of the US stock market—the world's largest—corresponded to 50 per cent of US total economic activity (GDP). In 2020, when interest rates hit their lowest point, it had increased to 250 per cent of US GDP.

## Trend 4: More Inequality

Inequality refers to an uneven distribution of income and wealth within societies. The four-decade decline in interest rates from 1980 to 2020 contributed to a persistent rise in inequality in many countries.

Interest rates influence inequality not least through their impact on housing and asset prices. As mentioned above, lower interest rates contribute to driving up the prices of real estate and stocks. These assets are predominantly owned by affluent households, meaning that when interest rates decrease and asset prices rise, income and wealth inequality increase, a fourth global trend over the 1980–2020 period.

Inequality is a complex and sensitive topic with many dimensions. The book delves into some of these issues, exploring, for instance, whether increased paper wealth from rising asset prices translates into disparities in consumption possibilities. Additionally, while lower interest rates may exacerbate inequality, the book also examines the possibility that inequality might contribute to falling interest rates because affluent individuals have higher savings rates, thus discussing the direction of causality between interest rates and inequality.

## Trend 5: More Financial Risk-Taking

When interest rates are low, returns to safe investments are low. In a low-interest-rate environment, investors may seek higher returns by taking on riskier investments in a so-called 'reaching for yield'. This increases the risk in the financial system. Increased risk-taking is a fifth trend caused by lower interest rates.

Overall, the book argues that the sustained decline in interest rates from the early 1980s to the pandemic in 2020 contributed to five global trends during the same period: more debt, higher house prices, higher stock prices, more inequality, and more financial risk-taking.

## The 2020 Pandemic and Its Immediate Consequences

The four-decade decline in interest rates ended abruptly following the Covid-19 pandemic in early 2020, as inflation subsequently flared up.

The book examines what caused the post-pandemic inflation shock. It also discusses how higher post-pandemic inflation prompted central banks worldwide to raise their monetary policy interest rates, which in turn caused other interest rates to rise, including those on sovereign bonds, mortgages, and corporate loans, thereby breaking the long-standing trend of ever-lower rates from 1980 to 2020. Just as declining interest rates during that period had elevated levels of indebtedness, house and stock prices, and inequality, the rapid increase in rates after the pandemic reversed these patterns, leading to lower house and stock prices and reduced inequality, at least temporarily.

## The Post-Pandemic World

An essential question in the book is whether the post-pandemic surge in inflation and interest rates marks the beginning of a new era characterized by persistently higher interest rates, or if it was merely a temporary spike that will diminish as the pandemic's effects fully recede. Based on an analysis of the factors that drove interest rates lower over the 1980–2020 period, the book posits that the future trajectory of interest rates will be shaped by six key trends. Of these, four trends suggest a future of low interest rates, while two indicate the possibility of higher rates.

The four trends that could lead to low future interest rates are:

1. Interest rates have been on a downward trajectory for 700 years.
   - Despite notable fluctuations, both nominal and real interest rates have exhibited a consistent and gradual decline over the past seven centuries. This remarkable pattern suggests that it is reasonable to hypothesize that interest rates may continue to fall in the future.
2. Population growth rates are projected to continue declining.

**6  How Low Interest Rates Change the World**

- Economic models suggest that slower population growth leads to lower interest rates. As global population growth is expected to decline in the future, this trend is likely to contribute to keeping interest rates low.

3. Life expectancies are expected to continue rising.
   - As people live longer, their savings must stretch over extended periods. This tendency to save more patiently can, according to economic models, lead to lower interest rates.

4. Economic growth rates are expected to remain relatively low.
   - In economic models, slower growth means that interest rates do not need to be as high to incentivize saving and smooth consumption changes. Globally, real economic growth is projected to decline in the coming decades. This growth slowdown could cause low future interest rates.

On the other hand, several persistent trends could drive interest rates higher. The book highlights two such trends:

5. The proportion of elderly individuals is likely to increase relative to younger populations.
   - Younger people tend to save for retirement, while older individuals draw down their savings to fund consumption during retirement. As the global population ages and fertility rates fall—that is, as there will be fewer young people relative to the elderly—overall savings may decline. This reduction in global savings could lead to higher future interest rates.

6. Public debt levels are expected to keep rising in many countries.
   - Increasing public debt puts upward pressure on interest rates, and many countries face substantial increases in public debt burdens. This rising debt could push interest rates higher.

While other factors—such as the transition to a more sustainable economy and the integration of artificial intelligence (AI) into production processes—will most likely also affect interest rates, the book focuses on these six trends, eventually offering its tentative conclusions on the future trajectory of interest rates. Finally, the book briefly discusses how these interest rate scenarios might shape future societal outcomes, including debt levels, housing and stock prices, and inequality.

## Organization of the Book

The book consists of four parts.

Part I comprises two chapters that examine the significant decline in nominal interest rates, inflation rates, and real interest rates over the four decades from 1980 to 2020. The chapters highlight the magnitude of this decline, placing it within a broader historical context that spans several centuries, and noting the historically low levels of interest rates reached just before the onset of the Covid-19 pandemic in 2020. The analysis concludes that the interest rate decreases observed during the 1980–2020 period were both remarkable and unprecedented.

Part II contains five chapters that explore how the dramatic decline in both real and nominal interest rates has significantly influenced five global trends from 1980 to 2020:

- An increase in indebtedness.
- A surge in house prices.
- A rise in stock prices.
- Growth in inequality.
- An escalation in financial risk-taking.

While recognizing the impact of other contributing factors, the book argues that the decline in interest rates was an important driver behind these trends.

Part III consists of three chapters that delve into the causes behind the four-decade decline in interest and inflation rates from 1980 to 2020. This part identifies four key trends that played a crucial role in driving down rates during this period:

- A shift in monetary policy towards maintaining low and stable inflation.
- Slower economic growth.
- Increasing life expectancy.
- Declining population growth.

Additionally, this part of the book also examines the underlying factors behind the post-pandemic surge in inflation and interest rates.

Part IV comprises four chapters that explore the future trajectory of interest rates. The book posits that the evolution of six key trends will be critical in shaping the future path of interest rates. It identifies four trends that suggest rates could be low in the future:

8   How Low Interest Rates Change the World

1. A continuation of a century-long fall in interest rates.
2. Low population growth rates.
3. Longer life expectancies.
4. Low rates of economic growth.

The book also examines two trends that could raise future interest rates:

5. Fewer young people relative to elder people.
6. High levels of public debt.

Part IV carefully weighs the arguments, and while recognizing the inherent challenges of making long-term predictions of interest rates, it suggests that interest rates are more likely to remain relatively low compared to historical norms. It further notes that the primary risk to this outlook is the potential for unsustainable growth in public debt. Additionally, this part briefly explores potential future scenarios for indebtedness, asset prices, and inequality under various interest rate environments.

Table 0.1 presents an outline of the book.

**Table 0.1**  Outline of the book

| | |
|---|---|
| **Part I: Falling Rates** | |
| Chapter 1 | Chapter 2 |
| The Level of Interest Rates: Today and Historically | Inflation and Real Interest Rates |
| **Part II: Consequences of Falling and Low Interest Rates** | |
| Chapter 3 | Chapter 4 |
| Debt and Low Interest Rates | House Prices and Low Interest Rates |
| Chapter 5 | Chapter 6 |
| Stock Markets and Low Interest Rates | Inequality and Low Interest Rates |
| Chapter 7 | |
| Financial Risk-Taking and Low Interest Rates | |
| **Part III: What Caused a Four-Decade Fall in Interest Rates?** | |
| Chapter 8 | Chapter 9 |
| What Caused a Four-Decade Fall in Inflation? | What Caused a Four-Decade Fall in Real Interest Rates? |
| Chapter 10 | |
| What Caused the Rise in Inflation and Interest Rates after the Covid-19 Pandemic? | |
| **Part IV: What Does the Future Hold?** | |
| Chapter 11 | Chapter 12 |
| Trends That Could Keep Rates Low | Trends That Could Elevate Rates |
| Chapter 13 | Chapter 14 |
| Putting It All Together: What Is the Outlook for Rates? | Debt, Inequality, and House and Stock Prices Considering Interest Rate Scenarios |

## Writing Style and Readership

While academic in nature, the book is written in a style that is accessible to a broad audience. Written in plain language, and without relying on complex formulas or equations, it delves into academic theories and empirical facts in a way that helps readers better understand the impact of interest rates on important societal outcomes.

A key feature of the book is its empirical approach and reliance on data. Figures and tables richly illustrate and support the arguments and theories presented, making it a fact-based book. With a long-term perspective, the book analyses data that spans many decades, often centuries. It builds its arguments by presenting stylized facts and relating them to relevant theories and academic literature, enabling readers to grasp the context behind the key points.

Because of its fact-based approach, the book should speak to several audiences, including general readers, students of economics and finance, academic scholars, and central bankers.

Typical non-academic readers regularly read publications like *Financial Times*, *Wall Street Journal*, or *The Economist*, showing an interest in economic developments and their societal impacts.

With these introductory remarks complete, let us embark on the fascinating journey into the evolution of interest rates and their impact.

**PART I**

# FALLING RATES

# 1

# The Level of Interest Rates

## Today and Historically

The persistent and sustained decline in interest rates over the 40 years from 1980 to 2020 forms the backbone of this book, and the significant consequences this had will be thoroughly discussed in subsequent chapters. However, before delving into this, it is essential to understand just how much interest rates fell, both in absolute and historical terms. This is the focus of this chapter.

We distinguish between nominal and real interest rates. Nominal interest rates are the rates borrowers pay and lenders receive. Typically, when inflation—the rate at which prices in the economy change—moves, nominal interest rates will move as well. However, nominal rates can also change independently of inflation. This happens if the real interest rate changes.

The real interest rate is the nominal interest rate adjusted for inflation. While the nominal interest rate represents the monetary rate applied to loans, the real interest rate reflects the actual change in purchasing power resulting from paying interest.

This chapter will discuss the developments in nominal interest rates, while the next chapter will cover inflation and real interest rates. Notably, both inflation and real interest rates also declined until the pandemic; that is, nominal interest rates, real interest rates, and inflation rates all trended downward for the four decades leading up to the Covid-19 pandemic in 2020.

After the pandemic, inflation spiked, followed by an increase in nominal interest rates. It remains a critical question whether interest rates have risen to a permanently higher level or if the post-pandemic rise in interest rates was temporary. Part IV of the book addresses this question. This chapter and the next focus on the period before the pandemic.

This chapter and the next present historical stylized facts without attempting to explain why interest rates fell continuously for four decades; that analysis will come in Chapters 8–10.

The conclusions from this chapter are: (i) the decline in interest rates over the last four decades was unusually large and persistent from a historical

*How Low Interest Rates Change the World.* Jesper Rangvid, Oxford University Press. © Jesper Rangvid (2025).
DOI: 10.1093/9780198946410.003.0002

perspective and (ii) interest rates reached historical lows immediately before the pandemic. The rest of the book explores the consequences of this sustained drop in interest rates, why it happened, and what the future holds.

## 1.1 Interest Rates during 1980–2020

Interest rates in advanced economies experienced a persistent decline from 1980 to 2020, dropping from double-digit figures in the early 1980s to nearly zero just before the pandemic. Figure 1.1 illustrates this trend, depicting the average yields on long-term government bonds across 17 advanced economies since 1980.[1]

Figure 1.1 shows average yields on long-term government bonds, typically 10-year bonds. For example, a yield of 10 per cent means that the borrower must compensate the lender with a return of 10 per cent per

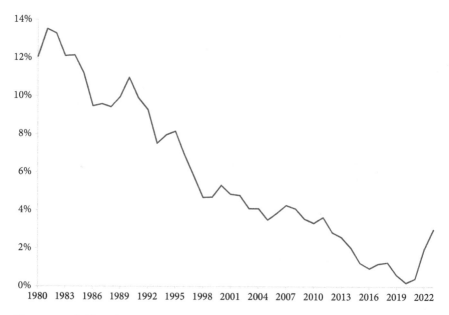

**Figure 1.1** Yields on long-term government bonds, 1980–2023. Average across 17 advanced economies.
*Data source:* FRED Database of St. Louis Fed.

---

[1] The 17 countries are Australia, Belgium, Canada, Denmark, Finland, France, Germany, Italy, Japan, Norway, Portugal, Spain, Sweden, Switzerland, The Netherlands, the UK, and the US. The book's focus is on advanced economies, where interest rates have exhibited similar trends over the past decades, as explored in Section 1.2.1. Parts III and IV of the book examine how specific trends in emerging markets have impacted interest rates in these advanced economies.

annum over the next 10 years. The decline in yields reflects a fall in interest rates. Box 1.1 reviews the difference between yields and interest rates. Generally, throughout the book, we will use these terms—yields and interest rates—interchangeably, making distinctions only when necessary.

In the early 1980s, governments that borrowed had to offer substantial compensation to lenders. In 1981, the average yield across advanced economies peaked at nearly 14 per cent. Put simply, this meant that advanced-economy governments on average had to compensate lenders by 14 per cent of the borrowed amount per year over the next 10 years.

Since the early 1980s, yields have consistently fallen. From their peak of 14 per cent in 1981, global yields declined by approximately 0.33 percentage points per year until the pandemic, corresponding to a fall in yields by one percentage point every three years.

In 2020, yields bottomed out near 0 per cent. Borrowing costs were negligible. In some cases, yields were even negative. In fact, this was the case in almost half (8) of the 17 countries used to create Figure 1.1. Negative interest rates can be perplexing. When lending money at a negative interest rate, lenders effectively pay the borrower in addition to providing the loan.

Typically, when borrowing something, such as a car or an apartment, one compensates the owner for its use. Similarly, borrowing money usually involves paying interest to the lender. However, with negative interest rates, the lender pays the borrower, which was the case for governments borrowing at negative rates in 2020.

After the pandemic, interest rates increased. However, from a historical perspective, they remained relatively low, as shown in Figure 1.1. We will revisit the post-pandemic development in rates in Part III.

## Box 1.1  Interest rates and yields

The interest rate is the percentage a borrower must pay to the lender as a fraction of the amount borrowed, typically quoted on a per annum basis. For example, if I borrow USD 100 for five years at an interest rate of 2 per cent, I must pay the lender USD 2 in interest each year for the next five years. The interest rate represents the cost of borrowing money, compensating the lender for the use of their funds. After five years, I must also repay the principal amount of USD 100.

Yields express the return the lender obtains over the investment period. Governments and corporations borrow money by issuing bonds. When I buy a government bond, I lend money to the government. Imagine I buy a one-year government bond today that promises to pay me USD 100 in one year. If the interest rate on the bond is 2 per cent, I

**16    How Low Interest Rates Change the World**

will receive USD 102 in one year, which includes the bond's face value (USD 100) plus the interest payment. If the bond's price is USD 99 today, the yield, or return, I receive from buying this bond is approximately 3 per cent (102/99–1 ≈ 3%).

Yields are correlated with interest rates. If the government promises to pay USD 3 in interest payments (an interest rate of 3 per cent), and I can buy the one-year bond for USD 99, the yield is approximately 4 per cent (103/99–1 ≈ 4%). In this example, the yield increases by about one percentage point when the interest rate increases by one percentage point. Because yields and interest rates are correlated, we will use the terms interchangeably when describing long-term historical developments in the cost of borrowing money.

## 1.2 Long-Term Developments in Global Interest Rates

This book frequently uses historical data extending back to 1870 for the 17 countries featured in Figure 1.1. This extensive dataset is available thanks to the remarkable efforts of economists Òscar Jordà, Moritz Schularick, and Alan M. Taylor. They have dedicated significant time and effort to collecting historical data on yields, interest rates, and numerous other economic variables, generously making this data freely accessible.[2]

Figure 1.2 illustrates the developments in global yields on long-term government bonds since 1870. It depicts the year-by-year average yield of long-term government bonds across the 17 countries mentioned in footnote 1.

Figure 1.2 conveys two crucial messages for this book:

1. The decline in yields from 1980 to 2020 was substantial from a long-term historical perspective, with yields falling by more than 10 percentage points.
2. In 2020, yields reached historically low levels, unprecedented in the past 150 years.

The figure also indicates that, even after the post-pandemic increase, yields remain low by historical standards. Before the global financial crisis of 2008–2009, global yields had never fallen below 3 per cent. The previous low

---

[2] The Jordà-Schularick-Taylor Macrohistory Database is available at www.macrohistory.net/database. For the book, the data has been updated by the author until 2024, which is when the book went to press.

**Figure 1.2** Yields on long-term government bonds, 1870–2023. Average across 17 advanced economies.
*Data source*: Jordà-Schularick-Taylor Macrohistory Database and FRED St. Louis Database.

was in 1946, right after the Second World War, when yields bottomed out at 3.3 per cent. In this context, the average yields of around 3 per cent observed in 2023 across advanced economies are still comparatively low.

Figure 1.2 also reveals that global yields tend to move in persistent waves. From the 1870s until the early 20th century, yields were generally falling. Yields then increased around the First World War and declined again until the end of the Second World War. After the Second World War, yields embarked on a remarkable upward trend, rising consistently for three and a half decades until the early 1980s. Yields peaked at 14 per cent in 1981 before entering the four-decade decline that is central to this book.

## 1.2.1 Dispersion in Yields across Countries

Figures 1.1 and 1.2 show the overall movements in yields across advanced economies. However, not all countries follow the same pattern. At various times and for different reasons, some countries deviate from the global trend. Figure 1.3 illustrates these deviations by depicting country-by-country movements in yields since 1870, alongside the average yield (as shown in Figure 1.2) and the highest and lowest yields in any given year.

It is important to note that the country with the highest yield varies from year to year. For certain spikes in yields, Figure 1.3 highlights the specific countries experiencing significant increases.[3]

Figure 1.3 illustrates how some countries sometimes deviate from the global trend in yields. For example, during the 1870s, Spanish yields significantly exceeded those of other countries. A similar pattern occurred in Portugal during the 1890s, 1920s, and the European debt crisis in 2012.

Yield spikes often coincide with debt crises. A debt crisis arises when a country cannot meet its obligations to bondholders. Spain faced such a crisis in the 1870s, and Portugal encountered a similar situation in the 1890s. In 2012, during the European debt crisis, Portugal did not default, but investor concerns led to higher yields, Figure 1.3 shows.[4] Notably, debt crises

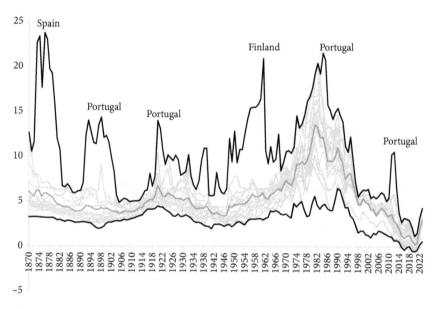

**Figure 1.3** Yields on long-term government bonds in 17 countries, 1870–2023. The figure shows the average of all 17 yields (darker line), and the highest and lowest yield in any given year (black lines).

*Data source*: Jordà-Schularick-Taylor Macrohistory Database and FRED St. Louis Database.

---

[3] Sometimes, data is missing. For instance, the Jordà-Schularick-Taylor Macrohistory Database does not include German yields during the German hyperinflation of 1921 and 1922. Consequently, some extreme cases might not be represented in Figure 1.3. However, this omission is not significant for the purpose of this book, which focuses on long-term trends rather than individual short-term anomalies. If an individual extreme case is relevant, it will be explicitly addressed in the book.

[4] In Greece, yields increased even more. Box 3.3 in Chapter 3 analyses the Greek debt crisis in the early 2010s.

The Level of Interest Rates    **19**

primarily impact the defaulting country and typically do not significantly affect overall global yield levels.[5]

Even when some countries occasionally deviate from the global trend, the central theme of this book is that all advanced economies studied here experienced persistently declining yields since 1980.

## 1.2.2  Long and Short Yields

In Figure 1.3, we observed yields on long-term government bonds, typically associated with maturities of 10 years or so. While strict definitions are elusive, short-term government bonds typically involve repayment of borrowed money within the next three months, one year, or a couple of years.

Yields on bonds with different maturities are related, but do not necessarily move in lockstep. For instance, central banks, as we will delve into later, exert more influence over short-term interest rates than long-term rates, influencing the wedge between the two.

Figure 1.4 illustrates the year-by-year movements of yields on global (averaged across 17 advanced countries) short- and long-term government bonds since 1870.

Figure 1.4 shows that yields on short-term global bonds usually exhibit a close relationship with yields on long-term bonds. Similar to long-term yields, short-term yields experienced an upward trend during the 1950s, 1960s, and 1970s, followed by a persistent decline spanning four decades from 1980 to 2020. Although short-term yields in 2023 are not as low as they were in 2020, they remain subdued from a long-term perspective.

Before the pandemic, several countries encountered negative short-term yields. In 2019, 11 out of the 17 countries represented in Figure 1.4 reported negative yields on their short-term debt.

Theoretically, yields of different maturities are interconnected. The yield on a long-term loan can be expressed as the average of the current short-term yield, expected future short-term yields, and a risk premium:

$$Long-term\ yield = Short-term\ yield\ today + expected\ future$$

$$short-term\ yields + risk\ premium$$

---

[5] Reinhart and Rogoff (2011) contains a thorough analysis of debt crises.

**Figure 1.4** Yields on long-term and short-term government bonds in 17 countries, 1870–2023. Averages across 17 countries.
*Data source*: Jordà-Schularick-Taylor Macrohistory Database and FRED St. Louis Database.

The risk premium compensates investors for the risk associated with holding a bond and is typically positive. Consequently, when the risk premium is positive and future yield expectations are ignored, long-term yields tend to exceed short-term yields—an empirical observation supported by Figure 1.4.

The difference between yields on long- and short-term debt is known as the 'slope of the yield curve'. An 'upward-sloping' yield curve occurs when long-term bond yields surpass short-term yields. Over the 154-year period from 1870 to 2023, the yield curve was upward sloping for 117 years. Since the mid-1990s, except for the years preceding the 2008 financial crisis, the yield curve has been notably steep.

In contrast, during 37 of the last 154 years, the yield curve was 'downward sloping', indicating that short-term yields exceeded long-term yields. This typically occur when people anticipate a decline in future short-term yields; that is, when 'expected future short-term yields' are lower than current short-term yields.

While fluctuations occur in the relationship between long and short yields, the main point to emphasize here is that both short and long yields have declined since the early 1980s, and, despite the recent rate increases post-pandemic, they remain at the time of writing relatively low in historical terms.

## 1.3 Yields on Corporate Bonds

It was not only yields on government bonds that fell from 1980 to 2020. The costs of borrowing for households and firms did so too. Rates on mortgage loans, credit card loans, student loans, deposits, and corporate loans all fell persistently. To illustrate this, Figure 1.5 shows developments in yields on US corporate bonds, which are bonds issued by corporations to fund their operations and investments.[6] Specifically, the figure considers two types of firms:

- AAA-rated firms: these are companies with a relatively low likelihood of defaulting on their loans.
- BAA-rated firms: these firms face a higher risk of loan repayment difficulties.

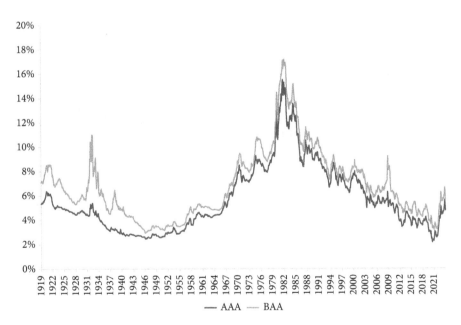

**Figure 1.5** Yields on US corporate debt, 1919–2023. AAA-rated firms and BAA-rated firms.
*Data source*: St. Louis FRED database.

---

[6] While extensive historical data for government bonds exists, information on international corporate bond yields is less comprehensive. Consequently, Figure 1.5 presents data related to US corporate bonds, a country for which such data is available.

## 22 How Low Interest Rates Change the World

Comparing Figures 1.2 and 1.5, one sees that the overall movements in corporate bond yields mirror those of government bond yields. In particular, both government and corporate bond yields declined during the interwar years, rose after the Second World War and up until approximately 1980, and declined again from 1980 to 2020. Hence, the cost of borrowing for corporations also fell persistently for four decades, from 1980 to 2020.

Figure 1.5 also reveals that BAA-rated firms (lower-rated) pay higher yields when borrowing compared to AAA-rated firms (higher-rated). This is natural because lending to BAA-rated firms carries a higher risk—the lenders face a greater chance of not receiving their money back. Investors demand compensation for this risk, which pushes up yields on BAA-rated bonds relative to AAA-rated bonds. But, again, the main point of Figure 1.5 is to document that not only government faced persistently lower borrowing costs from 1980 to 2020. Firms did as well, both higher- and lower-rated firms.

## 1.4 Very Long-Term Interest Rates for the UK

In 2020, global yields reached their lowest point in 150 years (Figures 1.1–1.4). One hundred and fifty years is a long period, but are we sure that rates were not lower further back in history? While the data we have for the 17 countries used in previous figures of this chapter extend back to 1870, we have data extending further back for a few selected countries. For example, the UK boasts a remarkable dataset on yields and interest rates spanning the past three centuries.

Figure 1.6 presents the monetary policy rate of the Bank of England, known as the 'Bank Rate'. This time series has been available since the Bank's founding in 1694, making it an impressive record of official monetary policy rates.[7]

For the first 250 years of its existence (until around 1960), the Bank of England maintained the Bank Rate at approximately 4–5 per cent. While there were fluctuations, the rate consistently reverted to this level.

However, the period since the 1950s stands out in a long-term historical context. During the 1950s, 1960s, and 1970s, the Bank Rate experienced significant growth, eventually reaching double-digit levels around 1980. Conversely, since 1980 and with only brief interruptions, the Bank Rate

---

[7] Founded in 1694, the Bank of England is the world's second oldest central bank, surpassed only by Sweden's Riksbanken, established in 1668. However, as far as the author is aware, no consistent time series of policy rates exists for Sweden for the whole period since its founding. This makes the Bank Rate time series shown in Figure 1.6 the longest available record of official monetary policy rates.

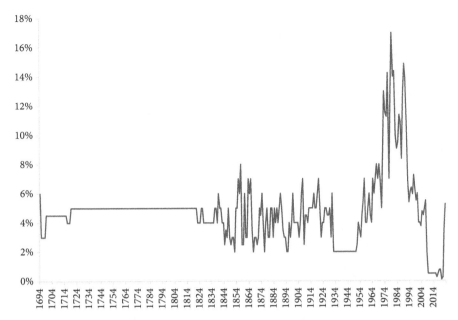

**Figure 1.6** The monetary policy rate, the Bank Rate, of the Bank of England, 1694–2023.
*Data source*: Bank of England.

has steadily declined. Specifically, the Bank Rate decreased by nearly 15 percentage points between 1980 and 2020.

Following the financial crisis and up until the pandemic, the Bank Rate remained at rock-bottom levels—significantly lower than at any previous point in history. Before 2008, the Bank Rate had never fallen below 2 per cent. Conversely, between the 2008 financial crisis and the pandemic in 2020, it did not exceed 0.75 per cent. Post-pandemic, the Bank Rate has been raised to its historical average of around 5 per cent. We can safely conclude that interest rates fell significantly between 1980 and 2020, reaching a historically low level before the pandemic.

## 1.5 Seven Centuries of Interest Rates

As part of his Harvard University PhD, Paul F. Schmelzing collected an impressive dataset of yields for seven countries dating back to the 1400s.[8] Although the dataset covers seven countries, full coverage is not available for all years.

---

[8] The dataset has been made accessible to other researchers by the Bank of England.

Figure 1.7 illustrates the global yield development since 1310, measured as the GDP-weighted average of nominal yields across France, Germany, Italy, Japan, the Netherlands, the UK, and the US. The figure also includes a trend line, representing the average long-term tendency of rate movements.

Figure 1.7 provides a remarkable insight: global yields have exhibited a persistent decline over the past 700 years. While fluctuations occurred, the overarching trend over seven centuries points towards falling yields. This is remarkable in light of the very different economic, democratic, and juridical regimes that obviously have prevailed over such long periods.

The period from 1980 to 2020 stands out. During these four decades, global yields dropped by more than 10 percentage points—an unprecedented historical decline. To emphasize this critical point, Figure 1.8 illustrates how global yields evolved in subsequent 40-year periods over the last seven centuries. Notably, the world never—that is, in the last 700 years—witnessed such a substantial fall in yields over a four-decade period as it did between 1980 and 2020.

The period from the end of the Second World War until 1980 stands out as well. During these decades, yields surged by almost 10 percentage points. Figure 1.8 confirms that this was also a unique experience. This means that

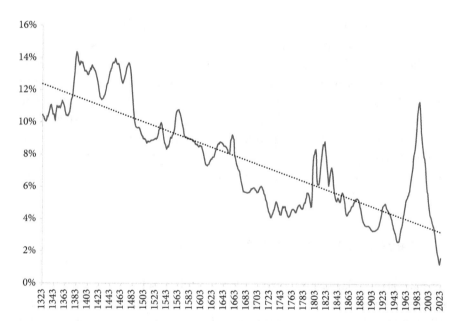

**Figure 1.7** Global yields, 1310–2023. Seven-year rolling average. Trend line included as a dotted line.

*Data source*: Bank of England/Schmelzing (2020).

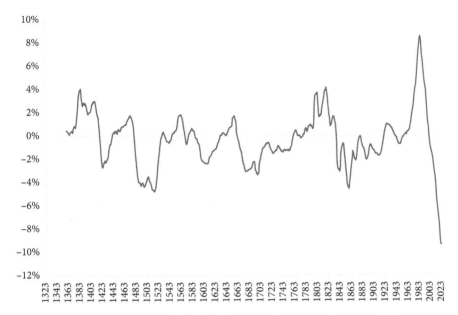

**Figure 1.8** Changes in nominal global yields over subsequent 40-year periods, 1310–2023.

*Data source*: Bank of England/Schmelzing (2020).

we had an era of unusually large yield increases from 1940 to 1980, followed by four decades of equally remarkable yield declines. These developments significantly impacted the global economy, as this book will argue.

While a 700-year time series is truly remarkable, Bank of England Chief Economist Andrew Haldane (2015) presented data showing short-term and long-term interest rates in the UK over nearly 5,000 years! Although the persistent multi-century decline in yields indicated by Figure 1.7 is not present in Haldane's analysis, three important stylized facts are shared: interest rates rose significantly between the Second World War and 1980, the decline in interest rates from 1980 to 2020 was historically large, and interest rates had never reached such low levels as they did just before the pandemic.

The overarching conclusion from studying data over the past 40 years, the past 150 years, and even across centuries and millennia for selected countries is that the drop in yields from 1980 to 2020 was unprecedented and yields in 2020 were historically low.

Why did yields decline so significantly from 1980 to 2020? One answer lies in the simultaneous fall of inflation and real interest rates, a topic explored in the next chapter.

## 1.6 Checklist

This chapter has illustrated the following key points:

- Yields and interest rates have steadily declined over the four decades from 1980 to 2020.
- Yields and interest rates reached historically low levels just before the pandemic.
- Over the past 150 years, government bond yields have moved in persistent waves, decreasing from the 1870s until the early 20th century, rising during the First World War, declining again until the end of the Second World War, increasing from 1945 to 1980, and then decreasing from 1980 to 2020.
- Similar historical patterns are observed in short-term global government bond yields and US corporate bond yields.
- In 2020, just before the pandemic, yields reached their lowest levels in recorded history. This chapter examined various yield data covering different sets of countries and spanning 150 years, 700 years, and even 5,000 years. Across these different datasets, the conclusion is consistent: the decline in yields from 1980 to 2020 was historically large, and yields in 2020 were unprecedentedly low.
- Since the onset of the pandemic, yields have risen but remain relatively low or around the historical average, depending on the country.

# 2
# Inflation and Real Interest Rates

Chapter 1 examined trends in nominal interest rates, highlighting their persistent decline from 1980 to 2020. This period marked the most significant four-decade decrease in rates in history, with interest rates reaching historically low levels just before the pandemic in 2020.

Nominal interest rates are mainly determined by inflation and the real interest rate:[1]

$$Nominal\ interest\ rate = Real\ interest\ rate + inflation$$

To comprehend the four-decade decline in nominal interest rates from 1980 to 2020, it is thus instructive to understand how inflation and real interest rates behaved. But what exactly are inflation and real interest rates, and how do they influence nominal interest rates?

Inflation refers to the percentage change in the overall price level in the economy from one period to the next, such as from one year to the next. There are numerous prices in the economy—the price of milk, butter, cars, heating, housing, and so on. When discussing inflation, we refer to the collective movement of these prices, often represented by an index like the consumer price index (CPI). Annual inflation measures the percentage change in this index from one year to the next.

The nominal interest rate compensates lenders for allowing borrowers temporary use of their money. When money is lent out, the lender forgoes its immediate use. For example, if you lend $1,000 instead of buying a $1,000 bicycle today, you require to receive enough back to still be able to purchase the bicycle in the future. If the price of the bicycle—or prices in the economy in general—have increased, you would want the interest rate on the loan to at least cover this rise in prices. Thus, inflation or anticipated inflation plays a significant role in determining nominal interest rates.

---

[1] Sometimes a risk premium is added to the right-hand side of the equation. As real interest rates and inflation are the main determinants of nominal interest rates, discussions of the risk premium will be short in this book, which is why it is left out of the formula above.

*How Low Interest Rates Change the World*. Jesper Rangvid, Oxford University Press. © Jesper Rangvid (2025).
DOI: 10.1093/9780198946410.003.0003

**28** How Low Interest Rates Change the World

A key point of this chapter is that inflation has declined over the 1980–2020 period. Since inflation is a key determinant of nominal interest rates, the decrease in inflation is a major reason why interest rates have also fallen.

Another important message is that while inflation has decreased, thus lowering nominal interest rates, the decline in nominal rates during 1980–2020 outpaced the fall in inflation. In other words, besides the reduction in inflation, another factor driving down nominal interest rates is the decrease in the real interest rate.

Real interest rates are essentially given as nominal interest rates minus inflation. Real interest rates indicate how much more goods and services lenders can purchase in the future with the money they lend out today. For instance, if inflation is 2 per cent and the nominal interest rate is 3 per cent—meaning the real interest rate is 1 per cent—the lender gains 1 per cent in real purchasing power when the loan is repaid.

The chapter will show that real interest rates have also declined over the past decades. Consequently, inflation rates and real yields both declined from 1980 to 2020, helping us to understand the fall in nominal interest rates over the period.

As Chapter 1 explained, nominal yields reached historic lows in 2020. Real yields were also low, but they have been even lower during earlier periods such as the two World Wars and the 1970s. During these periods, inflation increased substantially, diminishing the real return on lending. In contrast, in the last four decades, inflation has been falling and so have real interest rates, marking a unique phase from a historical perspective.

The chapter is structured into two sections. The first details historical inflation trends and the second focuses on real interest rates. These sections present stylized facts. Chapters 8 and 9 will delve into an examination of the reasons behind the decline in inflation and real yields, and thus nominal yields.

Box 2.1 further explains the relationship between nominal interest rates, inflation, and real interest rates.

## Box 2.1 Inflation and nominal and real interest rates

Nominal interest rates or yields represent the returns received (for lenders) or paid (for borrowers). For instance, if you purchase a bond for USD 98 that matures in one year with a face value of USD 100 (and no interest payments), the nominal yield would be 100/98 −1 = 2.05 per cent.

Saving today allows us to enhance our future consumption possibilities. When I invest in a bond today for USD 98, I forgo immediate consumption of that amount. Instead, I receive USD 100 next year, which I can then use for future expenses.

Deciding whether to save today, thereby deferring consumption, hinges on what I can purchase with my money next year. For instance, if I consider buying a watch today priced at USD 98, I might choose to delay my purchase if I'm confident I can still afford it next year. However, whether I can indeed buy the watch then depends on its future price.

If the price of the watch rises to USD 99, I can purchase the watch and have funds left over, thanks to the USD 100 from the bond. The percentage change in the watch's price over the year is 99/98 ≈ 1 per cent. Therefore, I would only opt to buy the bond if its expected return is sufficient to cover the increase in the watch's price. In this case, the bond's return of 2.05 per cent exceeds the watch's price increase.

Thus, we refer to 2.05 per cent as the nominal return/yield on the bond. The real return, however, accounts for changes in prices. Here, the real return on the bond is calculated as (1 + 2.05 per cent) / (1 + 1 per cent) = 1.04 per cent, which can be approximated more simply by subtracting inflation from nominal returns; that is, 2.05 per cent − 1 per cent = 1.05 per cent.

While we use the example of a watch's price here, our broader interest lies in the changes in all prices across the economy; that is, inflation. Inflation is typically measured by the percentage change in the prices of goods and services consumed, captured, for instance, by the CPI (consumer price index).

Whether I'm willing to delay consumption today depends on expectations of inflation and my required real return. In equilibrium, the nominal interest rate thus equals the required real interest rate plus expected inflation:

*Nominal interest rate = Required real interest rate + Expected inflation*

Understanding what drives changes in inflation and real interest rates enables us to grasp the forces behind changes in nominal interest rates, something we return to in Chapter 8 which discusses the causes of inflation and Chapter 9 which discusses the determinants of real interest rates.

Future price changes are uncertain, constituting inflation risk. Investors often seek compensation for bearing this risk, known as an inflation risk premium. In this book, we focus primarily on inflation and real interest rates as drivers of nominal interest rates, meaning inflation risk premiums are not discussed here.

## 2.1 Global Inflation during the Past Four Decades

Figure 2.1 illustrates the medium annual rate of inflation, defined as the annual percentage change in the CPI, across 17 advanced countries from 1980 to 2023. It also includes the global nominal interest rate on long-term government bonds (similar to Figure 1.1 in Chapter 1).² Figure 2.1 shows that inflation and interest rates have both trended down over the past four decades.

Global inflation soared to double-digit levels in the early 1980s, mirroring the era when nominal interest rates also reached double digits. Over the subsequent decades, inflation markedly declined, reaching around 2 per cent by the turn of the millennium, accompanied by a corresponding decrease in nominal yields. From then until the onset of the Covid-19 pandemic, global inflation remained within a narrow band of 0–2 per cent.

The pandemic and its aftermath triggered a sudden and significant surge in global inflation, hitting 8 per cent by 2022. Concurrently, nominal yields also rose post-pandemic, as depicted in Figure 2.1. Chapter 10 will delve into a detailed analysis of the factors driving the post-pandemic inflation flareup.

While Figure 2.1 underscores the long-term correlation between inflation and interest rates, it also reveals the deviations between the two. Firstly,

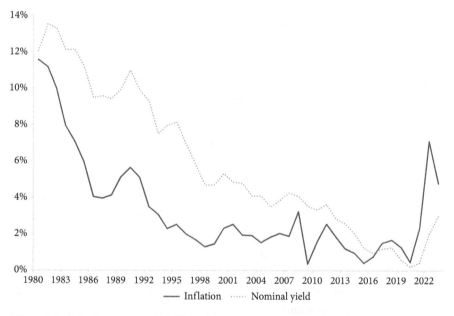

**Figure 2.1** Inflation rates and yields on long-term government bonds, 1980–2023. Average across 17 advanced economies.
*Data source:* OECD.

---

² Figure 2.1 presents the median inflation rates across 17 countries, rather than the average inflation rate. This choice is deliberate because some countries have experienced periods of extremely high inflation. In those instances, using the median provides a clearer indication of general inflation trends. Box 2.2 discusses such hyperinflationary episodes.

inflation decreased more rapidly than nominal yields during the 1980s and 1990s. Secondly, nominal yields typically exceed inflation, reflecting lenders' demand for a real return on their bond investments in addition to compensation for expected inflation.

Recent years, especially during the pandemic, have seen global inflation surpass global nominal yields. To understand this, remember that the yields in Figure 2.1 pertain to long-term rates, typically on 10-year government bonds, while inflation rates represent annual figures. If investors anticipate a decline in inflation, current nominal interest rates may be lower than current inflation rates because the low future inflation will ultimately yield a positive real return over the 10-year period.

## 2.2 Long-Term Trends in Inflation

While inflation and nominal yields have moved in tandem since the early 1980s, as indicated in Figure 2.1, their historical behaviour diverges when examined over longer periods. Figure 2.2 extends this analysis across 17 countries back to 1870, yielding several important insights.

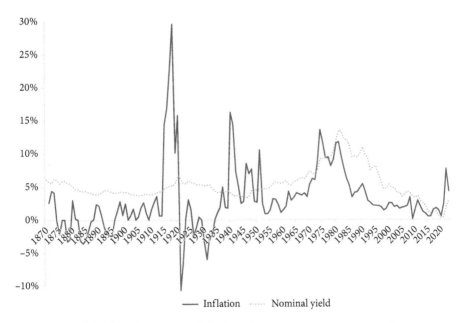

**Figure 2.2** Global inflation rates and yields on long-term government bonds, 1870–2023. Medians across 17 advanced economies.
*Data source:* Jordà-Schularick-Taylor Macrohistory Database and OECD.

Chapter 1 concluded that nominal interest rates had reached historic lows before the pandemic: just prior to the pandemic, nominal interest rates were at their lowest level in 700 years. However, inflation was not at historically low levels before the pandemic, despite consistently decreasing from 1980 to 2020. In earlier periods, inflation had been even lower than the near-zero inflation observed right before the pandemic. For example, during the 1880s, 1890s, and again in the 1920s and 1930s, inflation rates were frequently negative. In 1921, global prices plummeted by 11 per cent year on year.

Negative inflation—falling prices—is termed 'deflation'. Figure 2.2 illustrates that while inflation has been positive every year since the 1940s, it was often negative before that time.

The fluctuation of inflation around zero during the late 19th century—sometimes positive, sometimes negative—suggests that global prices remained relatively stable before the early 20th century. Prices for goods and services in 1914, at the outbreak of the First World War, were roughly equivalent to those of 45 years earlier, in 1870, as shown in Figure 2.3 which depicts the development of the global price level normalized to one in 1870, displayed on a logarithmic scale. Conversely, since the Second World War, prices have consistently risen each year, varying in magnitude but always trending upward.

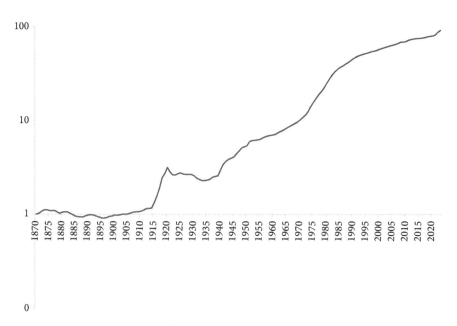

**Figure 2.3** Median price-level developments across 17 advanced economies, 1870–2023. Logarithmic scale.
*Data source:* Jordà-Schularick-Taylor Macrohistory Database and OECD.

Figure 2.3 illustrates a structural shift in inflation dynamics around the time of the Second World War, with prices being relatively stable from 1870 until the Second World War, with a notable exception of a sharp price increase during the First World War, and consistently trending upward since the Second World War.

Another significant observation from Figure 2.2 is the increased stability of inflation in recent decades. Over the past four decades leading up to the pandemic, inflation has remained low and positive, fluctuating around an average of approximately 1 per cent. Before the First World War, inflation was similarly low on average but exhibited much more variability, with periods of significant annual price declines followed by rapid increases.

Table 2.1 presents average global inflation rates during various periods alongside the volatility of inflation within those periods. Volatility measures how much inflation deviates from its average value. Lower volatility indicates inflation remains within a narrow range around the average, while higher volatility implies more significant fluctuations.

To interpret volatility, consider the complete 1870–2023 period in Table 2.1, where the average global inflation rate was 3.1 per cent with a volatility of 5.1 per cent. The interpretation of these numbers is that in two out of three years, inflation fluctuated within the range of −2 per cent (3.1 per cent − 5.1 per cent) to 8.2 per cent (3.1 per cent + 5.1 per cent). In the remaining one out of three years, inflation either dropped below −2 per cent or exceeded 8.2 per cent.

**Table 2.1** Average rates of inflation and volatility of inflation

|  | Mean | STD | Lower | Upper | Range |
|---|---|---|---|---|---|
| 1870–2023 | 3.1% | 5.1% | −1.9% | 8.2% | 10.1% |
| 1870–1914 | 0.4% | 2.1% | −1.7% | 2.4% | 4.2% |
| 1915–1949 | 4.7% | 8.5% | −3.8% | 13.3% | 17.1% |
| 1950–2023 | 4.0% | 3.2% | 0.8% | 7.1% | 6.3% |
| 1950–1969 | 5.0% | 3.5% | 1.5% | 8.5% | 7.0% |
| 1970–1989 | 7.8% | 3.0% | 4.9% | 10.8% | 5.9% |
| 1990–2019 | 2.0% | 1.1% | 1.0% | 3.1% | 2.1% |
| 1990–2023 | 2.2% | 1.5% | 0.8% | 3.7% | 2.9% |

STD = standard deviation. Lower and upper bounds are bounds within which two-thirds of inflation rates have fallen. 'Range' is the size of the range within which two-thirds of inflation rates has fallen; that is, Range = upper − lower.

Table 2.1 demonstrates that inflation has been remarkably stable since 1990. The volatility of inflation was only 1.5 per cent. Excluding the pandemic years (i.e. focusing on 1990–2019), inflation volatility drops even further to 1.1 per cent, marking it as a period with remarkably low and stable inflation.

Low and stable inflation prompts people and investors to adjust their expectations accordingly. When inflation remains predictably low and stable, there is a tendency to anticipate this trend will persist into the future, leading to a decrease in inflation expectations and thus in nominal yields on bonds. The sustained low and stable inflation experienced in recent decades, preceding the pandemic, has contributed to falling nominal interest rates during the same period.

## Box 2.2 Hyperinflation

In recent decades, we have grown accustomed to low and stable inflation, despite occasional flareups such as during the pandemic. However, throughout history, there have been periods of extremely high inflation known as hyperinflation.

One of the most infamous episodes of hyperinflation occurred in Germany during the early 1920s. Figure 2.4 illustrates German inflation trends since 1870.

During the German hyperinflation of 1923, prices skyrocketed by many thousands, potentially even millions, of per cent. For instance, a loaf of bread that cost 250 German

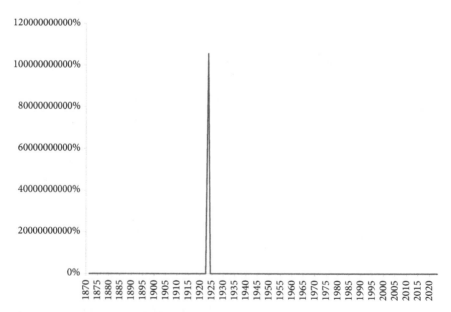

Figure 2.4 German annual inflation, 1870–2023.

*Data source:* Jordà-Schularick-Taylor Macrohistory Database.

marks at the beginning of 1923 surged to over 200 billion marks by the year's end (BBC Bitesize n.d.). Such rapid price increases inevitably lead to economic collapse.

The hyperinflation in Germany was precipitated by a drastic expansion of the money supply. The German Reichsbank, the German central bank at the time, printed vast quantities of money to fund government expenditures. Similar episodes of hyperinflation in other countries have also been attributed to excessive money printing. But why did central banks resort to such measures? Initially, increasing the money supply stimulates economic activity as people spend the newly available money. However, if the money printing continues unchecked, prices start to spiral upwards. This creates a vicious cycle where escalating prices necessitate even more money printing to sustain economic functioning, ultimately leading to severe economic repercussions.

Recent examples of hyperinflation include Venezuela (2016–2020) and Zimbabwe (2004–2009).

## 2.3 The Historical Behaviour of Real Interest Rates

Inflation has declined steadily from 1980 to 2020, and since inflation directly impacts nominal interest rates, this reduction in inflation is a significant factor contributing to the decline in nominal interest rates. However, nominal interest rates have fallen more than inflation; Figure 2.1 showed that interest rates exceeded inflation rates in the early 1980s but ended up being even lower than inflation rates before the pandemic. When nominal interest rates decrease by a greater extent than inflation, it indicates that real interest rates have also declined.

The real interest rate is calculated as the nominal interest rate minus inflation. Ex post, it represents the nominal yield (return) obtained from lending money minus the actual inflation experienced during the lending period. Ex ante, the real yield is the nominal yield expected from lending money minus the anticipated inflation over the investment period.

In long-term historical analyses, the real interest rate is often approximated by subtracting the most recent inflation rate from the nominal interest rate. This approach is used because data on expected inflation does not extend as far back in time as data on nominal interest rates and actual inflation.[3] Using this measure, Figure 2.5 illustrates the trajectory of real global yields over the past four decades; that is, it shows the difference between global nominal yields and global inflation rates depicted in Figure 2.1.

---

[3] The correct ex ante real yield over, e.g. the next 10 years is given by the nominal yield today minus expected inflation over the next 10 years. The correct ex post real yield is given by the nominal yield 10 years ago minus realized inflation over the past 10 years.

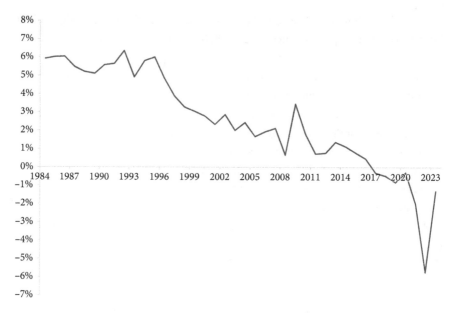

**Figure 2.5** Real yields on long-term government bonds, 1984–2023. Difference between median nominal yields and median inflation across 17 advanced economies. *Data source:* Jordà-Schularick-Taylor Macrohistory Database and OECD.

Like inflation and nominal yields, real yields have also experienced a downward trend since the mid-1980s. In the 1980s, real yields fell only little, but from the mid-1990s onward, there has been a significant and persistent decrease in real yields. During the mid-1980s, lenders required compensation at a rate of 6 per cent per annum above inflation, equating to a real yield of 6 per cent. Before the pandemic, the real interest rate had become negative. A negative real yield indicates that lenders are effectively paying borrowers in real terms to hold their money.

Moreover, the pandemic triggered a substantial drop in real yields. As shown in Figure 2.1, inflation increased more than nominal yields during and right after the pandemic, resulting in a pronounced decline in real yields.

Chapter 1 detailed how nominal yields reached historically low levels just prior to the pandemic, marking an unprecedented milestone in interest rate history. The narrative differs somewhat for real yields. Figure 2.6 illustrates the evolution of real yields over the past 150 years.

During the First World War, real yields plummeted to negative levels, reaching as low as minus 25 per cent. This occurred because, as discussed earlier, inflation surged to double-digit levels during the First World War, yet nominal yields did not rise correspondingly. Similarly, real yields were negative during the Second World War, in the early 1950s, and during the First Oil Crisis in 1973. In each of these instances, the primary driver was sharp increases in inflation. As depicted in Figure 2.2, nominal yields exhibit a smoother trend over time, whereas inflation has been volatile, occasionally spiking rapidly. Consequently, real interest rates have been equally volatile, closely tracking inflation volatility.

Figure 2.6 also presents the rolling average of real yields over the past decade (solid line), which smooths out short-term fluctuations. By eliminating these shorter-term fluctuations, Figure 2.6 demonstrates that the persistent decline in real yields over the last four decades is not unprecedented when viewed from a historical perspective. Real yields also declined persistently during periods such as the late 1800s to the First World War, the 1930s and 1940s, and the 1960s and 1970s. Conversely, real yields increased between the First and the Second World Wars, during the 1950s and the 1980s. In essence, real yields tend to fluctuate around an average of approximately 2 per cent over the long term.

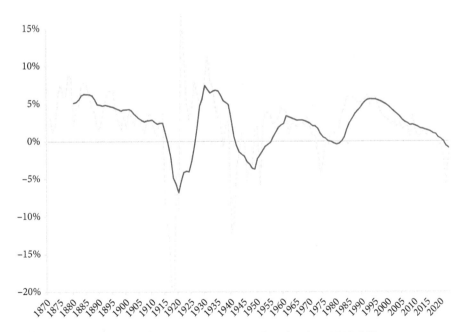

**Figure 2.6** Real yields on long-term government bonds, 1870–2023. Difference between median nominal yields and median inflation across 17 advanced economies. Annual real yield (dotted line) and rolling average of past 10 years' real yield (solid line).
*Data source:* Jordà-Schularick-Taylor Macrohistory Database and OECD.

Notice at the same time, though, that Figure 2.6 shows that the fall in real yields from 1980 to 2020 was rather smooth compared to the movements in real yields earlier in history.

It is important to note that while real yields were low both right before and in particular during the pandemic, real yields were not at all-time historical lows. This contrasts with nominal yields, which Chapter 1 explained were lower than at earlier points just before the pandemic. The historically low level of nominal yields before the pandemic was thus not 'only' due to historically low real yields. Instead, they were due to the combination of low real yields—although not historically the lowest—*and* low inflation.

## 2.4  Seven Centuries of Inflation and Real Rates

Chapter 1 concluded by examining the evolution of nominal interest rates over the past seven centuries. This chapter will do the same focusing on global inflation and real interest rates. As discussed in Chapter 1, the comprehensive data spanning seven centuries is derived from the meticulous research of Paul Schmelzing, available through the Bank of England. Global inflation and real rates are represented as GDP-weighted averages from France, Germany, Italy, Japan, the Netherlands, the UK, and the US. Figure 2.7 illustrates global inflation trends over the past 700 years.

Compared to global nominal yields, as depicted in Figure 1.7, global inflation has exhibited considerable volatility historically. Figure 2.7 displays rolling seven-year averages of inflation, which partially smooths out short-term annual volatility. However, even with this smoothing of annual inflation rates, they are still volatile, with periods of positive inflation followed by deflation, and then followed again by inflation of a similar magnitude. We conclude that inflation has been considerably more volatile than nominal interest rates throughout history.

A further notable historical stylized fact is the prevalence of deflation up until the early 19th century. Approximately one-third of the 600-year period from the early 13th century to the early 19th century experienced falling prices, while inflation was positive in the remaining two-thirds of the years.

This trend changed significantly over the past century. Since the Great Depression in the 1930s, where prices fell by 3 per cent per year on average from 1926 to 1933, there has been no extended period of deflation. Over the last 100 years, prices have consistently increased.

Figure 2.7 also highlights that the high inflation rates during the First and Second World Wars, as well as the inflationary period of the 1970s, were

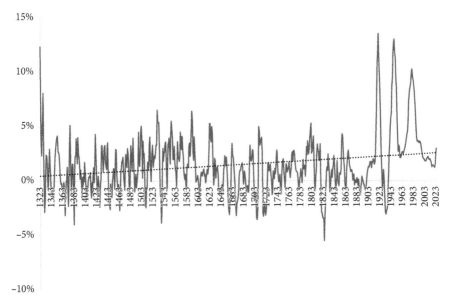

**Figure 2.7** Global inflation, 1310–2023. Seven-year rolling average.
*Data source:* Bank of England/Schmelzing (2020).

unprecedented in historical context. Never in history had global inflation reached such heights.

In summary, global inflation over the past century has differed from earlier episodes along two main dimensions. First, prices have generally trended upwards. In contrast, earlier historical periods often saw deflation; that is, falling prices. Second, there have been episodes of significant inflation flareups, which were less prevalent before the First World War.

A final observation about global inflation over the last seven centuries is the absence of a clear trend. While the trend line in Figure 2.7 shows a slight upward slope, indicating that average inflation rates may be marginally higher today compared to 700 years ago, inflation is so volatile that it is challenging to assert with certainty that inflation has exhibited a discernible upward trend over the last seven centuries.

## 2.4.1 Real Rates

Real interest rates are derived by subtracting inflation from nominal rates. Given the smooth downward trend of nominal rates depicted in Chapter 1, and the volatile nature of inflation (without a clear trend) illustrated in

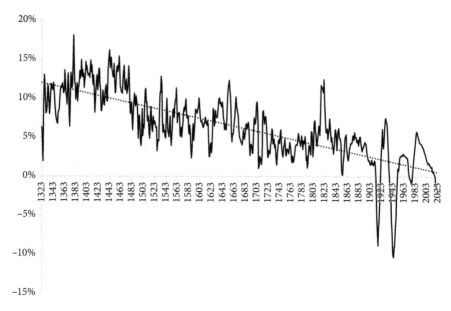

**Figure 2.8** Global real yields, 1310–2023. Seven-year rolling average.
*Data source:* Bank of England/Schmelzing (2020).

Figure 2.7, it turns out that real rates have followed a volatile downward trajectory over the last seven centuries. Figure 2.8 visually represents this.

Seven hundred years ago, global real interest rates were around 10 per cent. Over the past century, they have been close to zero on average. We conclude that real interest rates have fallen over the past seven centuries.

Real interest rates are volatile, though. For instance, we have seen significant episodes of very low real interest rates during the last century, particularly during the two World Wars. These low rates were driven by exceptionally high inflation, as already mentioned.

The behaviour of real interest rates over the past four decades stands in contrast to earlier periods. The last four decades have witnessed a prolonged and steady decline in real interest rates year after year. Earlier, real interest rates have been very volatile. Such a sustained period of declining real rates for four decades is thus unprecedented.

## 2.5 Checklist

This chapter has illustrated the following key points:

- Inflation has significantly declined since the early 1980s and has remained low and stable since the early 1990s.

- The pandemic in 2020 caused a brief surge in inflation, followed by a rapid decline, to be explored further in Chapter 10.
- Nominal interest rates are the sum of real interest rates and inflation.
- The prolonged period of low and stable inflation has been a key factor driving down nominal interest rates over the past four decades.
- Nominal interest rates have fallen more than inflation, though, meaning that real interest rates have also declined over this period.
- Real interest rates were low in 2020, right before the pandemic, but not at their lowest level ever. Lower real rates were observed during the First and Second World Wars and in the 1970s, caused by high inflation during these episodes.
- The reason for the low nominal interest rates before the pandemic was the combination of low inflation and low real interest rates, not the fact that real interest rates in themselves were historically low.
- Over the past seven centuries, global inflation has historically been volatile. Up until the early 20th century, periods of deflation, or falling prices, were common, while inflation has been the norm for the past 100 years.
- Since the 14th century, real interest rates have followed a downward trend similar to nominal rates but with significant fluctuations.
- The behaviour of real interest rates in the last four decades has been particularly unusual due to their smooth and persistent decline.

In total, inflation, real interest rates, and nominal interest rates have been steadily falling for four decades, from 1980 to 2020, with profound implications for societies, as the subsequent chapters will explore.

**PART II**

# CONSEQUENCES OF FALLING AND LOW INTEREST RATES

# 3
# Debt and Low Interest Rates

Interest rates play a critical role in shaping the affordability of debt for borrowers. When interest rates are lower, borrowers do not have to allocate as large a portion of their income towards servicing debt, improving their ability to borrow.

Between 1980 and 2020, interest rates fell significantly as demonstrated in previous chapters. This decline enabled increased borrowing capacity. Households, firms, and governments alike took advantage of lower interest rates to accumulate more debt, thereby causing a surge in global indebtedness.

This chapter focuses on the evolution of global debt levels. The key takeaway is that global debt escalated as interest rates fell from 1980 to 2020. In 1980, when interest rates were high, total debt in advanced economies averaged 135 per cent of their GDP. By 2022, when interest rates were much lower, this figure had more than doubled to approximately 300 per cent of GDP.

The chapter begins by examining developments in public debt. Over the past four decades, public debt levels have soared. Historically, governments borrowed primarily for wartime expenditures, aiming to reduce debts during peacetime. This is not the case anymore, where budget deficits have persisted even outside of wartime, contributing to persistent increases in public debt. Lower interest rates have arguably incentivized governments to increase borrowing further.

Like public debt, household and corporate debts have also surged over the past four decades. In advanced economies, household debt relative to GDP more than doubled, while corporate debt nearly doubled after 1980.

After the financial crisis of 2008 and the Covid-19 pandemic in 2020, government debt continued to rise, while household and corporate debt ratios stabilized. These crises prompted governments to increase spending significantly, financed by additional borrowing, whereas private sector borrowing growth moderated.

While there are valid reasons to borrow, such as mitigating economic downturns, buying a home, or funding investments that promote future

*How Low Interest Rates Change the World*. Jesper Rangvid, Oxford University Press. © Jesper Rangvid (2025).
DOI: 10.1093/9780198946410.003.0004

growth, high debt levels incur costs. These include higher interest rates when perceived risk by investors increases, which can dampen consumer spending and corporate investments, thereby slowing economic growth. Moreover, if public debt levels become unsustainable, it can lead to sovereign debt crises that further disrupt economic stability.

Overall, persistent declines in interest rates over the past four decades have contributed to a profound increase in global household, corporate, and government indebtedness. The future implications of these trends depend largely on how interest rates and government deficits evolve, topics that subsequent chapters of this book will delve into.

## 3.1 Sovereign Indebtedness in Advanced Economies

Many nations have significantly increased their indebtedness over the past four decades, coinciding with the global decline in interest rates. This trend is illustrated in Figure 3.1, depicting the evolution of global (advanced economies) sovereign indebtedness since the Second World War in relation to global interest rate trends. Indebtedness is measured as the ratio of

**Figure 3.1** Public debt in relation to GDP together with the nominal yield on long-term government bonds, 1946–2022. Average across 17 advanced economies.
*Data source:* Jordà-Schularick-Taylor Macrohistory Database and OECD.

public debt to GDP within each country. Figure 3.1 tracks global indebtedness, which is the average of sovereign indebtedness across 17 advanced economies.

The key takeaway from Figure 3.1 is the shift in global public indebtedness: it declined until the mid-1970s but has risen markedly during the period of falling global interest rates from 1980 to 2020. The magnitude of the rise is remarkable. Public debt-to-GDP ratios have climbed from approximately 30 per cent in the 1970s to nearly 100 per cent by 2022, marking a three-fold increase in indebtedness.

Immediately following the Second World War, global indebtedness stood at around 100 per cent of global GDP. Over the ensuing three decades, as interest rates on public debt increased, countries reduced their debt burdens, resulting in a nearly 70 per cent decline in the global debt-to-GDP ratio. This was a period characterized by significant fiscal discipline and debt repayment.

This fiscal prudence was crucial. Had countries not reduced their debt levels, they would have faced substantially higher interest expenses because interest rates rose during the 1950s, 1960s, and 1970s. Interest rates peaked in the early 1980s, as Chapter 1 explained, and fell persistently for four decades. This extraordinary decline in interest rates made borrowing cheaper and encouraged governments to accumulate debt. The feasibility of this is explored further in Box 3.1, which explains the interplay between interest rates, debt levels, and the burden of interest payments.

To understand the historical drivers of public debt, it is insightful to examine the experiences of two countries with long-term data: the US and the UK. These case studies shed light on why governments historically incurred debt and how these practices have evolved.

## Box 3.1  Interest rate, debt levels, and debt burden

Consider a scenario where you earn USD 100,000 annually and carry a debt equivalent to 40 per cent of your income, amounting to USD 40,000. At an interest rate of 14 per cent, you pay USD 5,600 annually in interest. This represents 5.6 per cent of your income.

Now, imagine if your debt were to more than double, increasing to USD 100,000, which matches your annual income, but the interest rate drops to 2 per cent. In this case, your annual interest payments would decrease significantly to just USD 2,000, equivalent to 2 per cent of your income. The lower interest rate means that servicing a larger debt is less burdensome.

These figures mirror trends observed in advanced economies over recent decades. In the early 1980s, global debt levels were approximately 40 per cent of global GDP, as depicted in Figure 3.1. This debt level corresponds to 40 per cent of total income in a country, akin to the example above, with an interest rate of 14 per cent.

By 2022, global debt levels had risen to nearly 100 per cent of global GDP, but the interest rate had plummeted to 2 per cent. The substantial decline in interest rates outweighed the increase in debt levels, resulting in reduced debt-servicing costs relative to income.

## 3.2 Historical Debt Developments: Two Case Studies—The US and the UK

### 3.2.1 The US

The US boasts data series on public debt levels dating back over two centuries to 1800, owing to the extensive data-collection efforts of the International Monetary Fund (IMF). Figure 3.2 illustrates the evolution of US public debt relative to US GDP since that time.

Figure 3.2 illustrates that the US in 2020 had reached its highest level of indebtedness to date. At the end of the Second World War, public debt was

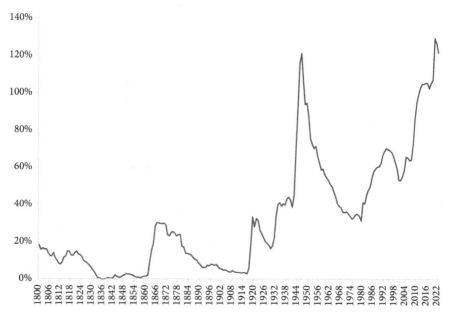

**Figure 3.2** US public debt relative to US GDP, 1800–2022.
*Data source:* IMF Historical Public Debt Database.

comparable to 2020 levels, though marginally lower. By 2020, US public debt had exceeded 120 per cent of GDP, marking an unprecedented accumulation in the nation's two-century history.

Figure 3.2 also identifies six significant episodes that drove substantial increases in US public debt:

- The American Civil War (1860–1865), escalating US public debt from approximately 0 per cent to around 40 per cent of US GDP.
- The First World War, where public debt similarly surged from nearly 0 per cent to about 40 per cent of GDP.
- The Great Depression in the early 1930s, witnessing a doubling of debt from roughly 20 per cent to 40 per cent of GDP.
- The Second World War, the peak until recently, when debt soared from around 40 per cent to approximately 120 per cent of GDP.
- The global financial crisis of 2008, seeing debt rise from about 60 per cent to nearly 100 per cent of GDP.
- The Covid-19 pandemic in 2020, pushing debt levels from around 100 per cent to about 130 per cent of GDP.

Changes in debt levels primarily stem from shifts in the primary budget balance, which is the government budget balance excluding interest expenses (other key drivers of debt levels include interest rates and economic growth, as explained in Box 3.2). Figure 3.3 illustrates the US government's primary budget balance as a percentage of US GDP since 1800.

The public deficit resulting from the Second World War was staggering, exceeding 25 per cent of GDP in 1943. Coupled with deficits from other war years (i.e. 1940, 1941, and 1942), this caused US public indebtedness to rise from around 40 per cent of GDP to 120 per cent. Similar patterns of increased indebtedness occurred during the First World War, with a deficit of 17 per cent of GDP, and the American Civil War spanning 1860–1865, where deficits approached 10 per cent of GDP.

Prior to 1970, during peacetime intervals without wars, the US government generally ran budget surpluses. This disciplined approach helped reduce national indebtedness during those periods.

However, since the 1970s, there has been a fundamental shift in fiscal prudence. Fiscal policy has increasingly focused on supporting economic activity and funding welfare services such as unemployment benefits and child support. This means that except for brief intervals, the US government

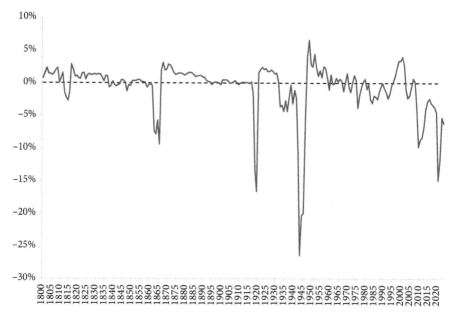

**Figure 3.3** Deficit/surplus on US government primary budget balance, 1800–2023.
*Data source:* IMF Public Finance in Modern History Database.

has consistently run deficits since the late 1960s/early 1970s, leading to a substantial accumulation of public debt. Major economic shocks such as the global financial crisis of 2008 and the Covid-19 pandemic in 2020 exacerbated this trend, prompting expansive fiscal policies aimed at stimulating economic recovery. In 2009, the deficit peaked at around 10 per cent of GDP, while the deficit resulting from the pandemic surged to 15 per cent of GDP in 2020, but even outside those periods, the US government ran sizeable deficits. For instance, during 2016–2020, a period with steady economic growth and low unemployment, the deficit stood between 3 per cent and 5 per cent of GDP every year, marking historically large deficits outside war years.

This significant shift in fiscal discipline is underscored by historical data: from 1800 to 1931, the US budget operated in surplus for approximately 75 per cent of the time, totalling 100 years out of 132. In stark contrast, from 1931 to 2022, surpluses occurred only 12 years, representing approximately 13 per cent of the time.

Several factors contribute to this shift, but an important one is the sustained decline in interest rates over the past four decades. Lower interest rates have facilitated easier financing of increasingly large debt burdens. Figure 3.4 visually illustrates this relationship, depicting the US debt-to-GDP ratio (from Figure 3.2) alongside US interest rates over the past two centuries.

Debt and Low Interest Rates 51

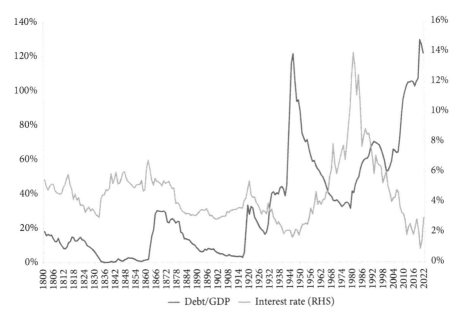

**Figure 3.4** US public debt relative to US GDP, 1800–2022.
*Data source:* IMF Historical Public Debt Database and Schmelzing (2020).

The figure prominently displays the prolonged and large decline in interest rates from 1980 to 2020, alongside a striking increase in indebtedness over the same period. Lower interest rates made borrowing more affordable, enabling the US government to sustain deficits without immediate fiscal strain. Conversely, from 1945 to 1980, rising interest rates prompted the US government to reduce its debt-to-GDP ratio. Had it not done so, the result would have been an escalation in interest costs because interest rates rose after the Second World War. Higher interest rates from 1945 to 1980 promoted fiscal discipline.

### Box 3.2 The dynamics of the debt-to-GDP ratio

The evolution of public debt as a fraction of GDP follows the formula:

$$\Delta(debt/GDP) = (R - G) \times (debt/GDP) - primary\ budget\ balance$$

where $\Delta(debt/GDP)$ represents the change in the public debt-to-GDP ratio from one period to the next, R denotes the interest rate paid on public debt, and G represents the growth rate of GDP. The primary budget balance signifies the deficit or surplus on the government budget before accounting for interest expenses.

## 52 How Low Interest Rates Change the World

This formula indicates that, assuming other factors remain constant, the ratio of debt to GDP will increase under the following conditions:

- $R>G$: When the interest rate exceeds the rate of economic growth.
- The primary budget balance is negative; that is, when there is a deficit on the primary government budget.

Therefore, the ratio of debt to GDP is primarily influenced by the following three key factors:

- Interest rate level: lower interest rates result in less rapid growth of indebtedness, all else being equal.
- Economic growth: higher growth rates in economic activity will decrease the debt-to-GDP ratio, assuming other factors remain unchanged.
- Government budget balance: a higher deficit on the primary government budget leads to an increase in debt, all else being equal.

### 3.2.2 The UK

The UK possesses historical data on budget balances and public debt levels dating back more than three centuries to 1690. Figure 3.5 depicts the deficit on the UK government budget as a percentage of UK GDP while Figure 3.6 shows UK public debt relative to GDP.

Figure 3.5 corroborates the narrative established by Figure 3.3 for the US, highlighting that government deficits in the UK historically stemmed predominantly from wartime expenditures. Significant budget shortfalls occurred during pivotal conflicts such as the Spanish Inquisition War in the early 1700s, the Seven Years' War around 1750, the Napoleonic Wars in the early 1800s, and, notably, during the First and Second World Wars. For instance, during the First World War, the deficit peaked at over 50 per cent of GDP in 1917.

The trajectory of UK public debt relative to GDP (Figure 3.6) reflects these wartime influences. Throughout the 1700s, the debt-to-GDP ratio surged with each conflict, marked by notable spikes. Post the Napoleonic Wars in the early 19th century, efforts were made to reduce public indebtedness. The First and Second World Wars precipitated substantial increases in public debt.

Since the Second World War, the UK has not engaged in major military conflicts. Despite this, akin to the US government, the UK government has consistently operated at a deficit nearly every year since the late

Debt and Low Interest Rates 53

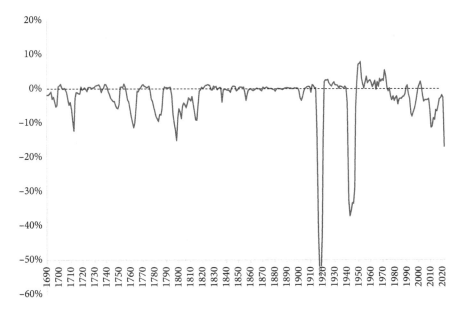

**Figure 3.5** UK government budget balance relative to GDP.
*Data source:* Bank of England.

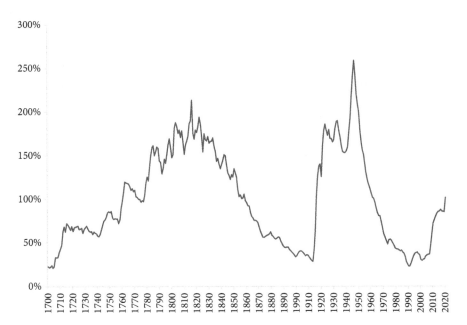

**Figure 3.6** UK government public debt relative to GDP.
*Data source:* Bank of England.

1970s. Deficits widened notably following significant economic shocks like the global financial crisis and the Covid-19 pandemic. This shift in the underlying causes of public deficits and debt accumulation is significant: historically, governments focused on debt reduction during peacetime, whereas in contemporary times, peacetime has seen governments accumulating debt.

## 3.3 Pros and Cons Regarding Public Debt

Public debt represents a collective responsibility and thus occupies a unique role in debt discussions. While low interest rates facilitate increased borrowing capacity, governments are not obligated to borrow. Therefore, the question arises: why have governments accumulated such substantial debt in recent peacetime periods, and what challenges accompany this accumulation? This section briefly presents arguments both for and against public debt, followed by an exploration of the implications of excessive debt.

### 3.3.1 Pros of Public Debt

Several arguments in favour of public borrowing can be made.

**Enhancement of long-term growth:** Borrowing to finance public investments that promote sustainable, long-term economic growth—such as in education, research, infrastructure, and transitioning to a sustainable economy—constitutes a sound rationale. If the returns on such investments outweigh borrowing costs, these expenditures are supported by robust economic arguments.

**Mitigation of economic downturns:** During recessions, governments can intervene to mitigate adverse economic impacts. By providing unemployment benefits to those displaced during recessions, governments bolster demand for goods and services, thereby attenuating the economic downturn. Such measures also prevent as severe a decline in employment levels, which is crucial as prolonged unemployment can erode workforce skills, complicating re-entry into the labour market. By curbing job losses during recessions, governments reduce the likelihood of long-term structural economic challenges.

The efficacy of such interventions is often evaluated in terms of the 'fiscal multiplier', which measures the increase in economic activity for each dollar injected into the economy by the government. While economists debate the exact size of the fiscal multiplier, there is consensus that it is larger during recessions than expansions (see, e.g. Auerbach and Gorodnichenko, 2011, 2012), underscoring the case for borrowing during economic downturns.

**Provision of a safe asset:** Public debt issued by safe-haven countries is considered a safe asset by investors. Countries with AAA credit ratings are deemed reliable borrowers who consistently honour their obligations. Some investors prefer safe assets for the security they offer over higher-yielding, riskier investments. Governments of such safe-haven countries may have a strategic advantage in providing these secure assets to meet investor demand.

**Provision of national security:** Historically, governments borrowed primarily to fund national security needs during wars or natural disasters. Ensuring national security remains a fundamental rationale for public debt issuance.

Thus, there are compelling reasons for governments to borrow. However, borrowing is not without costs. High levels of government debt incur significant expenses, as explained next.

## 3.3.2 Cons

**Limitations on governments' manoeuvrability arise from the necessity to service debt:** Borrowers must pay interest on their loans and eventually repay them, which places a strain on government budgets. When funds are allocated to debt servicing, they are unavailable for other critical areas such as education and healthcare, thereby constraining fiscal flexibility.

Governments have the option to raise taxes to fund expenditures and service debt. However, there is a limit to how much revenue can be generated from taxes, as higher tax rates can dampen economic activity. When a significant portion of income is collected in taxes, individuals may lose motivation to exert extra effort.

Confronted with high debt-servicing costs resulting from elevated debt levels and limited capacity to raise taxes, governments may opt to reduce expenditures. Yet, this course of action can be politically challenging, as voters may oppose austerity measures. Furthermore, cutting government spending, such as through layoffs of public workers, reduces income, diminishes consumer demand, and thereby negatively impacts overall economic activity.

Navigating these challenges involves trade-offs. In situations where government expenditures and tax rates are low, augmenting expenditures with slightly higher taxes can stimulate economic growth. Conversely, if expenditures and taxes are already high, further increases could stifle economic

## 56   How Low Interest Rates Change the World

activity. Economists refer to the 'Laffer curve', which illustrates that at low tax levels, raising taxes may increase total tax revenues, but at high tax levels, further increases could decrease revenues due to decreased incentives for economic activity (Wanniski, 1978).

**High levels of debt pose risks of sovereign debt crises:** When debt reaches unsustainable levels and a government cannot or will not raise taxes or cut expenditures, it may default on its debt obligations. This scenario deters investors from lending new funds to the government, leading to higher interest rates on new loans and further restricting fiscal flexibility. In extreme cases, investors may refuse to lend altogether, leaving the government facing a budget shortfall and forced to implement severe austerity measures or default on its debt, triggering severe economic repercussions.[1]

History is rife with examples of costly sovereign debt crises. Box 3.3 describes the Greek debt crisis of 2012 to illustrate how a sovereign debt crisis might unfold and its consequences. The crisis resulted in substantial losses for investors, posed a significant threat to the stability of the Eurozone, and proved costly for the Greek economy and society, with adverse impacts on income levels, increased unemployment, and social unrest, underscoring the profound consequences of unsustainable public debt levels.

## Box 3.3  The Greek sovereign debt crisis of 2012

The Greek debt crisis began in 2009, following the global financial crisis of 2008–2009. Greece, like other nations, experienced a severe economic downturn due to the financial crisis. In 2009, the newly elected government revealed that the previous administration had misrepresented the country's finances, disclosing a public deficit nearly twice as large as originally reported, amounting to close to 15 per cent of GDP. Subsequently, Greek public debt surged dramatically, climbing from around 100 per cent of GDP in 2008 to nearly 170 per cent of GDP by 2011, as depicted in Figure 3.7.

Investors became increasingly concerned about the sustainability of Greece's deficit and debt trajectory. Consequently, they hesitated to extend new loans to Greece unless they were compensated for the perceived risk. This caution led to a sharp increase in the yield on Greek government bonds, soaring to nearly 40 per cent by 2012, as depicted in Figure 3.8.

---

[1] Farah-Yacoub, Luckner, and Reinhart (2024) present comprehensive evidence on the repercussions of sovereign defaults over the past two centuries. According to their findings, 'sovereign defaults lead to significant adverse economic outcomes, with defaulting economies falling behind their counterparts by a cumulative 8.5 per cent of GDP per capita within three years of default. Moreover, output per capita remains nearly 20 per cent below that of non-defaulting peers after a decade. Based on the trajectory of the health, nutrition, and poverty indicators we study, we assess that the social costs of sovereign default are significant, broad-based, and long lived'.

Debt and Low Interest Rates 57

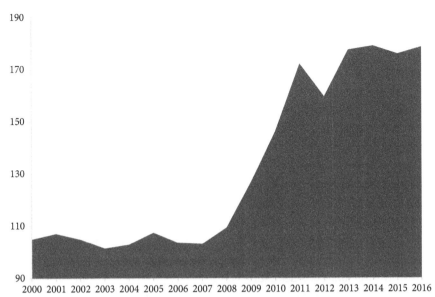

**Figure 3.7** Greek public debt relative to Greek GDP, 2000–2016.
*Data source:* European Union Database: Macro-economic indicators—indebtedness.

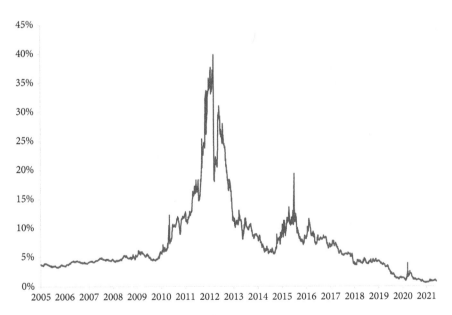

**Figure 3.8** Yield on Greek sovereign debt.
*Data source:* Datastream via Refinitiv.

## 58    How Low Interest Rates Change the World

The situation became untenable. Greece was unable to sustain its expiring debt obligations at such exorbitant interest rates. Essentially, Greece was on the brink of bankruptcy. The debt had ballooned to unsustainable levels, and the yields were unbearable.

However, Greece, as a member of the Eurozone, posed a critical challenge. Euro-area governments feared that Greece's difficulties could lead to its exit from the euro area, potentially reintroducing a national currency. Such a scenario would undermine the stability of the Eurozone: if countries could freely enter and exit the euro, was it truly a common currency or merely a fixed exchange rate regime?

In response, euro-area governments, alongside the European Central Bank (ECB) and the IMF, intervened to assist Greece. This coalition, known as the 'troika', provided substantial loans to Greece. In exchange, Greece committed to implementing rigorous fiscal reforms and austerity measures. These included pension reforms, tax hikes, public expenditure reductions, and other measures aimed at stabilizing public finances. Additionally, a restructuring of Greek debt was negotiated with private investors, who agreed to exchange existing bonds for new ones worth approximately 75 per cent less—a move that constituted the largest sovereign default ever.

While these measures stabilized the Greek situation, they came at a steep cost. Greek GDP contracted by 25 per cent, unemployment soared, salaries were cut, and pensions were reduced, exacting a heavy toll on Greek citizens. This episode underscored the profound consequences of excessive public debt.

Today, the Greek economy has improved, and investors are once again willing to lend Greece money at low interest rates, as illustrated in Figure 3.8. The remedy ultimately worked, but the sacrifices made were considerable.

---

**Reduce economic growth and crowd out private investments:** The interest rate that the government pays on its debt affects other interest rates in the economy, including the rates firms pay on their loans and households pay on their mortgages. For instance, Figure 3.9 illustrates the yield on US government debt alongside the yield on US corporate bonds, while Figure 3.10 illustrate yield on government bonds and mortgage bonds.

Yields on government bonds and corporate bonds are closely linked, as also discussed in Chapter 1. Since government bond yields set a minimum level for corporate and mortgage bond yields, yields on corporate bonds, both for highly rated and lower-rated investment-grade bonds (Figure 3.9), rise when government bond yields rise, and the same goes for mortgage rates (Figure 3.10).

**Figure 3.9** Yields on 10-year US Treasuries together with AAA-rated corporate bonds and BAA-rated corporate bonds, 1953–2023.
*Source:* FRED of St. Louis Fed.

**Figure 3.10** Yields on 10-year US Treasuries together with yields on 30-year mortgage bonds, 1971–2023.
*Data source:* FRED of St. Louis Fed.

## 60 How Low Interest Rates Change the World

When a corporation assesses an investment opportunity—such as new technology or equipment—it compares the potential returns with the financing costs. Higher financing costs decrease the likelihood that the investment will yield sufficient returns to justify the expenditure.

Similarly, higher mortgage rates increase the cost of borrowing for home purchases, reducing demand for housing among households.

In summary, elevated government debt may reduce private sector investment by raising interest rates (both government and corporate), thereby limiting economic growth. This phenomenon is known as 'crowding out', where increased government spending competes with and diminishes private sector investment and housing demand. Consequently, more resources are allocated to public investments at the expense of private sector opportunities.

## 3.4 When Is a Lot Too Much?

Sovereigns have increasingly accrued debt over the past four decades, aided by continuously declining interest rates. As discussed earlier, borrowing can yield benefits, but it is not without costs. So, when does debt become excessive?

Researchers have attempted to pinpoint thresholds beyond which public debt begins to adversely impact economic activity. Economists Kenneth Rogoff and Carmen Reinhart (2011) conducted widely referenced research suggesting that economic growth tends to decline once a country's public debt exceeds 90 per cent of its GDP. Figure 3.11 depicts the key findings of Rogoff and Reinhart's study.

Reinhart and Rogoff gathered data from numerous advanced and emerging countries, comparing debt levels relative to GDP with real GDP growth rates. Figure 3.11 illustrates that there is no discernible relationship between economic growth and debt levels until debt reaches around 90 per cent of GDP. The data shows that annual real growth remains around 3 per cent per annum (on average across countries) whether public debt is below 30 per cent of GDP, between 30 per cent and 60 per cent of GDP, or 60–90 per cent of GDP. However, in countries where debt exceeds 90 per cent of GDP, GDP growth slows significantly to around 1.5 per cent, half the rate observed in low-debt countries.

Other researchers have also identified a negative correlation between public debt and economic growth once a certain threshold is surpassed. For instance, Cecchetti, Mohanty, and Zampolli (2011) found a threshold of 85 per cent debt-to-GDP for advanced countries, while Patillo, Poirson, and

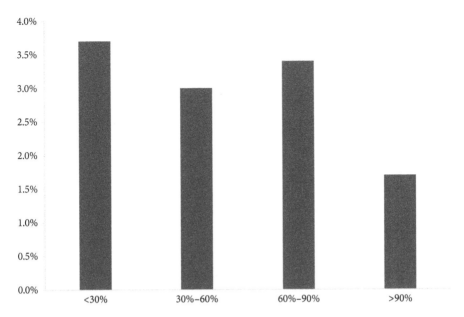

**Figure 3.11** Economic growth and debt-to-GDP ratios. Averages across many countries.
*Source:* Reinhart and Rogoff (2011).

Ricci (2002) identified a threshold of 35–40 per cent for emerging economies. On the other hand, some studies, such as Chudik et al. (2017), have found no clear threshold effects.

In conclusion, while there are benefits and drawbacks associated with public debt, excessive debt can reach a point where the disadvantages outweigh the advantages. However, pinpointing when this happens is challenging as it depends on various economic factors such as interest rates, economic cycles (recession vs. expansion), and political willingness to manage debt-servicing costs. Whether sovereign debt levels today are still far from, or getting dangerously close to, a point where costs outweigh benefits remains uncertain. Chapter 12 will delve deeper into the outlook for public debt.

## 3.5 Private Debt

The private sector comprises households and corporations. Similar to public debt, the levels of debt among households and corporations have risen dramatically over the past decades, as illustrated in Figures 3.12 and 3.13.

While private debt levels have been going up since 1950, the pace at which the private sector has accumulated debt has varied over time. Household

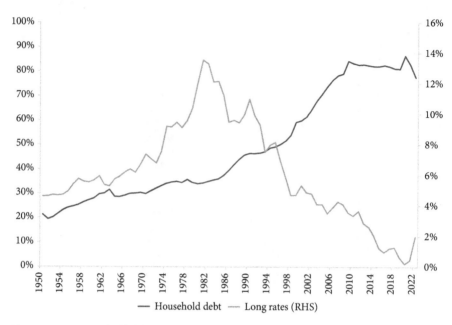

**Figure 3.12** Household debt relative to GDP, together with the nominal yield on long-term government bonds, 1950–2022. Averages across 17 advanced economies.

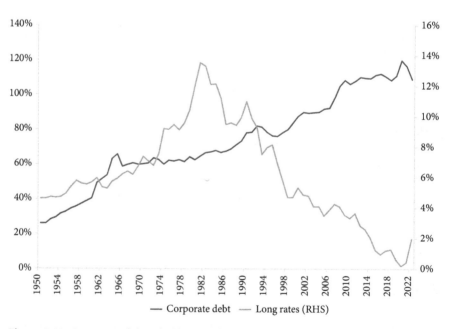

**Figure 3.13** Corporate debt relative to GDP, together with the nominal yield on long-term government bonds, 1950–2022. Averages across 17 advanced economies.
*Data source:* IMF Global Debt Database.

debt, for instance, notably escalated during the period coinciding with declining interest rates and up until the financial crisis. From a household-debt-to-GDP ratio of around 20 per cent in 1950, it has surged to approximately 80 per cent today, with a substantial increase occurring particularly between 1980 and 2008, when it climbed from 30 per cent to 80 per cent (Figure 3.12). The persistent decline in interest rates over the past four decades from 1980 to 2020 appears to have encouraged households to accumulate debt at a particularly high pace.

Similarly, the corporate sector has seen a significant rise in indebtedness, primarily from 1980 to 2008, a period marked by falling interest rates. Corporate debt as a percentage of GDP nearly doubled during this period, increasing from approximately 60 per cent in 1980 to about 110 per cent in 2008.

Since the financial crisis, both corporate debt and household indebtedness have plateaued. This contrasts sharply with the trajectory of public indebtedness post-crisis and during the Covid-19 pandemic, as illustrated in Figure 3.1. These divergent debt trends underscore the distinct roles of public and private debt.

Following the financial crisis in 2008–2009 and the pandemic in 2020, governments worldwide borrowed extensively to mitigate economic downturns through relief packages and stabilization measures. In contrast, private sector borrowing typically serves to fund consumption and investment. The financial crisis significantly disrupted the availability of private credit, influencing both the demand for credit from private entities and its supply from financial institutions. Moreover, firms and households became more cautious about taking on excessive debt, a lesson underscored by the crisis. Hence, since the financial crisis, private debt levels have not increased overall.

## 3.5.1 Pros and Cons of Other Private Debt

Many of the pros and cons associated with public debt also apply to private debt, whether it is household or corporate. For instance, debt can serve to smooth out temporary income fluctuations. If an individual loses their job and experiences a drop in income, they may take out a loan to maintain consumption levels. Similarly, corporations facing a temporary downturn in demand for their goods or services might borrow to bridge the gap. This mirrors the government's role in borrowing to stabilize economic activity during recessions.

**64** How Low Interest Rates Change the World

Another similarity lies in the fact that high levels of debt for individuals or corporations typically result in lenders demanding risk compensation, pushing up interest rates.

However, there are also crucial distinctions between public and private indebtedness. Firstly, governments have the unique ability to raise taxes, a power not available to private individuals or corporations. Additionally, some governments can issue safe assets, which has implications for financial markets and investor behaviour.

Perhaps most significantly, the government's actions regarding its debt position can have broad societal impacts. When a government borrows extensively, it can raise the overall interest rate level in the economy, as discussed in the previous section. This, in turn, affects the interest rates paid by households and firms. Moreover, sovereign debt crises can reverberate across large segments of society, posing challenges for businesses and households alike, as explained in Section 3.3. Conversely, the borrowing decisions of individual households or firms typically do not influence the economy-wide interest rate level.[2]

## 3.6 Total Debt

Let us tie everything together. Governments borrow, households borrow, and corporations borrow. The accumulation of all this borrowing constitutes the total debt in society. Since the 1980s, as interest rates began to decline, societies have experienced a significant increase in indebtedness, as illustrated in Figure 3.14. The figure illustrates the average ratio of total debt to GDP across 17 advanced economies.

Figure 3.14 underscores a critical trend: global indebtedness has surged since the 1980s, paralleling the decline in global interest rates.

In the early 1950s, total global debt hovered around 125 per cent of global GDP. By 1980, it had risen slightly, to about 135 per cent of GDP. From the 1980s onward, however, interest rates began a persistent decline, continuing for four decades. Societies responded by accumulating debt. Today, global indebtedness stands near 300 per cent of global GDP.

The dynamics of debt for households, corporations, and governments have varied across different phases due to their distinct needs, as explained in preceding sections of this chapter: households and corporations borrow

---

[2] When many or all households and all firms borrow too much, it might affect the overall level of interest rate, but not when a single firm or household does so.

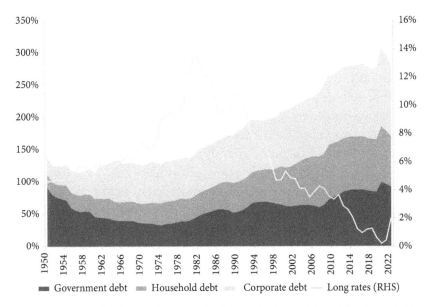

**Figure 3.14** Total debt (i.e. the sum of public and private debt, with private debt split into household and corporate debt, area graph and left-hand scale), as a fraction of GDP, together with the nominal yield on long-term government bonds (right-hand scale), 1950–2022. Average across 17 advanced economies.
*Data source:* IMF Global Debt Database.

to finance investments and consumption, while governments also provide economic support during crises. After the financial crisis, for instance, corporations and households restrained borrowing, whereas governments ramped it up.

If interest rates remain low, the debt surge may not pose an immediate issue. However, a rise in interest rates could make servicing all this debt challenging. Part IV of this book will revisit the outlook for interest rates and explore the potential consequences for global indebtedness.

## 3.7 Checklist

This chapter has illustrated the following key points:

- Sovereigns today are significantly more indebted than they were four decades ago, a trend largely driven by falling interest rates.
- Before the 1930s, nations typically balanced their budgets or ran surpluses during peacetime but resorted to heavy borrowing during wars.
- Since the 1970s in particular, advanced economies have increasingly borrowed for purposes other than wartime expenditures. Despite the

absence of major conflicts, public debt levels in advanced economies have surged since the early 1980s.

- Excessive public debt levels can lead to adverse consequences. High debt often results in higher interest rates, as investors demand greater compensation for the increased risk associated with lending to highly indebted borrowers. This, in turn, can dampen investments, consumption, and overall economic activity. Sovereign debt crises, where lenders refuse to extend further credit and sovereign defaults occur, are also risks associated with high levels of public debt.

- Academic research indicates that public debt does not necessarily hinder economic growth when it is at low levels. However, once debt levels become too high, economic growth tends to suffer. The threshold is not fixed, though, but varies based on economic conditions.

- Similarly, the private sector, including households and corporations, has also accumulated substantial amounts of debt since the early 1980s.

- Total societal debt—that is, the aggregate debt of sovereigns, households, and corporations—has risen significantly since the early 1980s. In the early 1980s, total global debt across advanced economies stood at approximately 135 per cent of GDP. Today, it stands close to 300 per cent.

- Ultimately, the decline in interest rates since the early 1980s has incentivized governments, households, and corporations alike to borrow more. This has resulted in societies being much more indebted today compared to four decades ago. Part IV of the book will revisit the potential future consequences of all this debt.

# 4

# House Prices and Low Interest Rates

Most people looking for a home need a mortgage to finance it. The interest rate on the mortgage is the most significant determinant of its cost. Over the past four decades, declining interest rates have reduced the cost of borrowing for home purchases. This has increased the demand for housing, leading to higher house prices.

This chapter explores the relationship between falling interest rates from 1980 to 2020 and house prices during the same period. It concludes that declining rates have significantly contributed to rising house prices in many countries. Academic research supports the finding that lower interest rates drive up house prices.

While interest rates have a primary influence on house prices, other factors play a role as well, such as income levels and access to credit. As people's incomes rise, they can afford more expensive homes, driving up housing demand. Similarly, easier access to mortgage credit increases demand for housing, which in turn pushes real estate prices higher. Demographic changes and shifting preferences, such as the increasing desire to live in cities, also influence house prices.

These factors are interrelated in equilibrium. Interest rates impact economic growth, which in turn affects interest rates. Similarly, interest rates influence credit availability, and the demand and supply of credit affect interest rates. To clarify the discussion, this chapter addresses these factors individually.

The chapter notes that house prices increased during the 1950s, 1960s, and 1970s despite rising interest rates. This was due to strong economic growth, which enabled more people to demand more homes.

The chapter also highlights a close relationship between outstanding mortgage credit and house prices over the past 150 years but recognizes that determining the chain of causality is challenging. Does mortgage credit increase because the value of collateral (house prices) rises, allowing people to borrow more against their homes? Or has easier access to credit led to higher house prices?

*How Low Interest Rates Change the World.* Jesper Rangvid, Oxford University Press. © Jesper Rangvid (2025).
DOI: 10.1093/9780198946410.003.0005

# 68 How Low Interest Rates Change the World

While acknowledging that interest rates are not the sole reason why house prices change, the chapter's main conclusion is that interest rates play a crucial role in house price movements and that falling rates in recent decades have contributed significantly to housing booms in many countries.

## 4.1 Developments in House Prices

House prices have increased in many, if not most, advanced countries in recent decades. Prices rose significantly before the global financial crisis of 2008. In fact, rising house prices and mortgage credit were key factors contributing to the crisis (see chapter 12 in Rangvid, 2021). Importantly, house prices had been rising since the early 1980s, with an acceleration in the years leading up to the crisis. After the housing-market slump following the financial crisis, house prices in many countries resumed their upward trend.

House prices have not always been on the rise. Over the past 150 years, house price trends can be divided into two distinct phases. Until the Second World War, house prices remained relatively stable in real terms; that is, after taking account of inflation. In contrast, since the mid-twentieth century, house prices have been on a consistent upward trajectory. This marks a significant and structural shift in the dynamics of global real house prices, first documented by Knoll, Schularick, and Steger (2017).

Figure 4.1 shows the developments in real house prices across 17 advanced economies since 1870.[1] When real house prices rise, house prices rise faster than the overall price level in the economy.

Figure 4.1 illustrates that global real house prices experienced several fluctuations from 1870 to 1950, but eventually stood at the same level in 1950 as in 1870: rising from 1870 to 1900, falling significantly during the First World War, rising again post-war, and then declining during the Second World War, ultimately bringing the real value of a house in 1950 back to its 1870 level.

However, from the mid-twentieth century onwards, house prices have consistently increased in real terms. Today, house prices are nearly five times higher in real terms than they were in 1950. This massive increase indicates a shift in the dynamics driving house prices over the past seven decades compared to the previous eight decades.

---

[1] A house price index generally tracks the sales prices of both new and existing dwellings, representing the overall trend in the cost of a typical home within a country. Real house prices are adjusted for general inflation by deflating nominal house prices using the consumer price index.

**Figure 4.1** Average of real house prices across 17 advanced economies, 1870–2022. Real house prices are normalized to '1' in 1870.
*Data source:* Jordà-Schularick-Taylor Macrohistory Database and OECD.

House prices have not risen steadily every year since 1950. There have been fluctuations. For example, house prices declined from the mid-1970s to the early 1980s due to significantly increased interest rates and uncertain economic conditions. Conversely, house prices surged dramatically before the financial crisis of 2008 and fell sharply afterwards. On average, though, over the period, house prices have trended upwards.

Global real house prices have grown by 1.1 per cent per year on average over the last 150 years. From 1870 to 1950, real house prices grew by an average of 0.4 per cent per year. Since 1950, the growth rate has been around five times higher, at 2.1 per cent per year.

Wars and their aftermaths have had a detrimental impact on house prices. From their peak in 1911 to their trough in 1920, global house prices fell by almost 50 per cent, a consequence of the First World War. During the Second World War, house prices declined by nearly 25 per cent.

Conversely, periods of financial excess have seen significant house price booms. For instance, house prices rose by 75 per cent during the decade leading up to the financial crisis of 2008. Similarly, the decade preceding the 1929 Wall Street Crash saw house price increases of nearly 60 per cent.

### 4.1.1 Different Countries

While house prices in most countries remained relatively stable until 1950 and have generally increased since then, the patterns of these developments vary across nations, as shown in Figure 4.2. The figure presents the cumulative percentage change in house prices for 16 different countries since 1980. All countries, except Italy and Japan, have experienced increases in real house prices.

In some countries, the rise has been dramatic. For instance, by 2022, real house prices in Norway were nearly 300 per cent above their 1980 levels. In most countries, real house prices have more than doubled.

## 4.2 Interest Rates and House Prices

This book explores the consequences of low interest rates. Has the fall in interest rates over the past decades contributed to the rise in house prices?

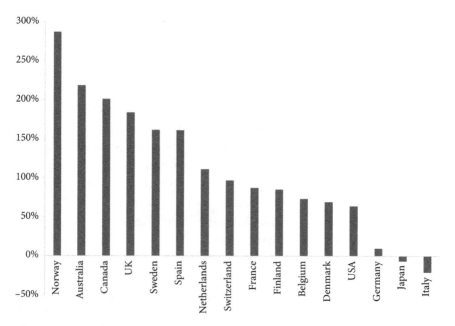

**Figure 4.2** Cumulative increases in real house prices, 1980–2022.
*Data source:* Jordà-Schularick-Taylor Macrohistory Database and OECD.

## 4.2.1 Why Should Falling Interest Rates Push Up House Prices?

It is natural to expect interest rates to influence house prices. Buying a house is the largest investment most households make, requiring substantial borrowing. Interest rates directly affect the cost of servicing a mortgage loan. Given a household's income and other expenses, lower interest rates enable households to afford larger loans. When households can borrow more, they are willing to pay more for houses, increasing housing demand and driving up house prices.

House prices are determined by the demand and supply of houses. Low interest rates might also affect housing supply. Investors can borrow more to finance new construction when interest rates are low, increasing the supply of houses. An increased supply of houses, all else being equal, tends to lower house prices.

This supply effect assumes that the primary constraint on house building is financing costs. In some cases, the constraint might be the availability of land. If many people want to live in a specific area, there might not be enough space for new construction, regardless of financing costs.

Urbanization, a major global trend identified by the United Nations (2020), has driven demand for housing in big cities.[2] In such areas, it may not be possible to build enough new houses to meet demand quickly, even when interest rates are low. Thus, lower interest rates likely affect demand more than supply, pushing up house prices.

From an asset pricing perspective, a house is both a place to live and an investment; that is, a house is both a consumption good (we buy a house to live in, i.e. to consume the housing services our house provides) and an investment good (we can save in our house). There are few similar cases.[3]

Buying a house today and selling it later for a higher price generates a return on investment. The value of an asset is determined by its discounted cash flow, a concept explained further in the next chapter. The cash flows from a house are the housing services it provides, equivalent to the rent saved by owning instead of renting. The present value of a house is found

---

[2] The United Nations (2020, p. 73) writes: 'A little more than 55 per cent of people now live in urban areas, about 4.2 billion people in 2018. In 1950, about 30 per cent or over 750 million people lived in urban areas, while two thirds remained in rural areas. By 2050, about 68 per cent or two thirds of the global population will have settled in urban areas, bringing the population there to about 6.7 billion.'

[3] Art, wine, cars, etc. are sometimes also viewed as providing both a savings and consumption purpose. For most people, these reflect considerably smaller investments than that of buying a house.

by discounting these future cash flows. The interest rate influences the discount rate; when interest rates are low, the discount rate tends to be low too, increasing the discounted value of cash flows and thus the value of the house. Therefore, falling interest rates increase house values.

### 4.2.2 Do Interest Rates Affect House Prices?

The previous section explained several mechanisms through which interest rates affect house prices. This section and the next discuss the empirical evidence.

Figures 4.3 to 4.5 present global house price developments since 1870 alongside long-term interest rate trends, divided into three subperiods: 1870–1945 (Figure 4.3), 1946–1979 (Figure 4.4), and 1980–2002 (Figure 4.5). In each figure, the interest rate is plotted on the right-hand axis, which is inverted, with lower values at the top. This inversion makes it easier to illustrate the relationship between house prices and interest rates.

Figure 4.3 shows that prior to 1945, interest rates and real house prices moved inversely in sync. When interest rates fell, such as during the periods 1870–1900 and 1920–1935, house prices rose. Conversely, as interest rates rose during the 1900–1920 and 1935–1940 periods, house prices fell. Over the seven-decade period from 1870 to 1945, house prices systematically

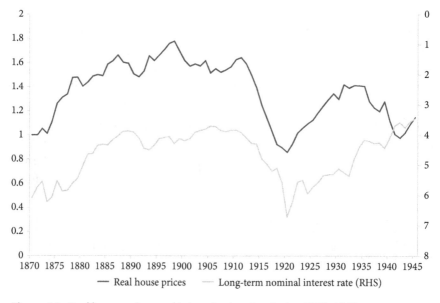

**Figure 4.3** Real house prices and interest rate rates during 1870–1945.

House Prices and Low Interest Rates 73

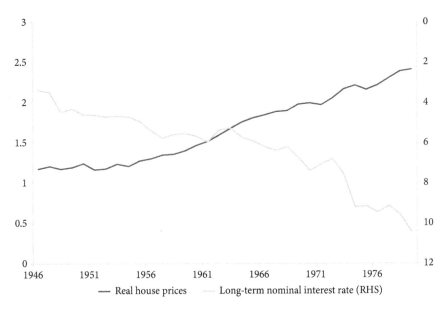

**Figure 4.4** Real house prices and interest rate rates during 1946–1979.

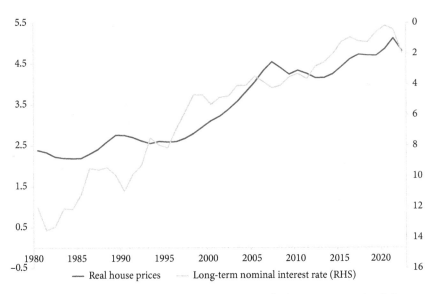

**Figure 4.5** Real house prices and interest rate rates during 1980–2022. In all three figures, interest rates are on the right-hand scale, and the scale is inverted.
*Data source for all three figures:* Jordà-Schularick-Taylor Macrohistory Database, OECD, and FRED St. Louis Database.

followed interest rate movements: higher interest rates led to lower house prices, and lower interest rates led to higher house prices.

A similar pattern has emerged over the past four decades (1980–2022), as depicted in Figure 4.5. During this period, real house prices and interest rates have been negatively correlated. Since 1980, falling interest rates have coincided with rising house prices, particularly from 1995 onwards. Also, the rise in interest rates during 2022 led to a decrease in house prices.

Academic research confirms that house prices react negatively to interest rate changes; that is, they rise when interest rates fall. Jorda, Schularik, and Taylor (2015) find that house prices fall following increases in interest rates in long-term international datasets. Sutton, Mihaljek, and Subelyte (2017), studying a shorter period, also find that falling interest rates lead to higher house prices. Kuttner (2014) surveys the literature, reporting that interest rate increases negatively affect house prices but also emphasizing the importance of credit availability in influencing house prices.

The figures in this chapter relate nominal interest rates and real house process. Why do nominal interest rates correlate with real house prices? Research such as that by Brunnermeier and Julliard (2008) indicates that individuals often experience money illusion when making decisions about purchasing homes. Money illusion refers to the tendency to interpret changes in nominal interest rates as changes in real interest rates, leading people to react to nominal rate fluctuations even when real rates remain unchanged. Consequently, when nominal interest rates decrease, there is a tendency for increased borrowing and subsequently higher house prices, even if real interest rates have not changed.

So, there is ample evidence that interest rates affect house prices negatively. However, the interest rate is not the only factor affecting house prices. Consider the 1946–1980 period (Figure 4.4), for instance. During this period, both interest rates and house prices were increasing; that is, house prices continued to climb throughout the 1950s, 1960s, and 1970s despite rising interest rates.

## 4.3 Economic Growth and Credit Growth

While interest rates are arguably a significant determinant of house prices, how much people can spend on housing, which is largely determined by their income, itself influenced by economic growth, also matters. Additionally, credit availability is crucial since most people need to borrow to buy a house.

## 4.3.1 Economic Growth

A booming economy leads to rising incomes. When economic activity is expanding, payrolls increase, allowing people to afford more expensive homes. Consequently, we would expect house prices to rise during periods of economic prosperity. Conversely, during economic downturns, house prices tend to fall.

Figure 4.6 illustrates the annual growth in global real per capita gross domestic product (GDP) across 17 advanced economies, broken down into different subperiods:

- The period before the First World War.
- The period between the First and Second World Wars.
- The period between the Second World War and 1973.
- The period after 1973.

Figure 4.6 reveals that global real economic growth has hovered around 2 per cent per annum for most of the last 150 years. Before the First World War, global economic growth averaged around 2 per cent annually, a rate that was

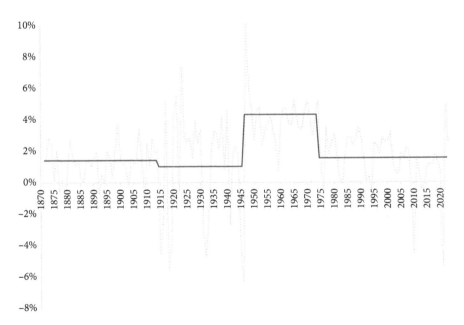

**Figure 4.6** Annual growth in global (average across 17 advanced economies) real per capita GDP and average growth across subperiods.
*Data source:* Jordà-Schularick-Taylor Macrohistory Database and FRED St. Louis Database.

maintained, though slightly lower, during the interwar years. Over the past four decades, growth has also been around 2 per cent per annum.

However, from 1945 to 1973, global growth was exceptionally high, averaging more than 4 per cent annually. This was more than twice that of the other periods. The 1950s and 1960s were marked by the establishment of welfare states in many countries, increased female labour market participation, and the post-Second World War recovery, all contributing to making this a period of economic prosperity. This booming period ended with the first oil price shock in 1973.

With nations becoming substantially wealthier, it is reasonable to assume that people desired larger and better homes. It seems plausible that during the 1950s and 1960s, people were willing to pay more for houses despite rising interest rates, driven by the era's economic prosperity.

Conversely, during periods of 'normal' economic growth of around 2 per cent per year, interest rate movements have a significant impact on house prices. This explains the negative relationship between global interest rates and global house prices outside the booming 1950s and 1960s. In particular, the large and persistent fall in interest rates over recent decades has contributed significantly to the consistent rise in house prices during this period.

## 4.3.2 Mortgage Debt

Most people need to borrow to purchase a house. The accessibility of financing plays a crucial role in determining house prices. When more individuals can secure loans, demand for housing typically rises, which, all else being equal, leads to higher house prices.

Figure 4.7 illustrates the close relationship between global house prices and global mortgage debt relative to global GDP.

In Figure 4.7, real house prices are normalized to '1' in 1870, following the convention of previous figures in this chapter. At that time, mortgage debt accounted for less than 10 per cent of GDP across the studied countries.

From 1870 to 1900, both house prices and mortgage debt as a fraction of GDP increased. However, during the First World War, both indicators declined, only to rebound during the interwar years, before falling again during the Second World War.

Since 1945, the trajectory has been notably different. Both house prices and the ratio of mortgage debt to GDP have shown persistent growth.

**Figure 4.7** Real house prices and mortgage debt as a fraction of GDP; mortgage debt refers to right-hand axis, 1870–2020. Averages across 16 countries.
*Data source:* Jordà-Schularick-Taylor Macrohistory Database and FRED St. Louis Database.

Across countries, there is a discernible relationship between the growth in mortgage debt and house prices. For instance, Norway and the UK have seen a rapid expansion in credit alongside substantial rises in house prices, whereas countries like Germany and the US have observed more modest growth in both house prices and the use of mortgage credit.

While Figure 4.7 demonstrates a strong correlation between mortgage credit and house prices, it does not provide insight into causality; that is, whether (i) rising house prices drive mortgage debt or (ii) expanding mortgage debt drives house prices. High house price growth could stimulate credit expansion, as banks are more willing to lend against higher collateral values. Conversely, increased mortgage availability could fuel house price growth by boosting housing demand.

Jorda, Schularick, and Taylor (2015, 2016) have conducted an extensive analysis on this issue using the same dataset as referenced in this chapter. Their findings suggest that mortgage credit plays a role in driving house prices. They argue that housing policies since 1945 have encouraged banks to issue more mortgage debt, with relaxed financial regulations enabling expanded mortgage lending. Additionally, Bordo and Landon-Lane (2013) note in their research that bank credit has been a significant factor influencing house price trends in international data since 1920.

## 4.4 Checklist

This chapter has demonstrated several key points:

- Falling interest rates over the last four decades have significantly contributed to the substantial increase in house prices across many advanced economies during this period.
- Throughout the past 150 years, higher interest rates have generally had a negative impact on house prices.
- Economic growth and the availability of credit also influence house prices.
- The period following the Second World War until the 1970s saw exceptionally strong economic growth in advanced economies, which helped drive up house prices despite rising interest rates.
- There is a strong correlation between growth in mortgage credit and house prices. This relationship is logical since higher house prices often necessitate larger loans. However, it is also plausible that easier access to credit fuels demand for housing, thereby pushing prices higher. Academic research suggests this latter direction of causality.
- Overall, while various factors contribute to fluctuations in house prices, the persistent decline in interest rates from 1980 to 2020 has been a significant factor driving the surge in house prices across many advanced economies during this period.

# 5

# Stock Markets and Low Interest Rates

Owning a stock means having a stake in a company's ownership. Interest rates influence the value of stocks through various channels:

- Interest rates influence the discount rate used to calculate the present value of future profits of the company.
- They impact economic activity, affecting the demand for products or services of companies and their profitability given production costs.
- Interest rates influence the return investors can expect from bonds. When investing in stocks and bonds, investors compare their return characteristics. Changes in demands for stocks and bonds affect their valuations.

All three channels suggest a negative relationship between interest rates and stock values. Persistent declines in interest rates, such as those observed from 1980 to 2020, should boost stock values.

This chapter explores the impact of interest rates on stock markets. The main conclusion is that the prolonged decline in interest rates over recent decades has coincided with a substantial increase in stock prices and stock market valuations.

Current valuations serve as a signal for future stock performance. All else being equal, higher prices paid for stocks today imply lower future returns from stock investments. Similarly, the chapter briefly discusses how falling interest rates affect bond returns. As interest rates drop, bond prices rise, thereby reducing future bond returns.

Combined with the previous chapter, which discussed the impact of interest rates on real estate prices, it becomes evident that falling interest rates from 1980 to 2020 led to elevated valuations of stocks, bonds, and housing. These dynamics have broader implications for inequality and financial risks, topics addressed in subsequent chapters. Also, while investors benefitted as interest rates fell, lower interest rates indicate lower prospective returns. Investing in stocks, bonds, or housing today faces different challenges than it did four decades ago when interest rates were much higher.

*How Low Interest Rates Change the World.* Jesper Rangvid, Oxford University Press. © Jesper Rangvid (2025).
DOI: 10.1093/9780198946410.003.0006

## 5.1 How Interest Rates Affect Stock Markets

Owning a stock means owning a part of a company, entitling shareholders to certain rights such as influencing corporate strategy through voting at general assemblies, and receiving a share of the company's profits commensurate with their ownership stake. These profits can either be reinvested in the company as retained earnings to fund future growth or distributed to shareholders as dividends or through share buybacks.

The value of a stock hinges on the anticipated future profits of the company. Since profits cannot remain within the company indefinitely, they are eventually distributed as dividends. Therefore, the value of a company today is determined by the expected future earnings, which dictate future dividends. This means that the value of a company today is determined by discounting future cash flows to investors to their present value:[1]

*Value of stock today = Expected value of future cash flows/Discount rate*

The discount rate reflects the return investors require to compensate for the time value of money and the risks associated with the investment. In essence, the discount rate converts future expected cash flows into current values.

Interest rates exert influence over both components on the right-hand side of this equation: they affect the expected profitability of the corporation by influencing economic conditions, consumer demand, and the cost of debt, and they also impact the discount rate.

### 5.1.1 Interest Rate and Earnings

Interest rates play a pivotal role in shaping a corporation's earnings, and thus ultimately the cash flows to investors, through their impact on both costs and revenues.

Firstly, lower interest rates directly reduce the cost of debt financing for firms. When interest expenses decrease, all else being equal, the firm's net earnings increase. This improvement in profitability tends to enhance the overall value of the firm and consequently supports higher stock prices.

---

[1] We must discount cash flows in one year back one year, cash flows in two years must be discounted back two years, etc. The full formula thus looks like: Value today = (Cash flow in one year)/(1+r) + (Cash flow in two years)/(1+r)$^2$ + (Cash flow in three years)/(1+r)$^3$ + ....

Additionally, lower interest rates stimulate economic activity by reducing borrowing costs for households and businesses alike. This typically leads to increased borrowing, higher consumer spending, and expanded investment by firms. As demand for goods and services rises in response to increased economic activity, firms can sell more products, thereby boosting their revenues and ultimately their profits. This positive effect on corporate earnings also contributes to higher stock prices.

## 5.1.2 Interest Rate and Discount Rate

To determine the value of a firm and its stock price, future cash flows are discounted back to their present value using a discount rate, typically expressed as:

$$Discount\ rate = 1 + r = 1 + risk\text{-}free\ interest\ rate + risk\ premium$$

The risk-free interest rate represents the economy-wide rate that applies uniformly to all firms. This rate directly influences the discount rate used to calculate the present value of future cash flows, thereby impacting the overall value of the company.

A lower risk-free interest rate results in a lower discount rate, given the risk premium. This means that future cash flows are valued more highly today, increasing the value of the firm. Consequently, when interest rates decline, the value of all firms in the stock market tends to rise, boosting the aggregate stock market.

In contrast to the risk-free rate, the risk premium is specific to each firm. It reflects the additional return investors demand for bearing the uncertainty or risk associated with investing in that particular company. Investors seek this premium because the outcome of their investment in a company is uncertain—profits could exceed expectations or fall short. This compensation ensures investors are adequately rewarded for the risk they bear beyond what a risk-free investment would yield.[2]

---

[2] This book focuses on analysing the aggregate stock market; therefore, detailed discussions of firm-specific risk premiums are beyond its scope. However, for reference, one commonly used model for determining firm-specific discount rates is the Capital Asset Pricing Model (CAPM). In the CAPM framework, an essential parameter is 'beta', which quantifies the relationship between the return of a firm's stock and the return of the overall stock market. Beta serves as a measure of the firm's relative riskiness compared to other firms within the broader market. When a firm's stock price tends to decline significantly when the overall market experiences downturns, its beta value is higher, indicating greater risk. This elevated risk profile leads to an increased risk premium that investors demand when considering investments in the firm.

### 5.1.3 Interest Rate and Aggregate Risk Premium

The aggregate stock market encompasses all individual firms trading within it. Investing in the aggregate stock market, such as through an index mutual fund, inherently carries risks. The aggregate risk premium of the stock market reflects the combined risk premiums of all individual firms, while cancelling out the unsystematic aspects of firms' riskiness. In financial terms, only aggregate systematic risk influences the market's risk premium.

The market risk premium is determined by the collective risk tolerance of investors. Theoretical models, such as those by Campbell and Cochrane (1999), suggest that aggregate risk tolerance depends on broader economic conditions. For instance, during recessions when job security is a concern, investors generally have lower risk tolerance. The interest rate plays a crucial role here by affecting aggregate demand in the economy and influencing the likelihood of entering a recession. Consequently, interest rates can impact aggregate risk premiums. A decrease in interest rates will typically lower the aggregate risk premium by improving broader economic conditions, potentially boosting the stock market.

In summary, changes in interest rates can affect the stock market value through various mechanisms. A reduction in the risk-free interest rate typically increases corporate profits, reduces the risk-free component of the discount rate used for valuing future cash flows, and diminishes the risk premium component of the discount rate.

Armed with insight into how interest rates can influence stock markets, let us turn to how the four-decade decline in interest rates from 1980 to 2020 impacted them.

## 5.2 Long-Term Evidence on the Global Relation between the Interest Rate and the Stock Market

Figure 5.1 illustrates the development of real stock prices across 16 advanced economies since 1900, alongside the global long-term nominal interest rate. Real stock prices are nominal stock prices adjusted for inflation using consumer price indices. Nominal stock prices are broad stock price indices from the different countries.

Global stock markets significantly declined during the First World War, followed by a flat trajectory with slight positive tendencies from 1920 to 1950. There was notable growth in the real value of stocks in the 1950s and 1960s, offset by a decline in the early 1970s due to substantial inflation

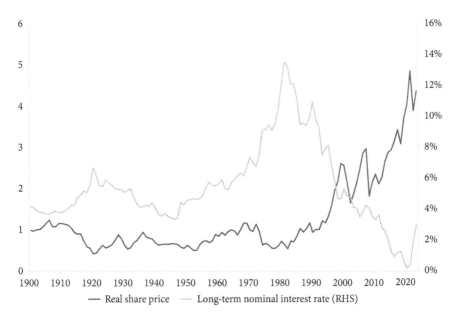

**Figure 5.1** Average of real stock prices across 16 advanced economies, normalized to "1" in 1900, together with the average of nominal long-term interest rates in advanced economies, 1900–2023. The interest rate refers to the right-hand scale (RHS).
*Data source:* Jordà-Schularick-Taylor Macrohistory Database and Datastream via Refinitiv.

eroding stocks' real value. Although nominal stock prices increased during this 1900–1980 period, they did not outpace consumer prices, resulting in minimal real stock price growth by 1980 compared to 1900.

Since the 1980s, however, the landscape has markedly changed. Real stock prices have embarked on an unprecedented upward trajectory, persisting for four decades. Remarkably, this sustained increase in stock prices aligns closely with the prolonged decline in interest rates over the same period. It suggests that falling interest rates have been a pivotal factor driving stock prices to historic highs during recent decades.

Interest rates and real stock prices have exhibited a predominantly negative correlation over the past 130 years, Figure 5.1 reveals. Between 1905 and 1920, interest rates rose while real stock prices fell. Conversely, from 1920 to 1940, interest rates declined, coinciding with rising stock markets. Since 1980, interest rates have consistently decreased, paralleling a continuous increase in stock prices.

An exception to this negative correlation occurred during the 1950s and 1960s, when stock prices rose despite rising interest rates. Readers may recall the analogous discussion from the previous chapter, which explored the correlation between house prices and interest rates. It was demonstrated in

Chapter 4 that house prices typically decline during periods of rising interest rates. This has been the case over the past 150 years, except during the prosperous 1950s and 1960s. This chapter reveals that the relationship between stock prices and interest rates mirrors that of house prices and interest rates; that is, stock prices have risen, like house prices, during periods when interest rates have fallen, except during the 1950s and 1960s.

Figure 5.2 compares the trends in real house prices and real stock prices over the past 130 years.

The overall movements in stock and house price over the past 130 years share similarities. Both house and stock prices experienced declines during the 1910s, followed by increases in the 1920s, and remained relatively stable through the 1930s and 1940s, before embarking on an upward trajectory. There are two notable periods where real house and real stock prices diverged: during the oil price shocks of the early 1970s and since the financial crisis of 2008. In the 1970s, the shocks led to high inflation rates that adversely affected stocks while real estate prices maintained their value. More recently, stock prices have surged considerably faster than house prices.

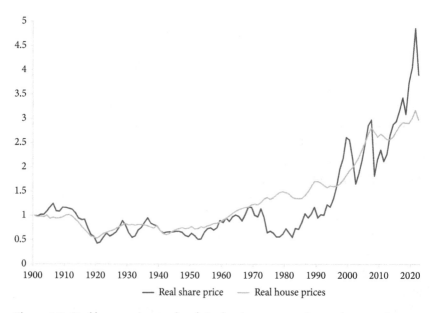

**Figure 5.2** Real house prices and real stock prices across advanced economies, normalized to "1" in 1900, 1900–2022.

*Data source:* Jordà-Schularick-Taylor Macrohistory Database, OECD, and Datastream via Refinitiv.

Stock prices are more volatile than house prices. This means they fall by more during setbacks, but also recover more rapidly from major downturns such as during the Great Depression in the early 1930s, the dot-com bubble of 2000, and the global financial crisis of 2008, where stocks experienced sharper declines but also quicker rebounds compared to house prices.

The previous chapter on house prices and interest rates discussed the divergence observed during the 1950s and 1960s from the general negative correlation between interest rates and house prices evident in other periods. Given the similar trends in stock and real estate prices, and considering that both are asset prices determined by discounted cash flows, it is reasonable to attribute the positive relationship between interest rates and stock prices during the 1950s and 1960s to the robust economic conditions of that era, like the previous chapter did for house prices. The economic expansion bolstered corporate earnings, thereby increasing cash flows for firms. This growth in earnings counterbalanced the effect of higher interest rates during the period.

## 5.3 Evidence from the US

While this book primarily focuses on global trends, examining specific markets for which we have more comprehensive data, such as the US stock market, can deepen our understanding of the link between interest rates and stock prices.

The US stock market holds special significance for several reasons. It boasts the world's largest stock market capitalization, the US economy remains the largest globally, and it serves as a leading stock market, influencing developments in other countries' stock markets. Moreover, Nobel Laureate Robert J. Shiller's extensive data collection efforts provide robust long-term data on US stock prices, earnings, and dividends since 1871. This data allows us not only to analyse how real share prices move in relation to interest rates over extended periods but also to assess whether the valuation of the stock market correlates with interest rates.

As discussed in Section 5.1, stock prices reflect investors' expectations of discounted future cash flows from firms. A high stock price suggests investors anticipate substantial future cash flows relative to the discount rate. A widely used metric is the price-to-earnings (P/E) ratio, which indicates how much investors are willing to pay for a company's earnings per share.

Earnings per share can be highly volatile, dropping significantly during recessions and surging in economic booms. For instance, the average earnings per share of major US firms in the S&P 500 plummeted from approximately USD 60 before the 2008 financial crisis to around USD 7 in the first quarter of 2009, marking an almost 90 per cent decline. In contrast, US GDP only contracted by less than 2 per cent over the same period. To provide a more stable measure of underlying earnings fundamentals, Robert Shiller introduced the Cyclical Adjusted Price Earnings Ratio (CAPE). CAPE smooths out earnings volatility by relating current stock prices to the average earnings over the past 10 years rather than just the most recent year. This metric has gained popularity as a gauge of the valuation of the US stock market.

Figure 5.3 visually represents CAPE for the aggregate US stock market, today represented by the S&P 500, in conjunction with the long-term US government bond yield since 1881, providing insights into how stock market valuations have responded historically to changes in interest rates.

To interpret Figure 5.3, let us consider the first observation of CAPE in January 1881. CAPE was approximately 18 at that time, indicating that the aggregate US stock market's share price in January 1881 was 18 times higher than the average earnings per share of the US stock market over the preceding 10 years.

The primary insight from Figure 5.3 is a negative relationship between the US long-term interest rate and the valuation of the US stock market,

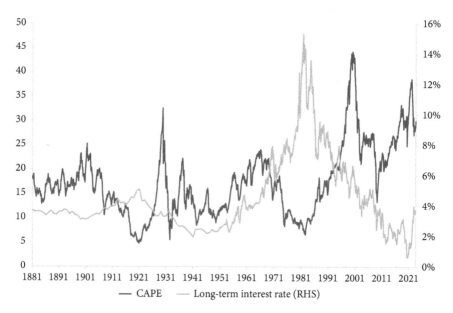

**Figure 5.3** CAPE and US long-term interest rate, 1881–2023.

*Data source*: Homepage of Robert J. Shiller.

with notable exceptions during the 1950s, 1960s, and immediately following the dot-com bubble around the turn of the millennium. Throughout other periods, CAPE tended to increase as interest rates declined. Particularly, the persistent decrease in interest rates over the past four decades has propelled the US stock market to unprecedented highs, only disrupted by the crash following the dot-com bubble in the early 2000s.

Earnings serve as the fundamental drivers of stock prices. However, earnings can be influenced by accounting regulations that may temporarily disconnect them from firms' underlying economic profitability. Siegel (2016) provides a comprehensive discussion on this issue concerning the US stock market and the CAPE ratio. While using a 10-year moving average of past earnings in CAPE helps mitigate the impact of accounting rules on stock valuation measures, it remains valuable to explore other valuation metrics to ensure the robustness of the insights from Figure 5.3.

Figure 5.4 presents the total market value of corporate equity in the US scaled by US GDP. This approach contrasts with CAPE in Figure 5.3, which scales stock prices with earnings. Rangvid (2006) examined the predictive power of these two measures for future US stock returns. His academic research demonstrated that scaling the stock market by GDP provides even more predictive information about future stock market returns, both domestically and internationally, compared to other metrics such as the price–dividend ratio (scaling stock prices by dividends) or the price–earnings ratio. Rangvid (2006) termed it the 'price–output ratio'. It is also known as the 'Buffet Indicator', as legendary investor Warren Buffett has used it to argue for or against the expensiveness of the US stock market. Figure 5.4 depicts the price–output ratio alongside the yield on long-dated US Treasuries. The time series tracking the value of all US corporate equity begins in 1953.

The narrative depicted in Figure 5.4 closely parallels that of global stock markets in Figure 5.1 and the CAPE of the US stock market in Figure 5.3. Generally, there exists a negative relationship between interest rates and the stock market's valuation: when interest rates decline, the value of the stock market tends to rise. The prolonged decline in rates since the early 1980s has notably propelled stock market valuations to unprecedented heights.

Also in Figure 5.4, the 1950s and 1960s deviate from this pattern due to robust economic growth, which pushed nominal yields higher and supported asset prices, as detailed in Chapter 4 and above. Conversely, following the dot-com bubble at the turn of the millennium, a substantial market correction occurred despite continued declines in interest rates.

The negative correlation between interest rates and the price–output ratio is underscored by recent events during the pandemic and its aftermath.

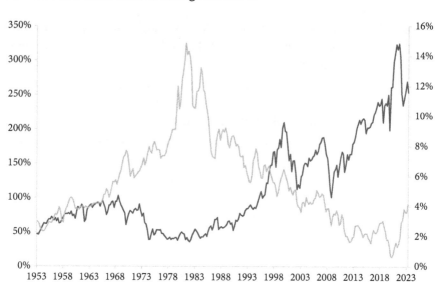

**Figure 5.4** Market value of US corporate equity relative to US GDP and US long-term Treasury yields, 1953–2024.

*Data source*: Fed St. Louis Database.

In early 2020, central banks swiftly lowered interest rates in response to the pandemic—a topic to be thoroughly discussed in Chapter 10—leading to a sharp increase in the stock market's valuation, as shown in Figure 5.4. Subsequently, as interest rates began to rise in 2022 amid post-pandemic inflation concerns, the valuation of the US stock market experienced a significant decline.

Figure 5.4 also highlights that US stocks reached an all-time high when interest rates hit bottom in 2020. At that time, total US corporate equity was valued at more than three times US GDP. Never in history had the stock market's valuation been so stretched, nor had interest rates been as low as they were just before the pandemic. In total, lower interest rates from 1980 to 2020 significantly lifted the value of the US stock market.

## 5.3.1 Interest Rates and Tax Expenses of US Corporations

Low interest rates contribute significantly to the rise in stock markets through several mechanisms, as discussed in Section 5.1. They reduce discount rates, thereby increasing the present value of future cash flows. They also bolster future economic activity, boosting expected cash flows. Additionally, low interest rates lower borrowing costs, reducing the cost of capital for companies. This, in turn, lowers interest expenses and enhances profits, thereby driving up stock prices.

In a notable 2023 paper, Federal Reserve economist Michael Smolyansky demonstrated that the decline in US interest rates over the past four decades has been a prime driver of the robust performance of the US stock market, as lower interest rates have reduced firms' interest costs, thereby accelerating their earnings growth. Furthermore, lower interest rates have decreased discount rates, leading to an expansion in price-to-earnings ratios.

Figure 5.5, based on Smolyansky's analysis, displays data illustrating the yield on 10-year US government bonds alongside the proportion of interest and tax expenditures in US corporate earnings. The figure demonstrates that lower interest rates have predictably reduced the portion of corporate profits allocated to interest payments. By alleviating debt-servicing costs for companies, lower interest rates have significantly boosted their profitability.

Smolyansky's findings indicate that lower interest rates (alongside reduced corporate taxes) can account for 40 per cent of earnings growth over the last four decades, and almost entirely explain the increase in price–earnings ratios.

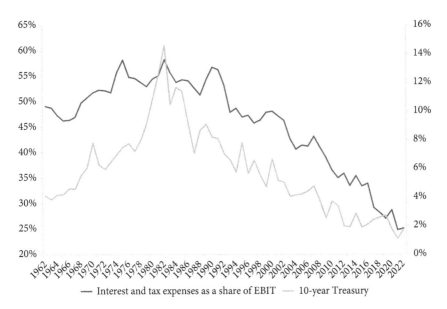

**Figure 5.5** Aggregate interest and tax expenses as a share of aggregate EBIT (Earnings Before Interest and Taxes) for S&P 500 non-financial firms. Annual data, 1962–2022.
*Source*: Smolyansky (2023).

## 5.4 Interest Rates and Expected Stock Market Returns

Valuation ratios serve an additional purpose: they indicate the future expected real returns from stocks. When investors are willing to pay high prices for stocks today, reflecting high valuations, there is a likelihood that prices may decrease in the future, resulting in lower expected returns. This foundational reasoning dates to Dow (1920) and gained rigorous academic attention through seminal works by Fama and French (1988) and Campbell and Shiller (1988a, 1988b). For a comprehensive exploration of how valuation ratios like the price–earnings ratio forecast future stock returns, see Rangvid (2021, chapter 18).

While the price–earnings ratio informs us about the premium investors are willing to pay for one dollar of earnings, its inverse, the earnings yield, tells us how much earnings investors receive per dollar invested in stocks. Consequently, the earnings yield serves as a predictor of future expected stock returns. Campbell and Shiller (1988a, 1988b) demonstrated how it and other valuation metrics effectively forecast real stock returns over extended periods. Typically, the earnings yield is considered a reliable estimate of the expected annual real stock return over the next decade. For example, an earnings yield of 5 per cent suggests that investors anticipate a real return of 5 per cent per annum from stocks over the coming decade.

Figures 5.6 and 5.7 illustrate the inverse of CAPE, known as CAPE-yield, alongside the long-term interest rate, segmented into two periods for clarity: 1881–1960 and 1960–2023.

Figure 5.6 illustrates a tenuous relationship between the CAPE-yield and long-term interest rates during the period from 1881 to 1960, whereas Figure 5.7 reveals a robust correlation between the two from 1960 to 2023.

Before 1960, while both the CAPE-yield and interest rates exhibited upward trends from 1900 to 1920 and declined from 1920 to 1940, their correlation was less pronounced compared to the post-1960 era.

On the other hand, the 1960s and 1970s saw a rise in both interest rates and the CAPE-yield. Notably, when US nominal interest rates peaked at 15 per cent in the early 1980s, the CAPE-yield followed suit. This alignment meant that investors anticipated real returns of 15 per cent per year from stocks over the following 10 years, mirroring the high returns offered by long-term US government bonds at the time.

Following their peak in 1980, long-term interest rates declined, leading to a corresponding decrease in expected returns from stocks. By the early 2020s, US stocks were anticipated to yield approximately 3 per cent annually in real terms over the subsequent decade.

Stock Markets and Low Interest Rates 91

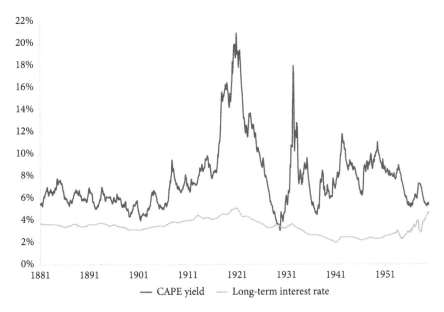

**Figure 5.6** CAPE-yield and US long-term interest rate, 1881–1960.

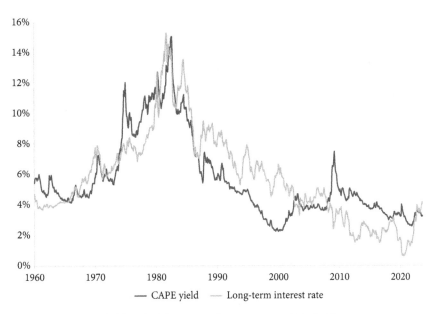

**Figure 5.7** CAPE-yield and US long-term interest rate, 1960–2023.
*Data source*: Homepage of Robert J. Shiller.

It is important to note that the earnings yield provides insights into expected real returns from stocks, reflecting returns adjusted for inflation. In contrast, government bond yields represent nominal returns. Economists have long debated why expected real returns from stocks should correlate with nominal bond returns. Fama (1981) and Bekaert and Engstrom (2010) explore various explanations for this relationship. One argument posits that expected inflation influences both nominal interest rates and real stock returns. The idea is that high inflation expectations might signal economic downturns, leading to lower expected real stock returns. Fama (1981) contends that inflation forecasts future economic activity, influencing real stock returns accordingly. Bekaert and Engstrom (2010) emphasize that periods of high inflation coincide with heightened uncertainty and risk aversion, which negatively impact real stock returns.

In summary, academic theories and empirical data over the past four decades indicate that low interest rates have diminished expected returns from stocks, underscoring the interconnectedness between nominal interest rates and stock market expectations.

## 5.5 Bond Returns

Interest rate movements exert significant influence over stock markets, as detailed in the preceding section of this chapter. Moreover, interest rates play a crucial role in shaping bond returns. While this relationship might appear self-evident, understanding the underlying mechanisms is relevant, not least for the following chapter that studies the relation between interest rates, asset prices (bond, stock, and other asset prices), and inequality. Before proceeding further, it is beneficial to introduce a few concepts, elaborated upon in Box 5.1.

### Box 5.1  Bond terminology

**Return from a bond investment**

The return from a bond investment comprises two components:

- The interest rate payments received from holding the bond.
- The change in the bond's price.

For example, if you purchase a bond with a 2 per cent coupon rate at USD 97 and sell it a year later when its price has risen to USD 98, the one-year return on your investment is calculated as:

$$2/97 + (98 - 97)/97 = 3.1\%.$$

## Yield to maturity

The yield to maturity, often referred to simply as 'yield' or 'effective interest rate', is the total return earned by purchasing a bond today and holding it until it matures at its par value, typically USD 100. This yield accounts for both any capital gain or loss and the periodic coupon payments received over its term.

Yield to maturity has been extensively used throughout this book.

The return from holding a bond until maturity equals the yield to maturity. However, if the bond is sold before maturity, the yield and the return typically differ due to fluctuations in the bond's market price relative to its par value.

## Bond price and yields

Bond prices and yields have an inverse relationship. When bond prices increase, yields decrease, and vice versa. For instance, consider a zero-coupon bond with a maturity value of USD 100 that was purchased for USD 96. The yield on this bond is calculated as: $100/96 - 1 = 4.2$ per cent.

More generally, for zero-coupon bonds held to maturity, the yield/return relationship is given by:

$$Yield = 100/Price - 1$$

Low yields reflect higher bond prices. Bond prices decline when yields rise.

## From yields to returns

In this section, we aim to describe how changes in yields affect bond investor returns, particularly amid the secular decline in yields observed over the past four decades. Historical databases typically record yield data rather than bond prices. How can we convert yields into bond returns?

As previously mentioned, bond returns encompass both coupon payments and capital gains or losses. Campbell, Lo, and MacKinlay (1996, chapter 10) illustrate how to convert a time series of yields into an approximate time series of returns, assuming a bond's duration. The approximate return can be calculated as:

$$Return \, (time \, t - 1 \, to \, time \, t) \approx yield \, (time \, t - 1) - duration \, x \, (yield \, (time \, t)$$
$$-yield \, (time \, t - 1))$$

The duration of a bond represents its weighted time to maturity and indicates the percentage change in bond price for a 1 per cent change in yield. Thus, the formula indicates that the return earned includes the yield from the previous period plus the capital gain over the investment period, with the capital gain calculated by multiplying the duration by the change in yield (with a negative sign due to the inverse yield–price relationship).

To calculate bond returns, assumptions about the bond's duration are necessary. This book primarily examines long-term bonds. The yield data typically represents the yield of the representative outstanding 10-year bond at the relevant point in time. Duration is shorter than maturity because duration is the weighted time to maturity. The duration used in calculations in this chapter assumes seven years. Conclusions are robust to this assumption.

---

Figure 5.8 illustrates bond returns and interest rates across 17 advanced economies since 1875. The methodology underlying the figure is as follows: for each country, bond returns are computed annually using the methodology outlined in Box 5.1. Subsequently, yearly averages are calculated across all countries. Given the high volatility of bond returns, the graph presents five-year moving averages to enhance readability.

Figure 5.8 highlights a clear positive relationship between yields and returns from bonds. When yields increase, bond returns also rise, and conversely so. Therefore, while rising interest rates can lead to capital losses on existing bonds, newly issued bonds at higher rates offer increased interest payments moving forward.

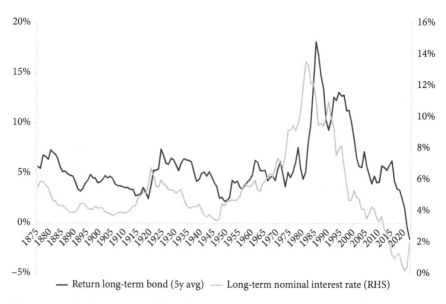

**Figure 5.8** Moving average of bond returns over past five years and yields on long-term government bonds (right-hand scale), annual cross-country averages, 1875–2023.

*Data source*: Jordà-Schularick-Taylor Macrohistory Database and FRED St. Louis Database.

Yields reached their peak around 1980. Following this period, bond investors enjoyed favourable conditions. Bonds were issued with relatively high coupons, and as yields declined, capital gains supplemented the high coupon payments. Bond returns were exceptionally strong in the early 1980s. Even though bond returns fell during the 1980s and 1990s, bonds still returned around 10 per cent per year.

Conversely, returns were notably low, even negative, in 2021–2022. This is due to bonds being issued with low coupon rates, resulting in minimal income from bond holdings. When interest rates subsequently rose during 2021 and 2022, causing capital losses, these losses surpassed the income generated by the bonds, resulting in negative returns.

## 5.6 Checklist

This chapter has established several key insights:

- Theoretical predictions indicate that stocks tend to perform well when yields decline, and conversely, they struggle when yields rise.
- Reduced funding costs and increased economic activity because of lower interest rates bolster firms' revenues and lift their stock prices, as do lower discount rates used to calculate the present value of firms' future cash flows.
- Empirical evidence strongly supports the notion that aggregate stock markets rise when yields fall. Over the past 150 years, except for the 1950s and 1960s, stocks have generally thrived during declining yield environments and suffered during rising yield periods.
- The 1950s and 1960s diverged from this pattern due to sustained economic growth that supported stocks despite rising yields.
- The prolonged decline in yields over the last four decades has driven stock market valuations to unprecedented levels.
- The earnings yield, inversely related to the stock-price-to-earnings ratio, serves as a gauge for expected future real stock returns. These expected returns have mirrored yield trends, declining alongside falling yields over recent decades.

# 6
# Inequality and Low Interest Rates

*Merriam-Webster* defines the 'essential meaning of inequality' as an 'unfair situation in which some people have more rights or better opportunities than other people'. This inequality can manifest in unequal outcomes, such as disparities in income or wealth distribution, or in unequal opportunities, such as differential access to education or the labour market.

This chapter explores how interest rates influence income and wealth inequality. Initially, it defines inequality and its typical measures, along with discussing reasons for tolerating some degree of inequality, for instance resulting from rewards to those who take risks that foster growth, while aiming to mitigate unjustifiable inequality, for instance arising from factors like unequal access to political power or market exploitation by corporations.

The chapter also examines trends in inequality over recent decades, revealing a general increase in both income and wealth inequality across most countries since the 1980s, contrasting with declining inequality trends in earlier periods.

The central thesis of the chapter correlates the trajectory of inequality with interest rate movements. It observes that inequality trends shifted around 1980, coinciding with changes in interest rate dynamics: a shift from rising interest rates and declining inequality before 1980 to falling interest rates and rising inequality thereafter. Empirical evidence suggests that the prolonged decline in interest rates over the past four decades has contributed significantly to the increase in inequality.

But why do falling interest rates exacerbate inequality? Lower interest rates, as detailed in previous chapters, elevate asset prices such as prices of stocks and real estate, thereby increasing wealth inequality. Additionally, lower interest rates decrease yields on bonds and other fixed-income investments, which are disproportionately held by lower-income groups reliant on interest income, thereby potentially increasing income inequality.

Monetary policy, particularly expansionary measures that lower interest rates to stimulate economic growth, can also affect inequality. While such

*How Low Interest Rates Change the World*. Jesper Rangvid, Oxford University Press. © Jesper Rangvid (2025).
DOI: 10.1093/9780198946410.003.0007

policies aim to curb unemployment during recessions, which impact lower-income groups disproportionately, they can also inadvertently contribute to rising inequality by boosting asset prices.

The chapter concludes by addressing whether higher wealth inequality resulting from falling interest rates significantly impacts consumption opportunities. The argument is that while falling interest rates may inflate asset values and widen wealth disparities on paper, the subsequent decline in expected future returns when interest rates fall can balance out these effects, thereby leaving people's relative consumption possibilities unaffected.

## 6.1 Is a Perfectly Equal Society Desirable? Or, When Is Inequality Too High?

Inequality in income and wealth refers to the disparity where some individuals earn more money and accumulate greater wealth than others. This discrepancy can be justified in economic terms under certain circumstances, while in others it cannot. When discussing inequality, the focus is less on striving for a perfectly equal society, where everyone earns and owns the same amount, and more on determining when inequality is excessive and when it arises from unjustifiable reasons.

Table 6.1 outlines the traditional arguments that defend why some individuals or corporations earn more than others, alongside reasons why inequality sometimes exists for unjustifiable economic reasons.

## 6.2 Trends in Inequality

This section introduces some key observations about global inequality trends. Figure 6.1 illustrates the distribution of wealth among individuals across 17 advanced economies in 2021.

Figure 6.1 underscores the significant disparity in wealth distribution. The figure is calculated as follows: for each country, individuals are ranked by their wealth, and the total national wealth is determined. Then, the share of total wealth held by the bottom 50 per cent of the population is calculated, as well as the share owned by the top 10 per cent with the most wealth.

Take the US as an example. The bottom 50 per cent of the population collectively owned just 1.5 per cent of the country's aggregate wealth in 2021. In stark contrast, the wealthiest 10 per cent controlled 70 per cent of the nation's total private wealth.

**Table 6.1** Arguments in favour of tolerating some degree of inequality and arguments against it

| Arguments why some people/firms might earn more than others | Market failures that cause inequality |
| --- | --- |
| **Reward for taking risks** | **Exploration of market power** |
| Society needs individuals willing to take risks to drive innovation, establish new businesses, and introduce new and better products and services. Initiating a new company or investing in innovative ventures involves significant uncertainty and risk. If these endeavours succeed—creating jobs and advancing society—the risk-takers deserve to be rewarded more than those who do not take these risks. | Some firms hold dominant positions in markets due to their innovative edge. However, there are instances where firms exploit their market power by setting excessively high prices, resulting in profits that exceed what would be fair compensation for their innovation. When firms maintain these high prices and are able to keep potential competitors out, consumers end up paying more than they should for products. Inequality stemming from the exploitation of market power represents a market failure. |
| **Reward for acquiring skills** | **Political and economic inequality** |
| Education plays a crucial role in equipping individuals with the competencies needed for complex tasks. However, pursuing education involves sacrifices, such as forgoing higher income during study years. To incentivize this investment in skills, individuals should be rewarded with higher salaries commensurate with their acquired expertise after completing their education. This ensures that the effort and time spent on acquiring skills are appropriately rewarded in the job market. | The concentration of economic power that translates into political influence represents another form of market failure. If large corporations have greater access to policymakers than smaller firms or workers, and if policy decisions are skewed in their favour, the owners of these firms benefit at the expense of others. This type of inequality arises when market dynamics fail to ensure equitable access to political decision-making processes and fair outcomes for all stakeholders. |
| **Incentivize hard work and effort** | |
| Efforts and diligence in work, regardless of the motivation behind them, should be acknowledged and compensated. Individuals who consistently go the extra mile contribute significantly to productivity and organizational success. Recognizing and rewarding hard work encourages continued dedication and a motivated workforce. | |

If wealth were distributed equally, each percentile group would hold a proportionate share—10 per cent of individuals would possess 10 per cent of wealth, 50 per cent would hold 50 per cent, and so forth. However, reality diverges sharply from this, demonstrating an unequal distribution of wealth.

This pattern extends beyond the US, although the US is one of the most unequal societies. Even in countries like Italy and The Netherlands, where

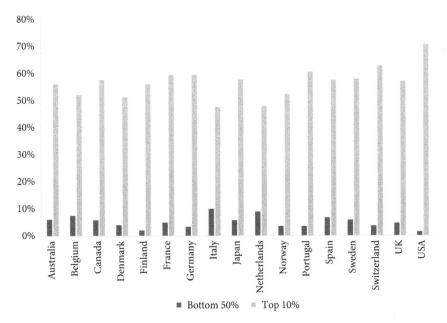

**Figure 6.1** Wealth distribution in different countries. Share of total wealth in a country accruing to the bottom 50 per cent and the top 10 per cent of the population, 2021.
*Data source:* World Inequality Database.

wealth inequality is comparatively lower, disparities remain significant. In Italy, for instance, the bottom 50 per cent of individuals own 10 per cent of private wealth, while the richest 10 per cent possess half of all wealth.

While wealth inequality tends to be more pronounced than income inequality, both are prevalent worldwide. Figure 6.2 illustrates income distribution across 17 advanced countries in 2021.

The top 10 per cent of earners in 2021 captured a disproportionate share of total income in their respective countries compared to the bottom 50 per cent of earners. Using the US as an example again, the highest-earning decile accounted for nearly half (45 per cent) of all income earned nationwide in 2021, whereas the bottom half collectively earned 13 per cent of the total income. This trend is consistent across various nations, even if the US is also topping the list when it comes to income inequality.

Wealth inequality, as depicted in Figure 6.1, surpasses income inequality (Figure 6.2). For instance, in the US, the wealthiest 10 per cent possessed 70 per cent of all wealth in 2021, while the top 10 per cent of earners claimed 45 per cent of total income. Conversely, the least wealthy 50 per cent held just 1.5 per cent of total wealth but the bottom 50 per cent of earners received 13 per cent of total income. Similar patterns are observed in other countries.

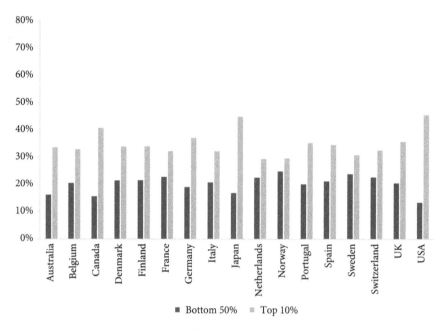

**Figure 6.2** Income distribution in different countries. Share of total income in a country accruing to the bottom 50 per cent and the top 10 per cent of the population, 2021.
*Data source:* World Inequality Database.

The disparity between wealth and income inequality arises from differing redistribution mechanisms. Income, to some extent, is redistributed through progressive tax systems and social benefits. High-income households typically face higher tax rates and fewer social benefits, while low-income households benefit from various forms of income subsidies and social welfare programmes. In contrast, wealth is less frequently redistributed, or at least to a lesser degree than income.

## 6.2.1 Inequality Has Increased during the Past Four Decades

Over the past four decades, inequality has increased across the globe. Figure 6.3 illustrates the proportion of total income earned by the top 10 per cent of earners in each country, comparing data from 1980 to 2021. The countries are ranked in descending order based on their 2021 income distribution.

Figure 6.3 illustrates that the top 10 per cent of earners claimed a larger share of total income in 2021 compared to their counterparts in 1980. For

Inequality and Low Interest Rates    101

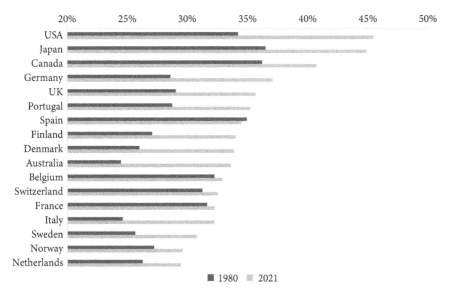

**Figure 6.3** Share of aggregate national income accruing to top 10 per cent income earnings in 1980 and 2021.
*Data source:* World Inequality Database.

instance, in the US, this group took home 35 per cent of aggregate income in 1980, whereas by 2021, they claimed 45 per cent.

By examining the fraction of total income earned by top earners as a measure of inequality, Figure 6.3 highlights that the US had the highest income disparity in 2021, followed by Japan. Conversely, The Netherlands exhibited the least unequal income distribution.

Figure 6.4 displays the trend from 1980 to 2021, detailing the fraction of aggregate income earned by the top 10 per cent in selected countries each year. This graph demonstrates a steady increase in inequality across most nations. Therefore, rising inequality has not been a result of a single event, such as a major recession, but rather a persistent trend unfolding over decades. This context is crucial to consider when examining the potential impact of interest rates on inequality in subsequent sections.

## 6.2.2  Inequality Fell Prior to 1980

The increase in inequality observed in most countries since 1980 does not simply extend a longer-term trend; rather, it marks a reversal. Before 1980, inequality decreased in many countries. This trend is evident in Figure 6.5, which charts the annual averages (across the 17 countries depicted in

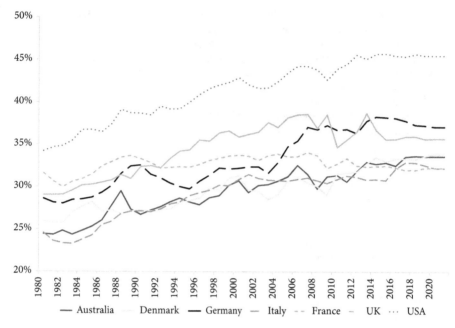

**Figure 6.4** Share of aggregate national income accruing to top 10 per cent income earners every year between 1980 and 2021.
*Data source:* World Inequality Database.

Figure 6.1) of total income garnered by the top 10 per cent earners since 1913, alongside the share of income held by the bottom 50 per cent of earners.[1]

Figure 6.5 illustrates that income inequality has been on the rise since 1980, whereas prior to that year, it either remained stagnant or decreased.

In more detail, between the First World War and the Second World War, inequality remained relatively stable across countries. On average, the top 10 per cent of earners received about 45 per cent of total income, while the bottom 50 per cent earned around 35 per cent.

Following the onset of the Second World War, inequality began to decrease. The share of total income held by top earners declined, while bottom earners saw their share increase. Although the Second World War had a significant impact on inequality, because wars destroy wealth, the trend of decreasing inequality persisted after the war, albeit at a slower pace. By 1945, the top

---

[1] During the early part of the sample period, data was available for only a limited number of countries. For example, in 1913, data was accessible for just three countries. By 1920, this expanded to six countries. From 1980 onward, data has been consistently available for all 17 countries. The pattern revealed by Figure 6.5 remains consistent when considering the median across countries, mitigating concerns about the representativeness of the sample.

**Figure 6.5** Share of aggregate national income accruing to top 10 per cent income earners and bottom 50 per cent income earners, 1913 through 2021. Average across 17 advanced economies.
*Data source:* World Inequality Database.

10 per cent earners accounted for 35 per cent of aggregate income across countries, which further reduced to 30 per cent by 1980.

While inequality focuses on income or wealth distribution among different groups of the population, it does not provide insights into how individual incomes or wealth levels themselves have evolved over time. To assess changes in the actual income levels of different segments of the population, one can examine trends in income levels. Figure 6.6, for instance, does this for the US, depicting the inflation-adjusted family incomes for the bottom 20 per cent and the top 5 per cent from 1966 to 2018, with data normalized to '1' in 1966.

Figure 6.6 reveals that the incomes of both the lowest- and highest-earning families grew at similar rates during the 1960s and 1970s. When high-earners experienced income gains, so did those with lower incomes. However, this pattern shifted after 1980. Since then, the incomes of the highest-earning families have surged considerably faster than those of the lowest-earning families. Remarkably, the real incomes of the bottom 20 per cent of US families have essentially stagnated since 1980—a span of six decades without improvement.

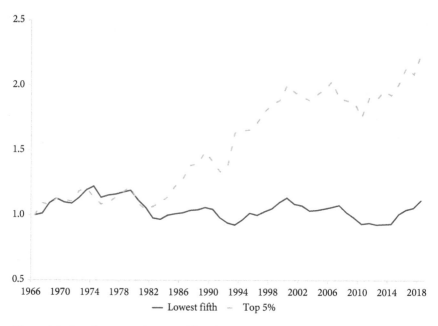

**Figure 6.6** Developments in US real family incomes. Real incomes for families in the bottom 20 per cent and the top 5 per cent of the income distribution, 1966–2018.
*Data source:* US Census Bureau.

In contrast, the purchasing power of the highest-earning families in 2016 was 150 per cent higher than it was in 1980. This stark contrast highlights the widening income inequality over time. The US Congressional Budget Office (CBO) underscored this trend in 2011: 'Between 1979 and 2007, income grew by: 275% for the top 1% of households; 65% for the next 19%; just under 40% for the next 60%; and 18% for the bottom 20%.'

## 6.3 Inequality and the Interest Rate

Given the observed trend of increasing inequality since the early 1980s and decreasing inequality before then, and considering earlier insights in this book that interest rates rose until 1980 and have fallen since, there is reason to explore the potential role of interest rates in shaping inequality trends. This section empirically examines the relationship between changes in interest rates and changes in inequality. Subsequently, the following section investigates the mechanisms through which interest rates influence inequality.

The correlation between interest rates and movements in inequality is robust. Figure 6.7 illustrates the share of total income accruing to the top 10 per cent earners across 17 advanced economies from 1980 to 2021. It juxtaposes this with the average long-term interest rates of these countries (shown on a vertical right-hand scale).

The correlation between interest rates and inequality developments since 1980 is striking. The rise in inequality across 17 advanced economies aligns closely with the decline in interest rates observed in these countries.

As highlighted in the previous section, the increase in inequality since 1980 marks a departure from the preceding trend of declining inequality. Figure 6.8 confirms that these long-term shifts in inequality correspond with movements in the interest rate over the same period.

The shift in inequality trends in 1980 corresponds with changes in interest rates. Before 1980, inequality was decreasing, paralleling a period of rising interest rates. However, in 1980, this pattern reversed: inequality began to rise while interest rates started to decline.

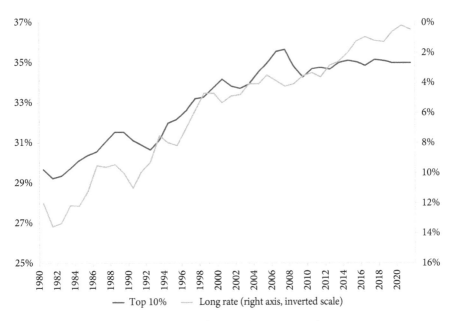

**Figure 6.7** Share of aggregate national pre-tax income accruing to top 10 per cent income earners and long-term interest rate. Averages across 17 advanced economies, 1980–2021.

*Data source:* World Inequality Database and Jordà-Schularick-Taylor Macrohistory Database.

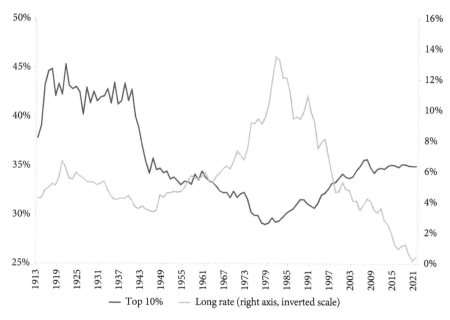

**Figure 6.8** Share of aggregate national pre-tax income accruing to top 10 per cent income earners and long-term interest rate. Averages across 17 advanced economies, 1913–2021.
*Data source:* World Inequality Database and www.macrohistory.net.

## 6.4 Why Do Interest Rates Affect Inequality?

A central point in this book is that the decline in interest rates since 1980 has driven up asset prices. Chapter 4 demonstrated how falling interest rates have fuelled housing booms, while Chapter 5 showed similar effects on stock prices.

Increased asset prices do not necessarily exacerbate inequality. For example, if both you and I own stocks and their value rises by the same percentage, we both benefit, maintaining the same wealth distribution between us, even if you hold more stocks than I do. If you own assets worth USD 200 and I own assets worth USD 100, and their value increases by 10 per cent, you gain USD 20 and I gain USD 10. Before the increase, you held 66.7 per cent of the total wealth (200/300), and I held 33.3 per cent. After the increase, the proportions remain unchanged: you hold 66.7 per cent (220/330), and I hold 33.3 per cent. Inequality has not changed.

However, inequality does increase if the assets you own yield higher returns than mine. For instance, if your assets appreciate by 10 per cent while mine appreciate by only 5 per cent, your share of total wealth increases from 66.7 per cent to 67.5 per cent, while mine decreases to 32.5 per cent.

Research, such as that by Campbell (2006) and Guiso and Sodini (2013), confirms that higher-income and wealthier individuals are more likely to invest in assets like stocks and real estate that on average deliver higher return than bonds and bank deposits that less affluent households hold more of. Wolff (2021) further supports this, showing that wealthier households predominantly invest in risky assets with higher long-run returns. Larsen, Munk, Nielsen, and Rangvid (2024) find similar patterns for real estate.

Chapter 5 highlighted that the persistent decline in interest rates since the early 1980s has significantly boosted stock market gains, primarily benefiting wealthy individuals who hold stocks. Conversely, low-income earners, who often rely mainly on labour income and may not own substantial assets, have seen lesser gains from rising asset prices (Owyang and Shell, 2016).

Changes in asset values not only impact wealth inequality but also income inequality because capital gains are considered part of income. As asset values rise, the income derived from these gains contributes to widening income inequality. This finding is supported by studies such as Berisha et al. (2018).

Greenwald et al. (2023) explore how falling interest rates amplify inequality in the US, emphasizing that affluent households benefit more from assets that appreciate with falling interest rates, while less wealthy households, who hold more deposits, do not see similar gains. Their research suggests that falling interest rates could explain up to 75 per cent of the rise in financial wealth inequality in the US over the past four decades.

## 6.4.1 Monetary Policy, Interest Rates, and Inequality

Central banks conduct monetary policy by adjusting the policy interest rates, which in turn influence other interest rates and asset prices. Therefore, an intriguing aspect of the debate on how interest rates affect inequality is whether monetary policy itself plays a role.

On the one hand, when central banks lower interest rates, stock markets tend to rise. Given that financial assets are predominantly held by the wealthy, this can exacerbate inequality, as described above. On the other hand, central banks reduce interest rates to stimulate economic activity and employment. This can mitigate inequality in several ways. First, the adverse effects of unemployment disproportionately affect low-income individuals (Schnabel, 2021; Ampudia et al., 2018; Bernanke, 2015). Thus, lowering interest rates to boost employment benefits low-income earners more, thereby reducing income inequality. Additionally, if lower-income individuals hold relatively more debt, which is supported by evidence (Schnabel, 2021; Ampudia et al., 2018; Bernanke, 2015), reducing central bank interest rates lowers their debt payments, further narrowing inequality.

The key question is whether a reduction in the monetary policy rate decreases inequality by stimulating overall demand in the economy, thereby increasing wages and creating jobs that primarily benefit low-income earners, or whether it increases inequality by inflating asset prices as discussed above.

Central banks argue that the former effect is dominant. They also argue that even if the latter effect were stronger, it is more important to prioritize job creation and reduce unemployment than to prevent a potential stock market boom. In essence, any resulting rise in inequality would be a justifiable trade-off if monetary policy helps more people secure employment. On the other hand, some criticize central banks for contributing to inequality; see, for instance, Weiss (2019).

When differing viewpoints exist, empirical evidence becomes crucial. Andersen et al. (2023), in a comprehensive study using detailed data on household-level impacts of monetary policy, conclude that expansionary monetary policy increases inequality. They find that while such policies boost salary income significantly for low-income households, other income components, such as business and stock market gains—concentrated among high-income households—grow even more. Moreover, they observe that high-income earners predominantly hold assets, which appreciate when monetary policy rates decrease. Additionally, debt burdens decline relatively more for high-income earners. Together, these factors contribute to an increase in inequality following a reduction in the monetary policy rate.

These findings contrast with those of Coibon et al. (2017) and Mumtaz and Theophilopoulou (2017), who assert that expansionary monetary policy reduces inequality. The discrepancies largely stem from Andersen et al. (2023) having access to more precise data, allowing for a clearer understanding of how monetary policy affects income and wealth disparities.

It is essential to note that this discussion on the impact of monetary policy focuses on short-term fluctuations within the business cycle—how monetary policy and interest rates influence inequality in the near term. Over the business cycle, central banks adjust interest rates to achieve their policy objectives, typically centred around maintaining low and stable inflation (Rangvid, 2021, chapters 10 and 11).

While short-term effects of monetary policy are interesting and important, they should not overshadow the broader context of the book's focus—analysing the long-term movements in interest rates and their enduring consequences. Specifically, the overarching theme remains the four-decade trend of declining interest rates coinciding with rising inequality.

## 6.5 Do Low Interest Rates Cause Rising Inequality or Does Rising Inequality Cause Low Interest Rates?

This chapter has focused on how lower interest rates, by boosting the prices of financial assets predominantly held by the wealthy, may exacerbate inequality. However, there is an opposing argument suggesting that the relationship between interest rates and inequality operates in reverse—namely, that inequality itself causes low interest rates. This hypothesis has been notably advanced by Mian, Straub, and Sufi (2021a, 2021b). Their reasoning is as follows: over the past four decades, increasing inequality has resulted in greater wealth accumulation among the already affluent. Wealthier households tend to save a larger portion of their income compared to less affluent households. Consequently, as inequality has risen, total savings in the economy have also increased. Since interest rates are influenced by the balance between savings and investments—see also Chapter 9—higher savings exert downward pressure on interest rates. Therefore, Mian, Straub, and Sufi argue that the surge in inequality explains the observed decline in interest rates from 1980 to 2020. They contend that lower interest rates do not drive increased inequality, contrary to conventional wisdom.

The idea that wealthier households save more has deep roots in economic theory dating back to pioneering works by Fisher (1930) and Keynes (1936), followed by contributions from Hicks (1950) and Pigou (1951). Empirical evidence supporting this notion was initially gathered by Duesenberry (1949) and Friedman (1957), and later verified by Carroll (1998) and Dynan, Skinner, and Zeldes (2004). The concept is straightforward: when individuals already possess sufficient income to meet their basic needs, additional income tends to be saved rather than spent (since these individuals already have what they desire). Conversely, individuals with lower incomes are more likely to spend additional income on necessities they previously could not afford. This principle is encapsulated in the idea of the marginal propensity to save, which reflects how much of an additional dollar of income is saved versus consumed.

Examining US data, Mian, Straub, and Sufi find that differences in savings rates are more pronounced across income groups than across age groups. For instance, the top 10 per cent of income earners have a marginal propensity to save of 0.21 (indicating they save 21 cents of each additional dollar of income), whereas the bottom 50 per cent have a marginal propensity to save of only 0.015 (saving 1.5 cents of each additional dollar). Conversely, differences in saving rates between older and younger cohorts are less pronounced.

Why is this distinction important? The literature argues that demographic changes, specifically longer lifespans, have led to an increase in aggregate savings and consequently a decline in interest rates—a topic to which Part III of this book will return. Mian, Straub, and Sufi counter that if elderly households' savings rates are not notably higher than those of younger households, increased longevity alone cannot explain rising savings or the decline in interest rates observed over the past four decades. Instead, they assert that rising inequality, and the resultant higher savings rates among the wealthy, have been the primary drivers behind the increase in total savings and the persistent decline in interest rates. In essence, according to Mian, Straub, and Sufi, it is inequality that has pushed interest rates downward, rather than interest rates driving up inequality.

As intriguing as Mian, Straub, and Sufi's hypothesis is, it faces at least two challenges. First, it is widely acknowledged that wealthier households tend to invest more in risky assets rather than safe ones, as discussed in Section 6.4. Therefore, even if inequality and savings rates among the wealthy increase, this may not necessarily translate into higher demand for safe assets and thus not a substantial decrease in their yields. Second, the decline in interest rates has been a global phenomenon, as highlighted in Chapter 1. While inequality has risen in numerous countries, as detailed in Sections 6.1, 6.2, and 6.3, the sharpest increases have occurred in the US. When inequality increases are more modest in many other countries, it raises doubts as to whether rising inequality alone can explain the widespread, four-decade decline in interest rates observed globally (see also the next section).

## 6.6 Other Factors Contributing to Inequality

While this chapter posits that falling interest rates have contributed to rising inequality over the past four decades, it does not assert that declining rates are the sole driver of increased inequality.

## Inequality and Low Interest Rates 111

To illustrate this, consider Figures 6.9 and 6.10. The two figures depict the share of national income accruing to the top 10 per cent of the income distribution in the US (Figure 6.9) and France (Figure 6.10), alongside the long-term interest rates in these countries. Notably, the movements in interest rates in both countries are nearly identical. However, the trends in inequality diverge significantly: inequality has surged in the US since 1980, corresponding with a decline in interest rates, whereas in France, inequality has remained relatively stable from 1980 to 2020, despite a persistent decrease in French interest rates over the same period. This divergence suggests that changes in interest rates do not invariably lead to changes in inequality; other factors also matter in shaping inequality dynamics.

This section explores two additional potential explanations for the increased inequality observed in many countries over recent decades.

First, the persistent rise in demand for skilled workers, driven by technological advancements, as discussed by Acemoglu (2002), has significantly raised wages for skilled workers relative to those of unskilled workers. This widening gap in wages contributes to growing inequality. The argument posits that during periods of substantial technological progress, such as the IT-based advancements of recent decades, individuals with the skills to adeptly utilize these new technologies are highly sought after, leading

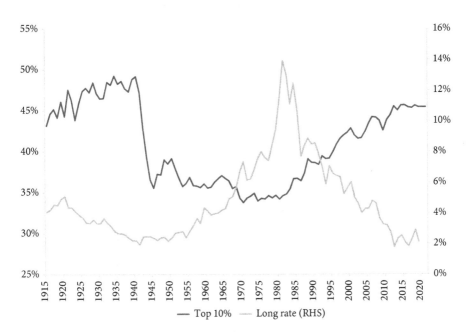

**Figure 6.9** Share of aggregate national pre-tax income accruing to top 10 per cent income earners and long-term interest rate in the US, 1915–2021.

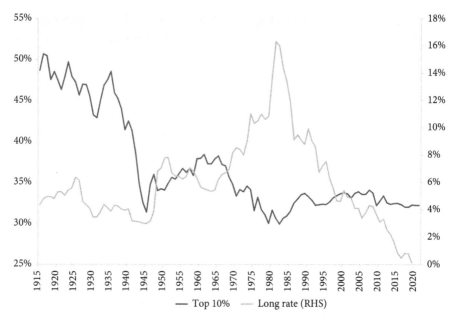

**Figure 6.10** Share of aggregate national pre-tax income accruing to top 10 per cent income earners and long-term interest rate in France, 1915–2021.

to increased returns on their skills. Conversely, individuals lacking these skills may experience stagnant wages or even job displacement, exacerbating inequality.

Second, a decline in workers' bargaining power has played a role. As documented by Stansbury and Summers (2020), the decline in union membership over the past decades has weakened unions' ability to negotiate for a fairer share of firms' profits on behalf of workers. Consequently, a smaller proportion of corporate profits now accrues to workers and a larger proportion to the owners of capital. Given that capital owners typically are already affluent, this shift exacerbates inequality. Moreover, reduced competition and increased market concentration allow large corporations to elevate prices without significant competitive pressure (Philippon, 2019), thereby bolstering corporate profits. As ownership of these corporations predominantly resides with the already wealthy, this trend further amplifies income disparities.

## 6.7 Has Inequality in Fact Increased? Debates about the Data

This chapter has presented numerous graphs documenting a marked increase in inequality over recent decades. Nevertheless, this evidence still remains subject to some debate. For instance, the groundbreaking work of Saez and Zucman (2016), who meticulously documented and analysed inequality trends in the US, has been revisited by Smith, Zidar, and Zwick (2023). While they agree that inequality has indeed increased, they argue that the magnitude of this increase is only half of what Saez and Zucman reported. In response, Saez and Zucman (2020, 2022) maintain their stance, asserting that inequality has risen significantly. Similarly, Auten and Splinter (2024) revisit the Piketty, Saez, and Zucman (2018) data, arguing that inequality has not risen as much as originally found, while Piketty, Saez, and Zucman (2024) argue that Auten and Splinter misinterpret data and that inequality has risen dramatically in the US. Notice that the debate referred to in this section relates to the US evidence, while increasing inequality is a global phenomenon, as described in earlier sections of this chapter.

## 6.8 A Final Word about Wealth Inequality

This chapter has argued that falling interest rates during the period from 1980 to 2020 have contributed to increased inequality in many countries, alongside other factors. The chapter has not taken a stance on whether higher inequality is problematic. This is a political question and thus outside the scope of this book. Nevertheless, it is important to clarify some dimensions in which rising inequality should not necessarily be viewed as problematic, and others where it should.

To illustrate one important point, consider a simple example. Imagine you own a business as the sole proprietor, with no other assets. This business generates a profit of USD 100,000 annually, indefinitely. Let us assume the interest rate is 5 per cent. According to the fundamental pricing formula in finance, also used in Chapter 5, the value of your business (an asset) can be calculated as:

$$Value \ = \ cash\text{-}flow \ / \ (interest \ rate \ - \ growth \ rate).$$

Given no growth in payouts (i.e. the growth rate is zero), the value of your business would be:

$$Value \ = \ 100,000/ \ (5\% - 0) \ = \ USD \ 2 \ million.$$

Now, imagine another person in the same country earns USD 100,000 annually through employment. Hence, both you and this person earn the same amount and can consume equivalently. This scenario represents an equal society.

If you were to sell your business, you would receive USD 2 million, which reflects its value based on the expected income stream. With this amount, you could invest in financial assets like bonds, yielding a 5 per cent return annually (USD 100,000), similar to your business income. This illustrates how asset pricing works.

Now, suppose interest rates decline from 5 per cent to 2 per cent, while everything else remains constant. The new value of your business would be:

$$100,000/ (2\% - 0) = USD\ 5\ million.$$

Your wealth has increased, while the other person's has not, assuming they do not own financial assets. This leads to increased wealth inequality.

However, despite the increased paper value of your business, your consumption possibilities remain unchanged. Even though you could sell your business for USD 5 million and invest in bonds yielding a 2 per cent return, your consumption capacity remains the same (still USD 100,000 annually).

This discussion underscores an argument made by Hoover Professor John Cochrane (2020), who posits that increases in wealth inequality, driven by changes in asset values due to interest rate fluctuations, may not significantly impact consumption possibilities.

### 6.8.1 An Example Where Inequality Matters

While the insight that paper gains on financial assets do not necessarily cause consumption inequalities helps sharpen our arguments, various factors can alter this conclusion, such as frictions. For example, individuals with high wealth may secure more favourable financial terms, like lower interest rates on loans. In such cases, wealth inequality becomes consequential.

Let us illustrate how inequality matters in the presence of frictions. Suppose you earn USD 50,000 annually and want to buy a house with a rental value of USD 10,000 per year. Assuming an interest rate of 5 per cent, the value of the house would be USD 200,000 (= 10,000/(5%-0)). You can purchase the house for USD 200,000 and reside there, saving the USD 10,000 annual rental expense.

Now, if the interest rate drops to 2 per cent, the value of the house would rise to USD 500,000 (= 10,000/(2%-0)). Despite this increase, your annual income remains USD 50,000. In a frictionless world, where borrowing terms perfectly adjust, you could borrow USD 500,000 as easily as USD 200,000 because the annual interest payment remains USD 10,000 (2 per cent of 500,000). However, in reality, banks might hesitate to lend you the higher amount, USD 500,000. This caution reflects a friction—specifically, bankruptcy costs.

Banks typically assess your creditworthiness based on your income relative to the loan amount, for a valid reason: if you lose your job, the bank risks greater losses with a larger loan. While theoretically, the bank could reclaim the house and sell it to recover the loan amount, real-world complications such as delayed possession or reduced property value could complicate this process. Consequently, the bank might prefer lending USD 200,000 over USD 500,000 in the above example, anticipating lower risk.

In such scenarios, changes in wealth due to interest rate fluctuations can have tangible consequences. It becomes an empirical question whether increasing wealth inequality resulting from falling interest rates translates into disparities in consumption possibilities or remains confined to paper gains. Greenwald et al. (2023), referenced in Section 6.6, delve into this issue for the US. Their study carefully explores how higher wealth inequality due to falling interest rates does lead to consumption inequality. Thus, the authors conclude that higher wealth inequality arising from lower interest rates does have real effects.

## 6.9 Checklist

This chapter has demonstrated several key points:

- No country exhibits a perfectly equal distribution of income or wealth. Discussions about inequality focus not on its existence but rather on its extent and whether it has increased or decreased over time.
- Economic inequality encompasses income inequality (a flow concept, indicating how much more one earns compared to others) and wealth inequality (a stock concept, reflecting the proportion of total wealth owned by different segments of the population). For instance, what fraction of total wealth is owned by the top 10 per cent of the population? What share of total income is earned by the highest earners?
- Rewards for working harder, starting new ventures, or pursuing higher education can contribute to inequality, meaning a certain degree of inequality is necessary to stimulate such entrepreneurial activities and incentivize individual effort.
- Excessive inequality can be detrimental, on the other hand. When inequality prevents social mobility, it is perceived as unfair. If someone earns nothing while a neighbour earns everything, with no prospect of

improving one's situation, inequality becomes unjust and discourages investments in education and entrepreneurship. Inequality can thus be seen as excessive or unfair depending on its origins.

- Wealth distribution is highly skewed in most countries, with a small fraction of the population owning most of the wealth. Income inequality, though still significant, tends to be lower due to income redistribution through taxes and social welfare programmes.
- Inequality has significantly increased over the past four decades, both in terms of income and wealth.
- The central argument of this chapter is that falling interest rates have been a major driver of increasing inequality.
- Since risky assets are predominantly held by the wealthy, and these assets tend to increase more in value when interest rates decline than do assets typically held by the less affluent, the resulting gains in stock and real estate disproportionately benefit the wealthy, contributing to rising inequality.
- In a frictionless economic environment, higher wealth inequality resulting from lower interest rates may not impact future consumption possibilities. While wealth levels may rise initially after a decline in interest rates, the subsequent lower returns on wealth could leave future consumption unchanged.
- However, in the real world, frictions exist. Changes in asset values can affect consumption possibilities. For example, individuals with greater wealth might secure more favourable loan terms. In such cases, rising inequality due to lower interest rates has tangible consequences.
- While falling interest rates have been identified as primary drivers of rising inequality, other factors such as increased demand for skilled labour and market concentration also influence inequality levels.

# 7
# Financial Risk-Taking and Low Interest Rates

Low interest rates may incentivize investors and financial institutions to take on greater risks, thereby contributing to making the financial system more fragile. When interest rates are low, the returns on safe investments diminish. Consequently, investors might be tempted to shift their capital from safe investments to riskier ones that promise higher expected returns but also come with higher risks. This phenomenon, known as 'search for yield', manifests in various ways: individual investors may increase their holdings in stocks and other volatile assets, pension funds and institutional investors might opt for riskier investments like illiquid assets, and banks may extend riskier loans due to reduced interest rate spreads—the traditional source of banks' income. Moreover, corporations may amplify their financial risks by reducing equity financing in favour of debt financing, thereby escalating their leverage when interest rates are low.

The search for yield can lead to asset-price misalignments or 'bubbles'. As investors pursue higher returns, they may drive asset prices above their intrinsic values, creating bubbles where prices are no longer justified by future cash flows. When these bubbles burst, holders of risky assets face substantial losses, potentially even triggering systemic financial crises if widespread.

Historical examples underscore these risks: low interest rates were implicated in the global financial crisis of 2008, as well as in preceding events like the stock market bubble before the Great Depression and the dot-com bubble of the early 2000s.

The repercussions of financial crises can be severe, often resulting in prolonged economic downturns. Recognizing the importance of preventing such financial excesses, policymakers have tightened financial regulations since the 2008 crisis. Robust financial and macroprudential regulations remain crucial measures to mitigate systemic risks when interest rates are low.

*How Low Interest Rates Change the World*. Jesper Rangvid, Oxford University Press. © Jesper Rangvid (2025).
DOI: 10.1093/9780198946410.003.0008

This chapter examines how low interest rates elevate systemic financial risks. It also evaluates whether low interest rates can precipitate asset bubbles, where asset prices deviate from their fundamental values. Finally, the chapter examines two instances where the accumulation of risks due to prolonged low interest rates ultimately led to significant financial disruptions. The first case explores how declining interest rates in the mid-2000s contributed to the onset of the global financial crisis in 2008, highlighting the crucial need for proactive measures to address the systemic financial risks posed by such conditions. The second case focuses on the liability-driven investment (LDI) crisis in the UK in 2022, providing further evidence of the challenges associated with sustained low interest rates.

## 7.1 Understanding How Low Rates Can Increase Financial Risk-Taking

Chapters 4 and 5 have illustrated how declining interest rates over the past four decades have driven up prices of real estate, stocks, and other financial assets. This development is natural because lower interest rates decrease discount rates and thus increase the present value of future cash flows. Therefore, a rise in house and stock prices due to falling interest rates need not be inherently alarming.

However, sustained declines in interest rates can lead to the accumulation of financial risk-taking through other channels.

### 7.1.1 Low Interest Rates Might Lure People into Investing in Financial Assets Using Borrowed Money

When the interest rate is low, the cost of using borrowed funds to boost return on equity is also low. This might lure people into leveraging up their investments using borrowed funds, thereby increasing leverage and heightening investors' vulnerabilities to financial shocks.

Distinguishing between situations where investors use their own capital only versus situations where they use borrowed funds is important. In the former, investors can potentially lose all their equity, but not more. In the latter case, declines in asset prices can surpass investors' equity, resulting in losses that extend to lenders as well. A society where low interest rates incentivize investors to borrow for financial market investments thus becomes more vulnerable to financial shocks.

### 7.1.2 Low Interest Rates Might Incentivize People to Invest More Riskily

In a society with low interest rates, individuals may become dissatisfied with the returns on their financial investments. Consider a saver who prefers low-risk investments and invests all savings in secure government bonds. As interest rates decline, the saver might find these investments no longer promise satisfactory returns. Consequently, the saver reassesses their portfolio allocation in response to the low-rate environment. This could lead to reallocating savings away from low-risk assets towards riskier investments. Risky assets offer higher expected returns to compensate for their inherent risk. Transitioning from a low-risk portfolio to a high-risk one can thus increase expected returns, but it also elevates exposure to market volatility. Therefore, if investors pivot towards riskier assets, they are likely to experience more frequent and significant portfolio losses. If such shifts occur widely, they can increase financial fragility within the society.

### 7.1.3 Low Interest Rates Increase the Risk of Overvalued Financial Assets and Financial Bubbles

Low interest rates can heighten the risk of financial bubbles. As discussed in Section 7.1.1, when low interest rates encourage borrowing for investments, or in Section 7.1.2, when they prompt a shift from safe assets to riskier ones, the demand for risky assets rises. With a limited supply of such assets, this can lead to higher asset prices. If demand surges excessively, investors may end up being willing to pay more for the asset than its fundamental value—a situation known as overvaluation.

Such conditions can foster financial bubbles, where investors bid up asset prices based more on expectations of future price increases rather than the intrinsic value derived from the asset's expected cash flows. This speculative behaviour is inherently risky because it sets the stage for prices to eventually correct. When shocks remind investors of the true fundamental values of assets, significant price adjustments—referred to as the bursting of the bubble—occur.

The repercussions from bursting bubbles can be severe. Investors suffer wealth losses, impacting consumption and investment decisions, thus affecting overall economic prosperity. Moreover, the bursting of a bubble can trigger panic among investors, leading to a cascade of selling that drives asset prices down further.

### 7.1.4 Low Interest Rates and Risk-Taking in Banks

Banks play a crucial role in market economies by taking deposits and use them to finance loans. Traditionally, banks' primary source of income is the interest rate differential between what they pay depositors and the higher rates they charge borrowers.

As the general level of interest rates declines, banks adjust deposit and lending rates accordingly. However, there is a practical limit to how much deposit rates can decrease because individuals have the option to hold cash rather than accept negative interest rates on their deposits. The level of deposit rates at which depositors choose to withdraw funds and store them outside the banking system is not precisely defined. Historically, it was commonly believed that 0 per cent marked this lower boundary, but central banks in Europe, prior to the pandemic, ventured into negative interest rate territory without triggering large deposit withdrawals. This suggests that the lower limit for deposit rates may be lower than previously thought, though its exact level is still unclear.

If interest rates persist at very low levels, banks may find their profitability squeezed. With lending rates declining more than deposit rates—because there is a limit to how low deposit rates can fall—the interest rate spread narrows, reducing banks' net interest income.

In response to diminished profitability, banks might seek higher returns by assuming greater risks. This could involve expanding into riskier loans or investing in more volatile financial assets. Both strategies increase the vulnerability of banks to adverse economic conditions.

Whether through reduced profitability or heightened risk exposure, persistent low interest rates can erode the resilience of banks. This weakened resilience heightens the potential for banking crises, underscoring the broader implications of prolonged low-interest-rate environments, an example of which is the financial crisis of 2008 which will be described in Section 7.4.

### 7.2 Do Low Interest Rates Lead to More Risk-Taking?

Several channels exist through which low interest rates might increase financial risk-taking, as the previous section discussed. The question is whether there is empirical evidence supporting the assertion that risk-taking increases when interest rates decline.

### 7.2.1 Retail Investors

Do retail investors increase their exposure to risk when interest rates are low? Lian, Ma, and Wang (2019) provide compelling evidence supporting this claim. In their study, participants were randomly assigned to groups where they had to decide how much of their wealth to allocate between a risk-free asset and a risky asset. Both groups were offered the same additional return from the risky asset, but one group faced a lower risk-free return. The findings showed that individuals allocated a significantly higher proportion of their wealth to the risky asset when interest rates were low, indicating a heightened appetite for risk in such situations. This pattern held across various demographic groups, including the general population and highly educated individuals, underscoring the robustness of the results.

Additionally, Lian et al. (2019) examined the actual portfolio allocations of members of the American Association of Individual Investors. They found that retail investors allocated less of their wealth to cash and more to equities when interest rates were low. Moreover, there was an observable increase in flows into risky assets and outflows from safe assets during periods of declining interest rates.

Further supporting this hypothesis, Daniel, Garlappi, and Xiao (2021) identified a related effect among individual investors. They observed that retail investors tended to favour riskier income-generating assets, such as high-dividend stocks and high-yield bonds, when interest rates were low and returns on safer investments, like bank accounts and bonds, were correspondingly low. This shift in portfolio allocation was attributed to some investors' preference for assets that provide steady income, even at the expense of higher risk.

In conclusion, the empirical evidence suggests that retail investors tend to take on more risk when interest rates are low. Is the same true for professional investors?

### 7.2.2 Pension Funds

Several studies indicate that institutional investors increase their allocation to riskier assets when interest rates are low. The International Monetary Fund (IMF) publishes the Global Financial Stability Report biannually, and its October 2019 edition focused on documenting how global financial institutions have heightened their risk-taking in response to declining global interest rates. According to the IMF (2019), various types of institutional investors have adjusted their investment strategies due to lower yields:

- Fixed-income mutual funds have shifted their portfolios towards riskier and less liquid investments.
- Defined-benefit pension funds are facing pressure to seek higher returns.
- Life insurers are also pressured to meet guaranteed returns on insurance policies in a low-interest-rate environment.

IMF (2019) demonstrated that pension funds experience increased liabilities when interest rates decrease. This phenomenon occurs because the present value of pension obligations rises under low-interest-rate conditions, as depicted in Figure 7.1. The question is whether the rise in liabilities affects how pension funds allocate their assets.

Pension funds aim to achieve solid returns on their investments to maximize payouts to their beneficiaries. When interest rates are low, returns from safe assets naturally decrease. In response, pension funds have increasingly turned to alternative assets such as private equity, infrastructure, and energy finance, as noted by the IMF (2019). The share of pension fund assets going to

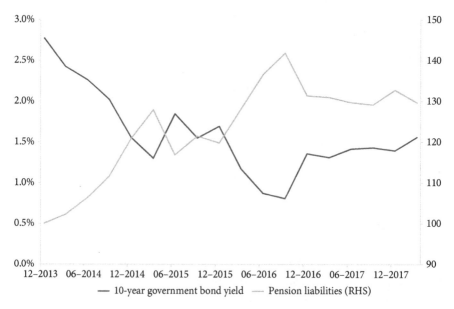

**Figure 7.1** Long-term interest rates and pension liabilities in pension funds (The Netherlands, the UK, and the US).
*Data source:* IMF (2019).

alternative investments has increased from around 5 per cent in 2007 to more than 20 per cent in 2018, the IMF shows. Such investments typically involve long-term commitments and limited liquidity, meaning they cannot be easily sold if needed. Consequently, pension funds, in addition to traditional risks like market and credit risks, expose themselves to the added challenge of illiquidity risk.

Illiquidity risk refers to the inability to sell an asset quickly without incurring significant losses. Pension funds (and other investors in illiquid assets) accept this risk in exchange for an 'illiquidity premium', which compensates for the lack of liquidity with potentially higher returns. While long-term investors like pension funds might be well suited to bear such risks, it is still important to recognize that this strategic shift away from safe assets like government bonds towards illiquid alternatives introduces new risks, particularly illiquidity risks, to pension funds.

Academic research corroborates a situation where pension funds increase their risk exposure in response to low interest rates. Andonov, Bauer, and Cremers (2017) demonstrate that US public pension funds increase their allocation to risky assets when long-term interest rates decline. The reason is that these pension funds may discount their pension liabilities with the expected return on their portfolios. If investments are predominantly in safe assets with low expected returns (because of low interest rates), the present value of liabilities is high. If the pension fund shifts towards riskier assets with higher expected returns, the present value of pension liabilities will fall. However, risks also increase.

Ioannidou, Pinto, and Wang (2022) focus on corporate pension plans in the US, finding that falling interest rates over recent decades have escalated their liabilities, leading many funds to confront funding and solvency challenges. In response, these plans have increased their exposure to equities to bolster anticipated returns. Ioannidou et al. (2022) underscore this behaviour by analysing a regulatory reform that adjusted discount rates used to calculate pension liabilities. This adjustment illustrates how low interest rates prompt pension funds to increase equity investments in pursuit of higher returns.

## 7.2.3 Mutual Funds

Not only pension funds increase their exposure to risky assets when interest rates are low; other institutional investors also exhibit similar behaviour.

Several studies have illustrated how mutual funds, particularly various types of fixed-income funds that invest in bonds and bills, have augmented their allocation to riskier assets in response to declining interest rates. Di Maggio and Kacperczyk (2017) provide insights into US money market funds, which, despite regulatory requirements to invest in safe short-term assets, have flexibility in choosing from a spectrum of assets including short-term government bonds (very safe) to somewhat riskier assets like bonds issued by banks. They observe that these funds increased their risk-taking post-financial crisis when monetary policy rates were reduced to near-zero levels.

Similarly, Choi and Kronlund (2018) analyse corporate bond funds and find comparable trends. Their research indicates that these funds tend to allocate more capital to risk assets during periods of low yields.

These findings underscore a broader pattern among institutional investors, namely that they adjust their investment strategies in pursuit of higher expected returns amidst low-interest-rate environments, thereby accepting higher levels of risk.

## 7.2.4 Banks

The traditional revenue model for banks relies on lending money at higher interest rates than they pay on deposits. This difference between lending and deposit rates directly impacts banks' profitability.

Empirical data consistently shows that the lending spread—that is, the difference between banks' lending and deposit rates—fluctuates in tandem with the broader interest rate environment in the economy. Figure 7.2, which utilizes long-term data from the UK where historical lending and deposit rates are well documented, illustrates this relationship. In this context, the lending spread is calculated as the gap between the interest rate charged on corporate loans and the rate paid on deposits by banks. It quantifies the profit margin UK banks earn (expressed in percentage points) when extending loans to corporations funded by household deposits.

To gauge the overall interest rate environment, Figure 7.2 references the Bank of England Bank Rate; that is, the central bank's policy rate.

Figure 7.2 illustrates that the lending spread increased alongside the rise in the central bank policy rate during the 1950s, 1960s, and 1970s. Furthermore, since 1990, the lending spread has declined in line with the overall decrease in the economy's interest rate levels, even when the fall in the Bank Rate all the way down to 0 per cent has been larger than the fall in the lending spread. Moreover, increases in the central bank policy rate during the recent

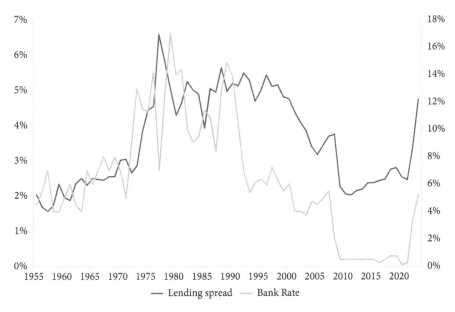

**Figure 7.2** The lending spread in UK banks, calculated as the difference between the corporate borrowing rate and the deposit rate together with the Bank of England Bank Rate (right-hand axis), 1955–2023.
*Data source*: A millennium of macroeconomic data, Bank of England.

post-pandemic recovery have corresponded closely with increases in lending spreads. Put simply, when interest rates in the economy change, banks' net interest income changes. So, when interest rates fell during 1980–2020, banks' interest income was squeezed (in the same way that it increased in the 1960s and 1970s).

In addition to the direct impact from changes in the general interest rate level to banks' lending spread, other factors can further compress bank revenues when interest rates decline. For instance, banks must maintain short-term liquid assets to manage potential liquidity withdrawals. The returns on these safe, short-term assets are heavily influenced by prevailing interest rates. As interest rates decrease, so do the returns on these assets, putting additional pressure on banks' income.

There are countervailing effects that mitigate the negative impact on bank profitability from lower interest rates. In particular, banks' funding costs also decline in tandem with interest rates.

The point here is that banks may react strategically to lower rates. If banks perceive that the overall effect of lower interest rates on their profitability is negative and persistent, they may seek to boost returns on their assets

## 126 How Low Interest Rates Change the World

by pursuing higher-yield opportunities.[1] This pursuit of higher returns often involves lending to riskier borrowers, thereby increasing the expected return per unit of lending but also elevating overall risk within the banking sector.

Academic research corroborates that banks, akin to retail and institutional investors discussed earlier, tend to take on more risk when interest rates are low. For instance, Maddaloni and Peydró (2011) demonstrate that European banks relaxed lending standards in response to low interest rates before the 2008 financial crisis. Similarly, Jiminez, Ongena, Peydró, and Saurina (2014) show that lower short-term interest rates prompt banks to increase lending to riskier firms. Moreover, Heider, Saidi, and Schepens (2019) investigate the behaviour of banks under negative interest rates in Europe during the 2010s, finding that deposit-funded banks are particularly reluctant to lower deposit rates below zero, fearing customer reactions. Consequently, deposit-funded banks may exhibit even riskier lending practices compared to their market-funded counterparts.

In summary, there is substantial reason to believe, supported by empirical evidence, that banks, pension funds, and other financial intermediaries, alongside retail investors, all tend to embrace riskier investments when interest rates are low. This heightened risk-taking contributes to increased systemic risks within the financial system, rendering it more fragile. The financial crisis of 2008 serves as a stark example of the consequences of such increased risk exposure during periods of low interest rates. However, before finishing the chapter with a discussion of the financial crisis of 2008, let us discuss how low interest rates may lead to mispricing of financial assets and bubbles.

## 7.3 'Mispricing' and the Level of Yields

The preceding sections have demonstrated how low interest rates prompt increased risk-taking among households and financial institutions. As outlined in Section 7.1, increased risk-taking induced by low interest rates drives up demand for risky assets. This phenomenon raises concerns that asset prices may be driven above their fundamental values. But what exactly constitutes the 'fundamental' or 'correct' price of an asset?

In theory, determining this seems straightforward: calculate the expected future cash flows and discount them back to the present. However, reality

---

[1] Banks might also compensate for the downward pressure of low interest rates on profits in additional ways, such as increasing commissions and fees.

complicates this simplicity. Future cash flows are uncertain—we cannot predict with certainty how a company will perform or what its future earnings will be. Moreover, choosing the correct discount rate is challenging as various models yield different outcomes. Hence, uncertainty surrounding both cash flows and discount rates makes identifying the 'right' value of an asset elusive.

Still, we can use models and informed assumptions to estimate expected cash flows and appropriate discount rates. Such models do not provide a definitive 'right' price, but the 'right' price given the specific assumptions.

This chapter employs a well-established model pioneered by Nobel Laureate and Yale economist Robert Shiller. Shiller's (1981) model centres on discounted cash flows, specifically dividends. His key insight was that rationality implies no systematic differences between ex ante expected dividends and realized future dividends. Under this assumption, Shiller posits that the rational stock price today can be calculated from backward induction using actual dividends, given an assumed terminal value for stock prices; that is, by discounting expected future dividends using a constant discount factor.

Figure 7.3 contrasts the actual US S&P 500 stock market index with its theoretical counterpart, the 'Fundamental stock price', which is, as mentioned, based on future dividends discounted by a constant discount factor under the rationality assumption. While the theoretical price evolves smoothly, the actual stock price exhibits significant volatility. Shiller's observation that actual stock prices fluctuate widely relative to their theoretical values led him to question the rationality paradigm, pioneering the field of 'behavioural finance'.

Figure 7.4 illustrates the main point of this section, showing the difference between the actual and fundamental stock prices alongside the US long-term yield (inverted). The discrepancy between the actual value of the S&P 500 and its theoretical counterpart serves as a measure of stock market mispricing, based on the specific model employed here.

When the S&P 500 exceeds its fundamental level, it indicates that the stock market is 'overvalued', meaning investors pay more for firms in the S&P 500 than their rational fundamental price. Figure 7.4 illustrates significant overpricing in the stock market during the peak of the late 1920s stock market frenzy in 1929, just before the crash that precipitated the Great Depression, and again in 1999 before the dot-com crash. Conversely, the US stock market was considered 'undervalued' immediately after the First and Second World Wars and during the late 1970s.

The primary message conveyed by Figure 7.4 is that there is a strong correlation between interest rates and stock market overvaluation. When interest

**Figure 7.3** Actual value of the S&P 500 together with its theoretical fundamental value, where the latter is based on future dividends discounted by a constant discount factor.
*Data source*: Robert J. Shiller's webpage.

rates rise, stocks tend to be underpriced, while falling interest rates tend to lead to stock market 'overvaluation'. This trend is particularly evident during the decades surrounding 1980. During the 1960s and 1970s, US interest rates rose steeply, causing the stock market to decline significantly and even drop below its fundamental value. By the peak around 1980, the fundamental value of the stock market was nearly double its actual value. Subsequently, as interest rates sharply declined after 1981, the stock market surged, ultimately resulting in a pronounced overvaluation leading up to the burst of the dot-com bubble around the turn of the millennium, before which stocks had become excessively expensive. The subsequent crash in stock prices was dramatic, followed shortly by the 2008 financial crisis which further exacerbated the decline. Since then, alongside the continual decline in interest rates, stocks have risen relative to their fundamental value.

A similar but less dramatic pattern was observed during the 1920s. Prior to 1920, rising interest rates led to a decline in stock prices relative to their fundamental value. After 1920, falling interest rates fuelled a bull market in stocks, where stocks became excessively overvalued, culminating in the stock market crash of 1929.

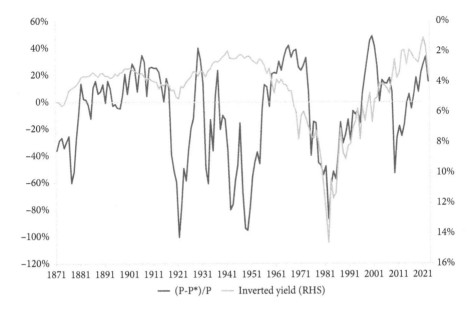

**Figure 7.4** Difference between the actual and the fundamental stock price, relative to the actual stock price (P-P*). The figure also includes the 10-year US Treasury rate, inverted right-hand scale, 1871–2023.
*Data source*: Robert J. Shiller's webpage.

In essence, the two most significant US stock market bubbles—the one preceding the 1929 crash and the dot-com crash of 2000—were both fuelled by declining interest rates. Furthermore, the four-decade-long fall in interest rates had taken stocks from being significantly undervalued in 1980 to significantly overvalued right before the pandemic. The conclusion is that persistent drops in interest rates can lead to misaligned asset prices and contribute to market instability.

## 7.4 Low Interest Rates and the Global Financial Crisis of 2008

The preceding sections of this chapter have detailed how low interest rates spur increased risk-taking in the financial sector and contribute to mispriced financial assets. These risks became apparent during the global financial crisis of 2008, leading to the most severe economic downturn since the Great Depression of the 1930s. The financial crisis serves as a stark reminder of the consequences when accumulated financial risks materialize.

**Figure 7.5** Federal Funds Rate in the years leading up to the global financial crisis in 2008.

*Data source*: FRED of St. Louis Fed.

This section focuses on explaining how low interest rates played a pivotal role in heightening financial risks prior to the 2008 crisis and contributed to its eventual collapse. It also outlines some of the profound repercussions of the crisis.

The crisis originated in the United States. The US Federal Reserve (the Fed) typically lowers the monetary policy rate during economic downturns to stimulate investment and consumption and raises it during strong economic periods to temper demand and inflationary pressures. Following the US recession of 2001, the Fed aggressively lowered its policy rate from 6.5 per cent in late 2000 to 1.75 per cent by late 2001, representing a nearly five-percentage-point decrease, as depicted in Figure 7.5. This was one of the most substantial cuts in rates over a one-year period since the Fed began setting a target for the Fed Funds rate in the early 1980s. The cuts were particularly noteworthy given the relatively mild nature of the 2001 recession.

As discussed earlier, house prices tend to increase when interest rates are lowered. Figure 7.6 illustrates the trajectory of real house prices in the US since 1970, normalized to a value of '1' in that year.

Between 1970 and 2000, US real estate prices typically increased, but not dramatically so. This changed after 2000 when house prices skyrocketed.

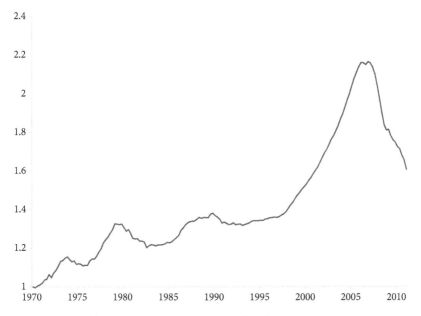

**Figure 7.6** Real house prices in the US, normalized to one in 1970.
*Data source:* OECD.

Lower interest rates enabled more people to afford larger loans, increasing demand for housing and consequently driving up house prices. The aggressive reduction in interest rates at the turn of the millennium helped fuel the housing boom.

Other factors also played a role, notably financial innovation. Structured credit obligations saw a substantial increase. In these, loans are bundled into tradable securities. This securitization not only enhanced liquidity but also facilitated risk diversification. By pooling loans, structured credit products bolstered funding availability and reduced mortgage costs.

Moreover, the emergence of shadow banks expanded financial intermediation beyond traditional regulated banks. Shadow banks facilitated the transfer of loans from regulated bank balance sheets, thereby lowering their capital requirements and reducing loan costs. This expansion in credit availability and reduced costs appeared beneficial initially.

However, these financial innovations also heightened opacity and risks within the financial system. In essence, low interest rates led to elevated risks in the household and banking sectors. This became apparent when the Federal Reserve began raising interest rates in the mid-2000s. Concerned about potential overheating in the economy, the Fed initiated rate hikes starting in 2004, as depicted in Figure 7.5. The hikes from 2004 to 2006 totalled almost five percentage points.

The consequences were profound. Many loans were adjustable-rate mortgages, meaning their interest rates fluctuated with prevailing market rates. Borrowers who had taken out loans at, say, 1 per cent found themselves unable to meet payments when rates climbed to 5 per cent. Defaults surged, leading to distressed property sales at significantly reduced prices as many sought to sell simultaneously. Banks incurred losses, becoming more hesitant to extend new loans, thereby tightening credit availability for potential homeowners. Ultimately, house prices plummeted, as illustrated in Figure 7.6. This downward spiral led to more defaults, foreclosures, job losses, and banking sector losses, culminating in the worst global recession since the 1930s.

This crisis serves as a reminder of the overarching theme in this chapter: persistent low interest rates can precipitate asset-price bubbles, increased leverage, and heightened systemic financial risks. Initially, the environment feels favourable—easy borrowing and low-cost loans spur investment and asset appreciation. Yet, as conditions shift, prices decline, defaults mount, and crises ensue. Low interest rates can catalyse such developments.

## 7.5 Low Interest Rates and the UK 2022 LDI Crisis

Another significant event where financial risks materialized due to financial institutions searching for yield in response to low interest rates was the LDI crisis in the UK in the autumn of 2022. The crisis was triggered by the presentation of the 'mini-budget' by the newly appointed UK chancellor, Kwasi Kwarteng, on 23 September 2022.

New UK prime minister Liz Truss had promised tax cuts, but the 'mini-budget' proposed unfunded tax reductions without offering a plan to address the resulting budget deficit. This lack of fiscal discipline unsettled financial markets, leading to a sharp increase in yields on UK sovereign bonds. While this alone was concerning, the situation escalated due to risky investment strategies employed by UK defined-benefit corporate pension plans, which had been implemented in response to the prolonged low-interest-rate environment.

Consider a pension fund that has committed to paying out GBP 100 in 30 years. The most effective way to hedge this liability is to purchase a bond with a face value of GBP 100 that matures in 30 years. However, since interest rates had been steadily declining since 1980, the yield on such bonds had remained low for many years, leaving pension funds underfunded. Instead of buying a bond with a face value of GBP 100 to match their liabilities, many pension funds opted to invest in a mix of bonds (with a face value less than GBP 100) and riskier assets, hoping that the higher returns from such a portfolio would cover the shortfall.

The problem with this approach is that deviating from the purchase of the 30-year bond with a face value of GBP 100 exposes the fund to the risk of being unable to meet its future obligations. This is where LDIs come into play.

To hedge against liability risks—specifically, the risk that pension funds may fail to meet their obligations due to fluctuations in interest rates and inflation—funds use derivatives. These derivatives require the posting of collateral, and pension funds typically use UK gilts (i.e., UK government bonds) for this purpose. The mechanics of these hedging contracts dictate that if the value of the collateral decreases, additional collateral must be posted, a process known as margin calls. In the case of LDIs, these margin calls required cash payments. BMO (2017) provides a detailed explanation of LDIs.

When interest rates rose in response to the 'mini-budget', bond prices fell accordingly. As a result, pension funds needed to raise cash quickly to meet margin calls, leading them to sell off UK gilts. However, because many funds had entered LDI contracts, the volume of gilts being sold was substantial. The market could not absorb this selling pressure due to insufficient liquidity, meaning that the funds could not offload these bonds without further depressing their prices. As bond prices continued to plummet, the value of the collateral also dropped, triggering even more cash calls. This led to a vicious cycle of forced selling, further price declines, and additional margin calls, creating a serious and escalating situation.

The increase in yields was striking, as shown in Figure 7.7. To highlight the impact of the 'mini-budget' on UK yields, Figure 7.7 shows the spread between UK and German yields. In the first half of 2022, the UK spread remained stable, even declining slightly. However, this changed dramatically with the introduction of the 'mini-budget', causing UK yields to spike significantly. On 26 September, the UK experienced its largest one-day increase in yields in 30 years, as noted by Rangvid (2022). UK bonds began trading at a premium of two percentage points over German bonds.

This was no minor disruption. The Bank of England (2022) issued a stark warning about a 'material risk to UK financial stability', a phrase that evokes concerns reminiscent of the 2008 financial crisis.

In response to the crisis, the Bank of England intervened, committing to purchase GBP 5 billion worth of gilts per day for a limited period. This intervention temporarily stabilized the markets, causing yields to fall

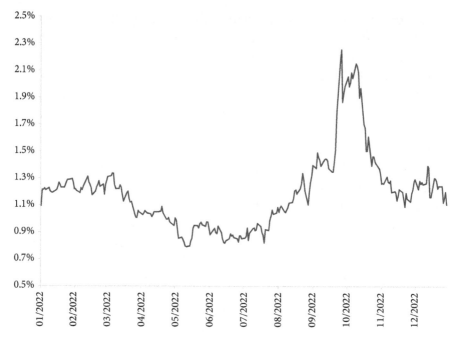

**Figure 7.7** UK–German yield spread (10-year bonds) during 2022.
*Data source*: Datastream via Refinitiv.

slightly. However, this relief was short-lived, as yields began to rise again after just a few days, prompting further intervention from the Bank of England. Eventually, the markets settled, aided by the resignation of Liz Truss, who ended up being the shortest-serving prime minister in UK history.

The LDI crisis ultimately served as a stark reminder that increased risk-taking driven by prolonged low interest rates can be costly when those risks materialize.

## 7.6 Checklist

This chapter has illustrated that:

- Low interest rates can heighten risk-taking in the financial system by:
    - Encouraging increased borrowing for investments.
    - Prompting investors to shift from safer to riskier assets, driven by 'search for yield' behaviour.
    - Potentially inflating asset prices, leading to financial bubbles.

- There is substantial evidence indicating increased risk-taking behaviour when interest rates are low:
  - Retail investors adjust their portfolios towards riskier assets.
  - Pension funds opt for riskier 'alternative' and illiquid investments while reducing exposure to safer assets.
  - Mutual funds tilt their holdings towards riskier assets.
  - Banks extend riskier loans.
- Persistent low interest rates may even contribute to asset mispricing.
- Overall, there is ample evidence suggesting that financial risk-taking rises when interest rates fall.
- A more fragile and risk-laden financial system has a stronger reaction when negative shocks occur, as evidenced during the global financial crisis of 2008.
- Preceding the 2008 crisis, low interest rates and financial innovation contributed to surging house prices.
- When interest rates began to rise in the mid-2000s, borrowers faced financial distress, leading to mortgage defaults, plummeting house prices, and substantial losses for banks. This chain of events precipitated the financial crisis, severely impacting the real economy with declining incomes and rising unemployment.
- The 2008 financial crisis and the UK LDI crisis in 2022 underscored how low interest rates can increase financial fragility and result in severe consequences.

## PART III

# WHAT CAUSED A FOUR-DECADE FALL IN INTEREST RATES?

# 8

# What Caused a Four-Decade Fall in Inflation?

Nominal interest rates, inflation rates, and real interest rates declined over four decades, from 1980 to 2020, as detailed in Part I, with immense societal consequences, as Part II explained.

Understanding why rates fell is important. Without comprehending the underlying reasons behind the 40-year decline in rates, evaluating future interest and inflation rate movements becomes challenging.

Chapter 2 illustrated that nominal interest rates are influenced by inflation and real interest rates. It also examined how inflation and real interest rates fell over the same four-decade period, thereby driving the overall decline in nominal interest rates. However, a key question remains: what were the causes of these declines in inflation and real interest rates, and consequently, nominal interest rates? This is the focus of the present and the subsequent chapter. This chapter delves into the factors influencing inflation, while the next chapter will address real interest rates.

Several factors contributed to the reduction in inflation from its peak around 1980 to the low and stable inflation environment that characterized the period before the pandemic of 2020.[1] These include not least shifts in monetary policy strategies but also globalization and other significant influences. This chapter explores these factors and their roles in lowering inflation rates, which contributed to the sustained decline in nominal interest rates between 1980 and 2020.

## 8.1 What Determines Inflation?

Broadly, there are two main schools of thought on what causes inflation:

- Monetary theory of inflation: this theory posits that inflation primarily stems from changes in the money supply.

---

[1] After the pandemic, inflation flared up. Chapter 10 will discuss why.

*How Low Interest Rates Change the World.* Jesper Rangvid, Oxford University Press. © Jesper Rangvid (2025).
DOI: 10.1093/9780198946410.003.0009

- Demand–supply theory of inflation: according to this perspective, inflation results from imbalances between aggregate demand and aggregate supply in the economy.

These two schools of thought provide contrasting frameworks for understanding the drivers of inflation. Let us review them.

### 8.1.1 Monetary View on Inflation

Nobel Laureate in economics (1976) and University of Chicago professor Milton Friedman famously articulated his view on inflation, based on his work with Anna Schwartz (Friedman and Schwartz, 1963), as follows:

> Inflation is always and everywhere a monetary phenomenon.

This sentence succinctly captures the essence of monetarism. It posits that over the long term, inflation primarily results from increases in the aggregate supply of money. An important implication of this theory is that the central bank, through its control of the money supply, can directly influence inflation rates. Another implication is that monetary policy's impact is limited to controlling inflation and does not extend to affecting real economic output.

At the core of the monetary perspective on inflation lies the Quantity Theory, expressed by the equation:

$$M \cdot V = P \cdot Y$$

Here, M represents the money supply in the economy, V denotes the velocity of money (the rate at which currency is exchanged in the economy over a period), P signifies the price level, and Y represents real economic activity. The theory traditionally assumes that V is constant and determined exogeneously, while Y is driven by non-monetary factors like population growth and productivity.

Under this framework, any change in M leads proportionally to changes in P, the price level. Inflation, the percentage change in the price level, therefore, results from changes in the money supply.

Modern economic thought has evolved from these foundational principles. Economists now recognize that in the short to medium term, both V and Y may be influenced by monetary policy rather than being solely exogenous.

For instance, changes in interest rates can affect the velocity of money as they alter the opportunity cost of holding cash. Moreover, it is believed today that central banks are capable of influencing economic activity in the short run through interest rate adjustments.

Thus, while the original monetarist formulation posited a straightforward relationship between money supply and inflation, contemporary understanding acknowledges that inflation dynamics are influenced by more than just the money supply. Thus, instead of expecting a one-to-one relationship between growth in the money supply and inflation every minute, every day, supporters of the theory expect a positive relationship, at least in the long run.

## 8.1.2 Inflation Caused by Demand and Supply

Another perspective contends that inflation arises from the interplay between demand and supply of goods and services, with monetary policy playing a pivotal role in balancing these forces, particularly in the short and medium term.

According to this viewpoint, inflation increases when aggregate demand in the economy rises, holding other factors constant. For example, during periods of economic prosperity with low unemployment and increased consumer spending power, demand for goods and services can exceed their available supply. Such excessive demand leads firms to raise prices, triggering inflation.

Monetary policy becomes crucial in managing inflation dynamics in this environment. If inflation is deemed too low, the central bank can stimulate economic activity by lowering interest rates, thereby encouraging borrowing for consumption and investment. This boosts aggregate demand and, consequently, inflationary pressures. Conversely, raising interest rates can dampen aggregate demand, helping to curb inflation when it exceeds acceptable levels. This mechanism is often referred to as 'Demand-Pull Inflation', where increases (or reductions) in demand drive inflation up (or down).

On the other hand, inflation can also be driven by supply-side factors. When the supply of goods or resources is constrained—such as during an oil price shock or in a tight labour market—production costs increase, prompting firms to pass these higher costs on to consumers through price hikes. This phenomenon, known as 'Cost-Push Inflation', highlights how increases (or reductions) in production costs affect inflation levels.

In addition to demand and supply dynamics, inflation expectations play a critical role in this theory. Anticipations of future price increases can spur current consumption, accelerating inflation. Similarly, if firms anticipate higher labour costs in the future, they may preemptively raise prices to offset expected expenses, thereby contributing to inflationary pressures.

## 8.2  Can Money Growth Explain the Fall in Inflation since 1980?

The monetary hypothesis can be explored by investigating whether a consistent positive relationship between inflation and the expansion of the money supply exists. Recall from Chapter 2 that inflation declined throughout the 1980s and 1990s, remaining low and stable in the subsequent decades up to the pandemic in 2020. Did the growth of the money supply follow a similar pattern? Figure 8.1 illustrates the median annual inflation rate alongside the median annual growth rate of the money supply across 17 advanced countries over the past 150 years.

Two main conclusions can be drawn from Figure 8.1. Firstly, significant fluctuations in inflation are often accompanied by corresponding fluctuations in the growth rate of the money supply. For instance, periods of rapid

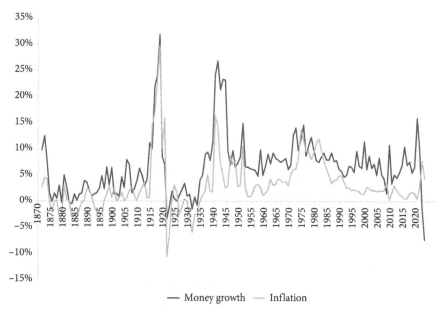

**Figure 8.1**  Inflation rates and annual growth rates in the narrow money supply, 1870–2023. Medians across 17 advanced economies.
*Data source:* Jordà-Schularick-Taylor Macrohistory Database and OECD.

expansion in the money supply, such as during the First and Second World Wars, typically coincide with high inflation. While this is in accordance with monetary theory, it is important to recognize that correlation does not necessarily imply causation. Inflation may increase due to a rise in the money supply, as the theory predicts, but conversely, an increase in the money supply could also be a response to rising inflation. Under constant velocity assumptions, as prices rise in the economy, more money is required for transactions. Therefore, periods of rapidly increasing prices are also periods of rapid money supply growth. Determining whether money causes inflation or vice versa remains a complex issue.

Secondly, Figure 8.1 illustrates the decline in inflation from the early 1980s through the mid-1990s, as discussed in Chapter 2, followed by a prolonged period of low inflation until the post-pandemic uptick in 2021–2022, the latter of which is further explored in Chapter 10. The figure reveals that while inflation has been falling, and eventually stable and low, since 1980, the level and volatility of money supply growth have not exhibited similar stability. In other words, the low and stable inflation environment that characterized the pre-pandemic period was not accompanied by a low and stable money growth process, as the monetary theory would have predicted. Inflation was low and stable even if money growth was not particularly low and stable.

Table 8.1 expands on these observations by presenting average growth rates and volatilities of the money supply over various periods. This data can be compared with Table 2.1 from Chapter 2, which detailed average inflation rates and volatilities during corresponding time spans.

**Table 8.1** Average rates of money growth and volatility of money growth in advanced economies

|  | Mean | STD | Lower | Upper | Range |
|---|---|---|---|---|---|
| 1870–2023 | 6.6% | 5.7% | 0.9% | 12.3% | 11.5% |
| 1870–1914 | 3.3% | 3.0% | 0.3% | 6.4% | 6.1% |
| 1915–1949 | 8.9% | 9.5% | −0.6% | 18.4% | 19.0% |
| 1950–2023 | 7.4% | 3.4% | 4.1% | 10.8% | 6.7% |
| 1950–1969 | 8.7% | 2.8% | 5.9% | 11.5% | 5.6% |
| 1970–1989 | 9.5% | 2.4% | 7.1% | 11.9% | 4.8% |
| 1990–2019 | 6.4% | 2.2% | 4.2% | 8.6% | 4.3% |
| 1990–2023 | 6.1% | 3.8% | 2.3% | 10.0% | 7.7% |

STD = standard deviation. Lower and upper bounds are bounds within which two-thirds of money growth rates have fallen. The range is the size of the range within which two-thirds of money growth rates have fallen; that is, Range = upper − lower.

Table 8.1 illustrates that money growth rates in advanced eeconomies were somewhat lower during the 1990–2019 period compared to the 1970–1989 period (6.4 per cent vs. 9.5 per cent), while volatility remained relatively constant (2.2 per cent vs. 2.4 per cent). This contrasts sharply with the behaviour of inflation. As shown in Table 2.1, inflation rates were significantly lower during the 1990–2019 period compared to 1970–1989 (2 per cent vs. 7.8 per cent), with inflation volatility also declining (1.1 per cent vs. 3.0 per cent). Moreover, when considering the post-pandemic surge in money supply; that is, comparing 1990–2019 to 1990–2023, money growth volatility increased noticeably, whereas inflation volatility did not (Table 2.1). These divergent trends suggest that explaining inflation purely through changes in the money supply is challenging.

The relatively weak relationship between money growth and inflation during the 1990–2023 period is further evident when examined on a country-by-country basis. Figure 8.2 depicts the relationship between average inflation and average money growth across countries from 1990 to 2023. Over these three decades, there is scant evidence of a strong correlation between a country's average inflation rate and its average money supply growth. At most, there is a slight tendency for countries with higher average money supply

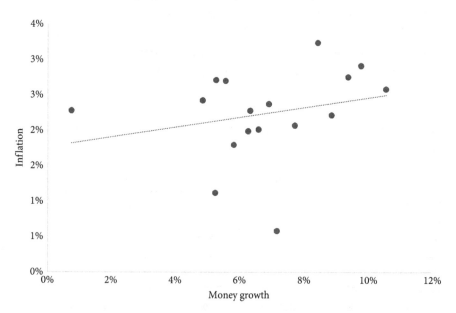

**Figure 8.2** Average rate of money growth versus average rate of inflation, 1990–2023, country by country.
*Data source:* Jordà-Schularick-Taylor Macrohistory Database and OECD.

growth to also experience slightly higher average inflation rates. Ultimately, these findings further suggest that attributing the decline and stability of inflation since 1980 solely to monetary factors is problematic. The conclusion that the monetary theory does not provide a full explanation for the behaviour of inflation is supported by academic studies; see, for example, Lucas (1980), McCallum and Nelson (2011), and Teles et al. (2016). To comprehensively understand the factors contributing to the decrease and stability of inflation before the pandemic, we must explore additional influences and dynamics beyond monetary factors.

## 8.3 Demand-Pull and Cost-Push Effects

Several factors have influenced the demand-pull and cost-push channels, contributing to changes in the inflation process over the past four decades. This section will examine and review some of these factors.

## 8.3.1 Monetary Policy and Central Banks

One of the key reasons for the low and stable inflation observed throughout much of the 1980–2020 period is the shift in monetary policy strategies compared to earlier decades.

In the 1960s and early 1970s, where inflation was high, there was a prevailing belief that controlling inflation would inevitably lead to high unemployment. As a result, central banks prioritized avoiding the tightening of monetary policy, even if inflation increased, because they believed that the cost of reducing inflation was too high.

Today, in contrast, central banks operate under inflation targeting frameworks where maintaining stable inflation around a specified target is their primary goal. If inflation increases, monetary policy is tightened. This shift represents a significant evolution in monetary policy, marking a deliberate effort to anchor inflation expectations and promote inflation stability.

### 8.3.1.1 Monetary Policy in the 1970s
To understand this shift in thinking, let us examine monetary policy in the 1970s using the example of the United States. Figure 8.3 depicts inflation trends in the US during the 1970s and early 1980s alongside the US monetary policy interest rate, the Federal Reserve (Fed) Funds Rate. As

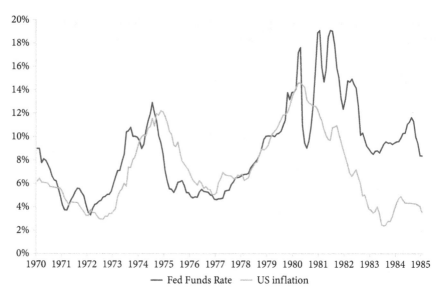

**Figure 8.3** Federal Funds Rate and US inflation.
*Source*: FRED of St. Louis Fed.

inflation climbed in the early 1970s, the Fed responded by raising interest rates. However, as signs emerged indicating a downturn in inflation by 1974, the Fed significantly and immediately lowered the monetary policy rate. Consequently, real interest rates (shown in Figure 8.4) were negative during much of the 1970s.

When the real monetary policy interest rate is negative—that is, when the monetary policy rate falls below the inflation rate—it stimulates aggregate demand in the economy, thereby potentially exacerbating inflationary pressures. This development implied that when new inflationary shocks struck in the late 1970s, inflation surged dramatically once again.

Why was monetary policy not tightened enough in the early 1970s? During the 1960s and 1970s, economists and policymakers, including then Fed chair Arthur Burns, adhered to the Phillips curve theory (Phillips, 1958). This theory suggests a trade-off between unemployment and inflation: lowering unemployment could be achieved by increasing inflation, and vice versa. Policymakers were afraid that tightening monetary policy to combat inflation would result in higher unemployment. Essentially, they believed that accepting a higher inflation rate was necessary to prevent unemployment from rising.

As De Long (1997, p. 264) highlights: 'Monetary policy did not effectively curb inflation in the early 1970s because it was not sufficiently pursued. The

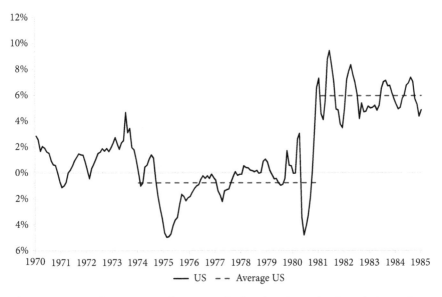

**Figure 8.4** US real monetary policy rate, calculated as the Federal Funds Rate minus inflation, including averages over 1974–1981 and 1981–1985.
*Source*: FRED of St. Louis Fed.

Federal Reserve chair at the time did not have confidence that such measures would be effective at an acceptable cost.' Consequently, monetary policy remained relatively loose throughout the high-inflation 1970s.

As depicted in Figures 8.3 and 8.4, inflation only began to decrease significantly after a severe tightening of monetary policy in the late 1970s and early 1980s. Real interest rates were raised sharply and maintained at elevated levels for several years. Unfortunately, this stringent monetary policy approach contributed to the severe recession of 1980. Reducing inflation after years of excessively loose monetary policy proved to be costly.

### 8.3.1.2 The Change in Views on Monetary Policy

The negative experiences of the 1970s caused a shift in monetary policy thinking. Instead of a belief that reducing unemployment in the long run can be brought about by accepting a permanently higher rate of inflation, consensus thinking today suggests there is a short-term trade-off between economic activity and inflation, but not a long-term trade-off. In fact, this short-term trade-off forms the cornerstone of modern-day monetary policy: Central banks adjust monetary policy rates to stimulate economic growth when inflation is too low and vice versa. On the other hand, economists today

**148** How Low Interest Rates Change the World

no longer see a persistent trade-off between inflation and unemployment; instead, they perceive the long-run Phillips curve as vertical.

These insights trace back to the influential work of Robert Lucas on rational expectations in the 1970s. According to this theory, if inflation remains high and the central bank fails to intervene, people adjust their expectations accordingly. People will in such situations anticipate higher inflation in the future, prompting them to demand higher wages. In response, firms raise prices further to cover increased wage costs, sparking a wage-price spiral. The key takeaway is that anchoring inflation expectations is crucial to preventing such spirals.

The experiences of the 1970s, marked by persistently high inflation and insufficient central bank action, also led to a heightened focus on central bank independence in the 1980s and 1990s. Independent central banks are granted clear policy objectives, such as achieving low and stable inflation, and are free from political influence when pursuing their goals. Research by Alesina and Summers (1993) demonstrated that independent central banks indeed delivered lower inflation rates during the 1970s and 1980s compared to their non-independent counterparts.

To anchor inflation expectations, central banks are encouraged to adhere to a credible rule aimed at controlling inflation. This principle was underscored by the insights of Nobel Laureates Kydland and Prescott (1977) and Barro and Gordon (1983) on rules versus discretion in monetary policy. When guided by monetary policy rules like the famous 'Taylor rule', proposed by John B. Taylor (1993), independent central banks can more clearly communicate their interest rate decisions.[2]

The emphasis on independent central banks and clear monetary policy frameworks has been pivotal in shaping the inflation dynamics observed over the pre-pandemic period. When individuals understand that central banks are committed to low inflation and comprehend their strategies to achieve this goal, they adjust their expectations accordingly, thereby anchoring inflation expectations. Overall, these shifts in monetary policy goals, frameworks, and procedures have been instrumental in maintaining low and stable inflation from 1980 to 2020.

---

[2] The Taylor rule suggests adjusting the policy rate based on deviations of inflation from a target level and economic activity from full employment. It advocates raising the policy rate by more than inflation increases to effectively curb inflationary pressures.

## 8.3.2 Globalization

The significant shift in monetary policy strategies highlighted in the previous section is not the only factor influencing inflation dynamics, even if perhaps the most important one.

The world also became increasingly interconnected over recent decades, with globalization playing a significant role in aligning inflation rates across countries and contributing to maintaining low inflation levels.

To demonstrate the synchronization of inflation rates across countries over the past three decades, Figure 8.5 depicts the highest and lowest inflation rates recorded each year across 17 advanced economies since 1870. Instances of hyperinflation and extremely high inflation rates (defined as inflation rates exceeding 30 per cent) have been excluded from the figure to enhance clarity and interpretation.

Figure 8.5 illustrates significant disparities in inflation rates among countries before the Second World War. For instance, during the 1870s and 1880s, some countries experienced substantial deflation, with prices declining by 10 per cent to 20 per cent annually, while others saw inflation rates as high as 20–30 per cent. Similar divergences persisted during the interwar years. Since

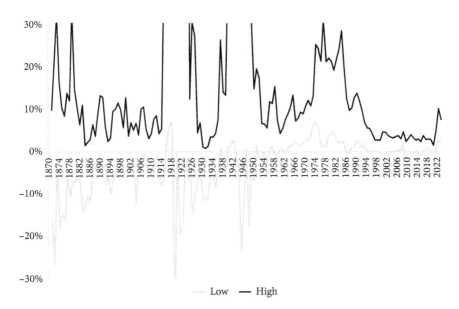

**Figure 8.5** The highest rate and the lowest rate of inflation among 17 advanced economies, year by year.
*Data source:* Jordà-Schularick-Taylor Macrohistory Database and FRED St. Louis Database.

the Second World War, deflation has largely vanished, as also emphasized in Chapter 2, yet significant variations in inflation rates persisted into the 1970s and early 1980s. Overall, prior to the early 1990s, there were wide disparities in inflation rates across countries.

In contrast, since the early 1990s, inflation rates have become more uniform across countries. As depicted in Figure 8.5, inflation rates have typically ranged from 0 to 3 per cent during the last three decades. This synchronization suggests that domestic economic developments alone have not been the only drivers of inflation rates; instead, global factors have played a crucial role.

One prominent global factor contributing to this synchronization, alongside changes in monetary policy strategies mentioned earlier, is globalization. A typical measure of globalization is countries' openness; that is, how much they trade with other countries relative to their total economic activity. Figure 8.6 illustrates the development in openness year by year across 17 advanced economies during the last 150 years.

Countries now engage in significantly more trade with each other compared to earlier periods. Since the early 1990s, foreign trade, defined as the

**Figure 8.6** (Export + imports)/GDP, 1870–2020. Medians across 17 advanced economies.
*Data source:* Jordà-Schularick-Taylor Macrohistory Database and OECD.

sum of exports and imports relative to GDP, has been notably high. On average, foreign trade constitutes more than half of GDP across countries, a trend that has persisted since the early 1990s.

Increased global trade prompts firms to seek the best deals globally, and not only locally, fostering heightened competition. For example, why purchase an expensive T-shirt from a local producer when an equally good and cheaper option is available from China? This global competition exerts downward pressure on prices and contributes to maintaining low inflation. Moreover, when globalization leads to T-shirts being sourced from the same country, price changes for that T-shirt will impact prices in all countries where it is sold. This interconnectedness underscores the growing importance of global factors in influencing inflation across different countries during 1980–2020, thereby synchronizing inflation processes internationally.

The hypothesis that globalization has acted as a check on inflation and has fostered greater alignment of inflation rates across countries during the period with falling inflation is supported by economic research. For instance, Forbes (2019) argues that globalization has influenced inflation dynamics in numerous countries.

## 8.3.3 Oil Prices

Changes in oil prices have historically been a crucial factor in economists' considerations of the cost-push effect on inflation. The substantial spikes in oil prices during the 1970s played a pivotal role in the high inflation observed during that era. However, recent years have seen oil price fluctuations that did not exert a comparable impact on inflation. To facilitate a discussion of oil prices' effect on inflation, Figure 8.7 illustrates the annual changes in oil prices since 1947.

During the 1950s and 1960s, oil prices remained stable. This stability abruptly changed in the early 1970s when major geopolitical events affected oil supply dynamics.

In 1973, during the Yom Kippur War, Middle Eastern countries, in response to Western support for Israel, formally embargoed oil exports. This led to a nearly 200 per cent surge in oil prices, Figure 8.7 shows, marking a significant shock after decades of price stability.

Oil was a critical production factor in the 1970s, and such a sudden price increase had profound impacts on businesses and households. Firms passed on these added costs to consumers, contributing to inflationary pressures.

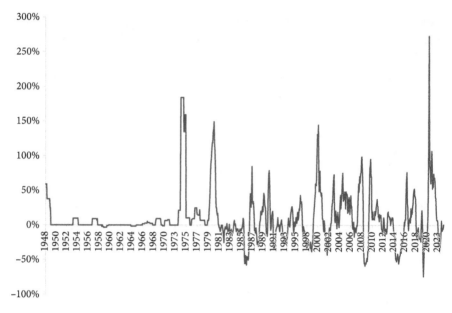

**Figure 8.7** Annual percentage changes in oil prices.
*Source*: FRED of St. Louis Fed.

Another spike in oil prices occurred in 1979 following disruptions from the Iranian Revolution. These events, alongside other factors like rising food prices, contributed to the high inflation of the late 1970s.

Since the 1970s, oil prices have been volatile, Figure 8.7 shows. In contrast, inflation has been stable since the 1980s, up until the pandemic, as discussed in Chapter 2. This disconnect between volatile oil prices and stable inflation rates since the 1980s means that today, increases in oil prices do not have the same inflationary impact as they did in the 1970s. There are most likely two reasons. First, the high volatility of oil prices means that shocks to oil prices will be short-lived. If firms perceive an oil price hike as temporary, they may refrain from passing it on to consumers. Moreover, global economic dynamics have shifted significantly since the 1970s. Modern advancements in energy-efficient technologies and a shift towards alternative energy sources like natural gas have reduced oil's overall importance in the global economy. For instance, the World Bank (2024) reported: 'The global economy's reliance on oil has diminished considerably since the 1970s. For instance, oil intensity, which measures the amount of oil required to produce one unit of GDP, declined from 0.12 tons of oil equivalent (toe) in 1970 to 0.05 toe in 2022.' For these reasons, inflation today is less susceptible to fluctuations in oil prices than during the turbulent 1970s.

### 8.3.4 Demographics and Labour Supply

In recent decades, significant demographic shifts have shaped global labour markets. The working-age population has grown both in absolute terms and as a proportion of the total population. Additionally, the integration of eastern European countries into the global economy after the fall of the Berlin Wall in 1989 has further expanded the global labour supply.

An expanded labour supply gives employers more leverage in wage negotiations with employees, exerting downward pressure on wages. With wage growth subdued, firms face less pressure to increase prices, thereby moderating inflationary tendencies. Goodhart and Pradhan (2020) argue that this expansion of the global labour supply over the past three to four decades has been a contributing factor behind the sustained low inflation observed during the period from 1980 to 2020.

## 8.4 Checklist

This chapter highlights several key points regarding inflation and its underlying causes:

- According to monetary theory, inflation results from an increase in the money supply.
- Over the past 150 years, periods of strong money growth have often coincided with high inflation rates. This long-term correlation suggests a relationship between money supply and inflation, but one must recognize that a correlation does not prove causation.
- Between 1980 and 2020, inflation initially declined and then stabilized, but money growth did not follow the same trajectory. Consequently, attributing low and stable inflation solely to monetary supply developments since the early 1980s is challenging.
- More importantly, monetary policy strategies have changed. Central banks have gained independence since the 1980s, with their primary objective being to maintain low and stable inflation. This has contributed to stabilizing inflation and keeping inflation expectations in check.
- Globalization has also played a role in maintaining low and stable prices.
- Oil price shocks were responsible for inflation spikes in the 1970s. However, today, oil plays a less critical role in economic activity and inflation dynamics.

- In summary, a combination of factors—independent monetary policies, reduced oil dependency, globalization, and a larger global labour force—has contributed to the sustained low and stable inflation observed between 1980 and 2020.
- Low and stable inflation has influenced nominal yields and interest rates over the past four decades, lowering them significantly.

# 9

# What Caused a Four-Decade Fall in Real Interest Rates?

Nominal interest rates have declined for four decades. Nominal interest rates are composed of real interest rates plus inflation. Chapter 2 demonstrated that both inflation and real interest rates decreased over this period, leading to the fall in nominal rates. The previous chapter detailed the reasons for the decline in inflation. This chapter focuses on why real interest rates declined.

Interest rates represent the return on savings in assets such as bank deposits and bonds, as well as the cost of borrowing. Borrowing enables investment today, while saving ensures funds for the future. On a macroeconomic level, total savings must equal total investments; what is used for investments must equal what is set aside for savings. The real interest rate makes sure this happens; that is, it balances the desired demand for investments and the desired supply of savings. If the supply of savings increases or the demand for investments decreases, real interest rates fall.

This chapter explores what contributed to reduced investment demand and increased savings supply from 1980 to 2020, leading to lower real rates.[1] These factors include demographic changes, shifts in wealth distribution, slower economic growth, reduced private fixed investments, lower population growth, a scarcity of safe assets, and central banks entering the safe asset market. Additionally, the chapter discusses the secular stagnation theory, which suggests that the equilibrium interest rate that secures desirable economic growth and stable inflation fell so much that the actual real interest rate remained too high to support sufficient growth and inflation.

The chapter begins with a brief explanation of the theory on how real interest rates balance the demand for investments and the supply of savings before analysing the factors that caused real interest rates to fall from 1980 to 2020.

---

[1] The chapter builds upon a vast academic literature examining the fall in real interest rates from 1980 to 2020, such as Bean et al. (2015), Carvalho, Ferrero, and Nechio (2016), Brand et al. (2018), and Obstfeld (2023).

*How Low Interest Rates Change the World.* Jesper Rangvid, Oxford University Press. © Jesper Rangvid (2025). DOI: 10.1093/9780198946410.003.0010

## 9.1 Theory: Determination of the Real Interest Rate

The real interest rate is the cost you pay for borrowing money, adjusted for inflation. Firms borrow money primarily to make investments, which generate returns. The lower the interest rate on borrowing, the more likely it is that the returns on these investments will exceed the cost of borrowing; that is, the interest rate. Essentially, the lower the real interest rate, the higher the demand for investments. In Figure 9.1, which shows the demand for investments and supply of savings in an economy on the horizontal axis against the real interest rate on the vertical axis, this is depicted by a downward-sloping line labelled 'II'. It is downward sloping because demand for investment is higher when the real interest rate is lower.

The interest rate also affects how much people want to save. The higher the real interest rate offered on a government bond, the more attractive it becomes to purchase that bond. Buying a bond means postponing consumption today for the future, essentially saving. Therefore, a higher real interest rate increases the desire to supply savings. Figure 9.1 illustrates this with an upward-sloping line labelled 'SS'. The 'SS' line represents the willingness to supply savings at various real interest rates.

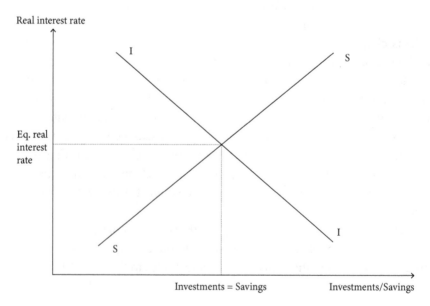

Figure 9.1 Determination of the equilibrium interest rate.

As shown in Figure 9.1, the equilibrium real interest rate balances the demand for investments with the supply of savings. For example, if more people wish to save at any given real interest rate (for various reasons that will be discussed later), the supply of savings (SS) curve shifts to the right, as shown in Figure 9.2. With more savings available at any given interest rate and no change in investment demand, the real interest rate must decrease to balance savings and investments. The lower interest rate stimulates more investments, thereby achieving equilibrium at a higher level of both savings and investments.

Alternatively, if the desired level of investments decreases, the investment demand (II) curve shifts to the left, as illustrated in Figure 9.3. In this scenario, the interest rate must also fall to encourage reduced savings, ensuring that savings and investments remain equal.

Of course, the lines can also move in opposite directions. A decrease in savings would shift the SS curve to the left, while an increase in investments would shift the II curve to the right, both resulting in higher real interest rates.

This chapter focuses on the reasons why real interest rates declined from 1980 to 2020. The primary implication of the framework presented here is that this decline must be due to a reduction in desired investments, an

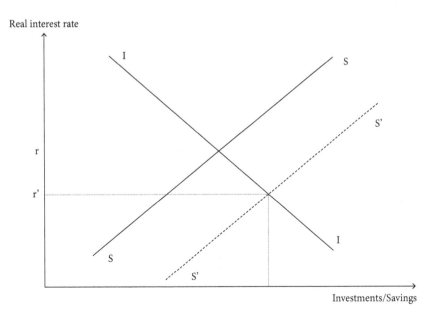

**Figure 9.2** SS curve moves to the right.

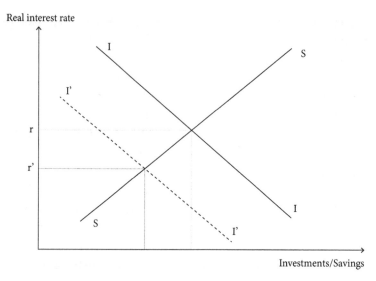

**Figure 9.3** II curve moves to the left.

increase in desired savings, or a combination of both. Therefore, the main empirical task is to identify why and to what extent desired investments fell, or why and to what extent desired savings increased. The framework outlined in this section does not address these specifics. The remainder of this chapter aims to do so, but before proceeding, the next subsection presents a stylized framework that links the real interest rate to specific economic variables.

### 9.1.2 Economic Growth and the Real Interest Rate

The framework presented above is valuable because it provides a consistent way to understand real interest rate movements. However, it is also somewhat generic in that it does not specify exact relationships between economic variables and the interest rate. For instance, it indicates that if desired investments drop, the interest rate will drop, but it does not explain the causes behind the drop in investments or quantify the resulting change in interest rates.

Fortunately, economic models exist that make clear predictions about the relationship between certain economic variables and the real interest rate. One key model is the Ramsey-Samuelson-Solow growth model, described in Box 9.1. This model posits a simple linear relationship between real economic growth and the real interest rate. While it is not a one-to-one relationship, as it depends on consumer/investor preferences such as risk aversion and rate of time preferences, the model predicts that a fall in economic growth should lead to a fall in the real interest rate. Additionally, the model suggests that the real interest rate should be lower if people expect to live longer and if the population size decreases.

Overall, based on the previous and this subsection, we would expect lower real interest rates in an economy characterized by:

- Lower rates of economic growth.
- Lower rates of population growth.
- Longer life expectancy.
- Higher desire for savings.
- Lower demand for investments.

The rest of this chapter will examine the extent to which these factors have contributed to the decline in real interest rates in recent decades, beginning with economic growth, population growth, and life expectancy, and then addressing other factors that could affect desired savings and investments.

## Box 9.1 Model-based theoretical arguments for lower interest rates

The Ramsey-Samuelson-Solow growth model is a fundamental framework in macroeconomics. In this model, individuals make consumption and saving decisions that maximize their lifetime utility. The basic premise is that people dislike situations where they can only afford minimal consumption and that increased consumption yields higher utility, albeit at a diminishing rate. This preference leads to a relatively stable consumption path, known as consumption smoothing. People smooth their consumption by saving when they have high income and borrowing when they have low income, which influences the real interest rate.

In this framework, the equilibrium or long-run real interest rate depends on economic growth, population growth, and people's rate of time preference. Economic textbooks explain that the equilibrium long-run real interest rate in this model can be expressed as:

$$r = \delta + \gamma\Delta c + n$$

where r is the equilibrium real interest rate, $\delta$ is an individual consumer's discount rate (the rate at which future consumption is discounted to the present), $\gamma$ represents the individual's risk aversion (with $\gamma$ being the inverse of the individual's intertemporal rate of substitution if there is no uncertainty), $\Delta c$ is the growth rate of per capita consumption, and n is the population growth rate.

**160** How Low Interest Rates Change the World

The equation states that if Δc and/or n increase (i.e. if there is a higher growth rates of per capita consumption and/or a higher population growth rate), r (i.e. the long-run real interest rates) increases.

The logic is as follows: if economic growth is high, future consumption will be higher than consumption today (higher economic growth means higher future income that finances higher future consumption). Therefore, the real interest rate must be high enough to persuade individuals to forgo consumption today in favour of saving for future consumption, which is already expected to be high. Essentially, the higher the expected future consumption growth, the higher the real interest rate must be in equilibrium.

This can also be explained by supply and demand for savings. If future consumption is expected to be high relative to today, the supply of savings today will be low as people prefer to consume now instead of saving. In Figure 9.1, the SS curve would move to the left. This low supply of savings pushes up the real interest rate.

The sensitivity of the interest rate to changes in economic growth depends on people's intertemporal substitution rate, or their risk aversion. If people are less willing to substitute consumption today for tomorrow (i.e. their rate of intertemporal substitution is low, represented by a high $\gamma$), the interest rate must be even higher to convince them to save more today.

Population growth also positively affects the real interest rate. In the Ramsey-Samuelson-Solow framework, savings finance investments in real capital, which is used in production. The return on additional capital, bought with extra savings, equals the marginal productivity of capital that in turn equals the real interest rate. However, this also depends on the capital–labour ratio. All else equal, when population growth is high, the capital–labour ratio falls, increasing the marginal product of capital and, consequently, the real interest rate.

Finally, $\delta$ is the individual's discount rate. If people are impatient, preferring current consumption over future consumption, a higher interest rate is required to encourage saving. Conversely, if people are patient and willing to postpone consumption, the interest rate need not be as high. Longer life expectancy can be viewed in this context. If people expect to live longer and spend more time in retirement, what they save today must be stored even longer to finance consumption late in life, which can be seen as increased patience.

In summary, in this workhorse model, the real interest rate is lower when:

- Economic growth is low.
- Population growth is low.
- People expect to live longer.

## 9.2 Real Economic Growth and the Real Interest Rate

Many economic models link real economic growth to real interest rates, as Box 9.1 explained. In such models, the real interest rate tends to be lower when per capita real economic growth is lower. This leads to a straightforward question: is the fall in real yields since the 1980s, as documented in Chapter 2, due to a decline in the growth rate of real economic activity? Two conclusions emerge:

- Over the past four decades, global real economic growth has indeed been persistently falling.
- However, from an even longer-term perspective, the relationship between real economic growth and real interest rates appears less strong.

Figure 9.4 illustrates developments in the growth rate of global (average across 17 advanced economies) real economic activity (GDP) per capita over the past four decades. The figure shows the yearly growth rate, its rolling 10-year average to smooth out short-term fluctuations, and a trend line fitted to the rolling average.

Figure 9.4 shows that annual real economic growth is volatile, with significant fluctuations from year to year. However, when smoothing out these short-term fluctuations, a persistent decline becomes evident. The downward-sloping linear trend line highlights this steady decline in underlying economic growth from the early 1980s to 2020. This trend is further underscored by decade-by-decade average growth rates: economic growth in advanced economies was 2.2 per cent per year on average in the 1980s, 1.8 per cent per year in the 1990s, and 1 per cent per year in the 2000s and the 2010s. Thus, despite significant annual fluctuations, there has been a small but persistent decline in economic growth over the past four decades.

The stylized fact that economic growth has been falling supports the theory that lower economic growth rates have contributed to the decline in real interest rates from 1980 to 2020. Furthermore, the relationship between economic growth and real interest rates is a key feature in empirical models that estimate underlying equilibrium real interest rates, as explained in Box 9.2.

While it is an important conclusion that lower economic growth has gone hand in hand with lower real interest rates during past decades, it should also be recognized that the significant yearly fluctuations around the growth trend mean that the empirical evidence is not definitive. This conclusion is consistent with academic studies, such as Hamilton et al. (2016), which found 'some evidence that higher trend growth rates are associated with higher average

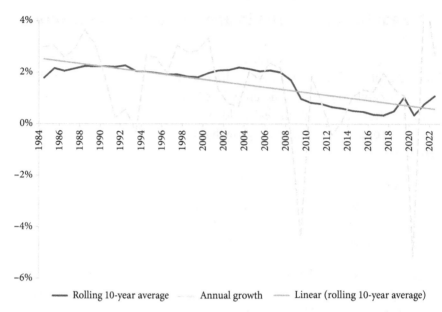

**Figure 9.4** Growth in real GDP per capita, 1984–2022. Annual global growth (dotted line), rolling average of past 10 years' global growth (solid black line), and a linear trend line (solid grey line). Annual global growth is the average across 17 advanced economies.

*Data source:* Jordà-Schularick-Taylor Macrohistory Database and OECD.

real rates' but also noted that 'this finding is sensitive to the particular sample of data that is used'. Hamilton et al. (2016) concluded that factors beyond changes in the trend growth rate are crucial for explaining shifts in the equilibrium real rate over time. This book shares that conclusion: lower economic growth rates help us understand the decline in real interest rates over recent decades, but other factors must also be considered.

### Box 9.2 Real economic growth and $r^*$

The theoretical link between real economic growth and real interest rates implied by economic models has been used by researchers to derive underlying fundamental real interest rates. These are often viewed as measures of equilibrium real interest rates, referred to as '$r^*$'.

$r^*$ plays a crucial role in economic analyses as it indicates the real interest rate when all temporary economic shocks have dissipated, essentially showing where interest rates are ultimately heading. $r^*$ is particularly significant in monetary policy analyses, as it informs us about the current stance of monetary policy: if the current (real) monetary policy rate is above $r^*$, monetary policy is tight; otherwise, it is not.

Different researchers and institutions define $r^*$ with slight variations: the Richmond Fed defines $r^*$ as 'a hypothetical interest rate that is consistent with economic and price stability', the New York Fed describes it as 'the real short-term interest rate expected to prevail when an economy is at full strength and inflation is stable', and the IMF defines it as 'the real interest rate that would keep inflation at target and the economy operating at full employment—neither expansionary nor contractionary'.

Since $r^*$ cannot be directly observed, it must be estimated. When $r^*$ is defined as the real interest rate prevailing when the economy is operating at full capacity and inflation is stable, researchers often first model the evolution of economic activity and inflation, then derive $r^*$ as the level of the real interest rate at which these variables are in equilibrium.

The New York Fed was the first to publish estimates of $r^*$ for the US, and it regularly updates these estimates. Figure 9.5 shows estimates of underlying economic trend growth in the US and the associated equilibrium interest rate, $r^*$.

The New York Fed estimates that underlying trend growth in the US has been lower post-1980, especially since the global financial crisis of 2008, which has consequently pulled down underlying equilibrium real interest rates.

Additional international evidence on falling equilibrium levels of real interest rates, or international $r^*$s, has been provided by researchers such as Jordà and Taylor (2019).

**Figure 9.5** $r^*$ and trend growth in the US, 1961–2024.
*Data source:* New York Fed.

**164    How Low Interest Rates Change the World**

They find that $r^*$ has been declining in Germany, Japan, the US, and the UK over the past several decades. The New York Fed also publishes estimates of underlying trend growth and equilibrium interest rates for the euro area and Canada, indicating a similar decline in these regions over recent decades.

## 9.3  Demographics

Global demographic shifts also provide insight into why real yields have declined in recent decades. As discussed in Box 9.1, when life expectancy increases and population growth slows, real interest rates should tend to decrease.

### 9.3.1  Life Expectancy

Increasing life expectancy tends to boost the supply of savings, as explained in Box 9.1. Figure 9.6 illustrates life expectancy at birth across low-, middle-, and high-income countries. In 1965, newborns in high-income countries could expect to live around 70 years. By 2021, this figure had risen to 80 years, marking a 14 per cent increase in life expectancy over that period. Similarly, life expectancy has significantly risen in low- and middle-income countries. In middle-income countries, it increased from 52 years to 70.5 years (a 24 per cent rise) from 1965 to 2021, while in low-income countries, it climbed from 42.6 years to 62.5 years (a 47 per cent increase relative to 1965 levels). When people live longer, savings made when young must last longer, reflecting a more patient attitude. When people are more patient, the interest rate does not need to be very high to persuade people to save, as Box 9.1. explained. In other words, higher life expectancy leads to lower real interest rates.

Former Princeton University professor and Federal Reserve (Fed) chair Ben Bernanke famously argued in 2005 that low interest rates were influenced by a 'Global Savings Glut'. His theory posited that the expanding populations and life expectancies, as well as growing economies, of countries like China and other emerging markets led to increased savings. As economic growth improves living standards, and people expect to live longer, more individuals can afford to save for retirement. This surge in global savings, according to Bernanke, found its way into safe bonds in advanced economies, driving

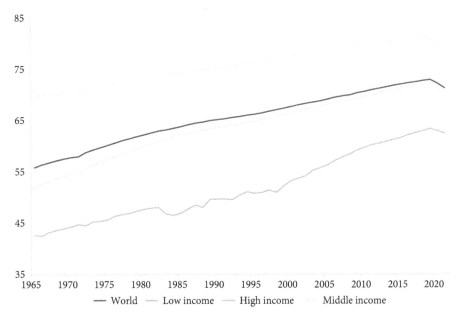

**Figure 9.6** Life expectancy at birth in low-, middle-, and high-income countries, as well as worldwide, 1965–2021.
*Data source:* World Bank.

down global interest rates. Goodhart and Prathan (2020) further develop this argument, suggesting that the fall of the Berlin Wall in 1989 and the subsequent integration of eastern Europe into the global economy similarly boosted global savings.

It is noteworthy that the Covid-19 pandemic led to a decline in life expectancies in 2020 across all countries, particularly affecting lower-income nations.

While longer life expectancies can help us understand lower interest rates, it is notable that life expectancies also increased during the 1960s and 1970s, a period when real interest rates were rising, as Chapter 2 discussed.

In this regard, another aspect to consider is how savings develop over the life cycle. People save during their working years to fund consumption in retirement, thereby smoothing out their life-long consumption patterns. The balance between saving while working and dissaving during retirement influences global savings trends. Figure 9.7 illustrates this by comparing the fraction of the global population aged 65 and over with those aged 25–65 since 1950.

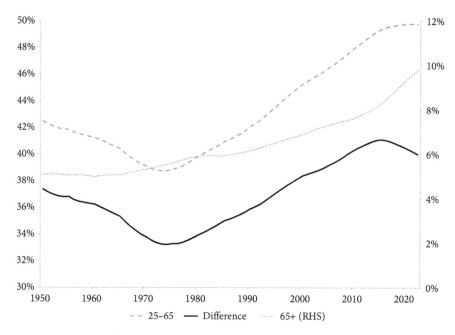

**Figure 9.7** Fraction of the global population aged 25–65, aged 65 and above (right-hand scale), and the difference between the two, 1950–2023.
*Data source:* World Bank.

Both the proportion of individuals aged 65 and over, who are assumed to have a higher tendency to dissave in retirement, and the proportion of those aged 25–65, who typically save while working, have increased over time. However, the share of the global population aged 25–65 has grown more rapidly than the share of those aged 65 and above during the period from 1980 to 2020 when interest rates declined.

Specifically, the percentage of individuals aged 65 and older has risen from approximately 6 per cent of the global population in 1980 to around 9 per cent in 2020, an increase of three percentage points. The percentage of those aged 25–65 has increased from about 40 per cent in 1980 to roughly 50 per cent in 2020, an increase of 10 percentage points. This demographic shift signifies an expansion in the portion of the population inclined towards saving relative to those inclined towards dissaving, contributing to an overall increase in global savings. This increase in savings has exerted downward pressure on real interest rates, thereby helping to explain the decline in interest rates observed from 1980 to 2020.

Interestingly, before 1980, when real interest rates were rising, the trend was the opposite. There were relatively fewer people in the working age, and the same number in retirement, meaning relatively fewer people who saved. This asserted upward pressure on real interest rates. In total, these demographic changes help explaining global real interest rate movements, both while they increased during the 1950s, 1960s, and 1970s and when they fell during the period 1980–2020.

## 9.3.2 Population Growth

The model presented in Box 9.1 suggests that a decrease in population growth rates should result in lower real interest rates. Figure 9.8 illustrates the annual growth rate of the total population across 17 advanced economies since 1870.

Figure 9.8 highlights that population growth experiences significant declines during major wars, such as the First and Second World Wars.

The figure also makes clear that population growth in advanced economies has been historically low in recent decades, when compared to other non-war periods. On average, from 1980 to 2022, the total population in the 17 advanced economies studied grew by 0.5 per cent per year. In contrast, from the end of the Second World War until 1980 (1950–1980), population growth was nearly double at 0.95 per cent annually, and from 1870 to 1910, preceding the First World War, it was 1.1 per cent per year. Thus, during the period

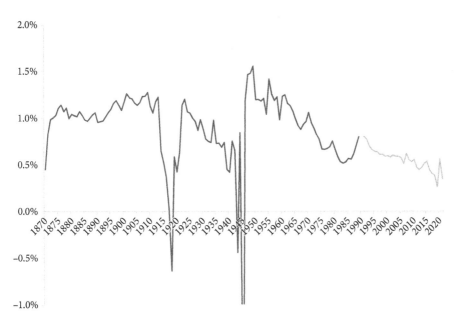

**Figure 9.8** Annual growth rate of total population in 17 advanced economies.
*Data source:* Jordà-Schularick-Taylor Macrohistory Database and World Bank.

when real interest rates have declined, population growth has also declined to historically low levels.

Moreover, the trends in population growth coincide with fluctuations in real interest rates around war periods. As shown in Chapter 2, real interest rates in advanced economies plummeted during wartime, mirroring the sharp declines in population growth during these periods.

## 9.4 Fewer Safe Assets

Some government bonds are considered 'safe assets' because they maintain their value and liquidity even during periods of widespread market turmoil. Certain investors have a strong preference for these safe assets, and some are even mandated by regulations to hold them. When demand for safe assets is high relative to their supply, their prices rise and their yields decrease.

Caballero, Farhi, and Gourinchas (2017) argue that one reason for the decline in government bond yields in recent decades is the reduction in the global supply of safe assets. They highlight that before the 2008 financial crisis, safe assets amounted to 37 per cent of global GDP, but by 2011, this figure had dropped to just 18 per cent due to many assets losing their safe-haven status during the crisis. They also suggest that the rate of economic growth in advanced economies, which issue safe assets, has not kept pace with economic growth elsewhere, especially in emerging markets, where demand for safe assets has risen, as also argued in the Global Savings Glut hypothesis of Bernanke (2005), mentioned in Section 9.3.1. Consequently, the supply of safe assets has not matched the increasing demand for them, helping to explain why yields in advanced economies have been declining, according to Caballero, Farhi, and Gourinchas (2017).

If this explanation holds true, the yields on safe assets should decline relative to yields on riskier assets. Caballero, Farhi, and Gourinchas (2017) analyse the expected returns on various risky assets and argue that yields on safe asset have fallen particularly steeply. Rachel and Summers (2019), meanwhile, observe declines in yields on risky assets such as earnings yields from stock markets and corporate bonds during the same period. They contend that factors like low economic growth and demographic changes discussed earlier in this chapter are more influential in driving these declines, rather than a shortage of safe assets.

The significance of the 'safe-asset channel' in explaining low interest rates during the 1980–2020 period remains a topic of debate. While this book acknowledges the relevance of this channel, it emphasizes that other factors play crucial roles in the downward trend of yields.

## 9.5 Central Bank Purchases of Safe Assets

After the 2008 financial crisis, central banks in advanced countries initiated large-scale asset-purchase programmes, commonly known as quantitative easing (QE) programmes. These initiatives became necessary because central bank interest rates had reached 0 per cent or even turned negative post-crisis; that is, interest rates could not be lowered further, yet inflation remained persistently low. With conventional interest rate tools exhausted, central banks sought alternative means to stimulate economic activity and encourage inflation.

The core mechanism of asset-purchase programmes involves central banks buying substantial amounts of government bonds. By doing so, they increase demand for these bonds, driving up their prices and consequently lowering their yields. Given that government bonds serve as benchmark securities, this reduction in yields on government bonds should transmit throughout the economy, leading to lower interest rates across various financial instruments and sectors. This, in turn, is intended to stimulate borrowing, investment, and overall economic growth.

When a central bank acquires bonds on the open market, those bonds become assets held by the central bank, thus enlarging its balance sheet. Figure 9.9 illustrates the expansion of the balance sheets of the European Central Bank (ECB) and the Fed relative to the Eurozone and the US economies, respectively. Prior to the financial crisis, central bank balance sheets were roughly proportional to the size of their respective economies. However, by 2020, the Fed's balance sheet had grown to 10 times the size of the US economy, while the ECB's had expanded to eight times the size of the Eurozone economy.

QE programmes were launched to reduce interest rates. However, there is ongoing debate about the extent and timing of their impact. In the United States, the Federal Reserve implemented QE across four phases, labelled QE1, QE2, QE3, and QE4. Early evidence by Krishnamurthy and Vissing-Jorgensen (2011, 2013) suggested that QE1 effectively lowered yields on both Treasuries and mortgage-backed securities. Yet, their findings on the effectiveness of QE2 and QE3 are more mixed.

Krishnamurthy, Vissing-Jorgensen, and Nagel (2015) studied the ECB's QE response during the sovereign debt crisis of 2010–2012. They concluded that

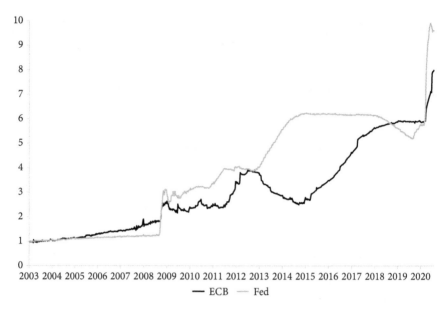

**Figure 9.9** Central bank balance sheets relative to GDP, normalized to one in 2003. Eurozone and the US, 2003–2020.
*Source:* FRED of St. Louis Fed.

ECB QE significantly reduced yields for countries hardest hit by the debt crisis, such as Italy, Spain, and Portugal. Additionally, research by Darmouni and Rodnyansky (2017) indicated a positive impact of QE on bank lending.

Regarding the broader economic effects of QE, such as employment and real economic activity, studies offer varied findings. Luck and Zimmermann (2020) found mixed evidence, noting that QE1 did not notably affect overall employment in the US, whereas QE3 showed some impact. In contrast, research by Levin, Lu, and Nelson (2022) on QE4 during the pandemic found only limited positive effects.

Central banks generally assert that QE has been effective; see, for instance, Luck and Zimmermann (2019). Fabo, Jancokova, Kempf, and Pastor (2021) provide an intriguing perspective on this. They examined 54 analyses from 2010 to 2018 on QE's effects in the US, UK, and Eurozone and found that studies authored by central bank researchers, who may have a vested interest in demonstrating QE's effectiveness, tend to report more favourable outcomes compared to independent academic studies.

While QE programmes might have contributed to low interest rates after the financial crisis of 2008, particularly the first QE programmes, it is important to emphasize that QE cannot explain the overall decline in real yields from 1980 to 2020, simply because QE programmes commenced only in 2009. Before the financial crisis, and probably also after, other structural factors mentioned in this chapter are responsible for yield declines.

## 9.6 Changes to the Income and Wealth Distribution

Chapter 6 extensively explored the relationship between inequality and interest rates, reaching the conclusion that declining interest rates contributed to heightened inequality from 1980 to 2020. The chapter also explained that higher inequality can depress interest rates.

Wealthier individuals tend to have higher savings rates. This means that overall savings in the economy increase as inequality rises because a greater portion of income and wealth is concentrated in the hands of those who save more out of additional income. This increase in total savings can lead to a decrease in interest rates. Since inequality has been growing since 1980, coinciding with a period of declining interest rates, this trend supports the idea that inequality might contribute to driving down interest rates.

## 9.7 Secular Stagnation

The secular stagnation hypothesis, originally introduced by Alvin Hansen in the late 1930s to explain the prolonged economic struggles after the Great Depression, was revisited in a modern context by Lawrence Summers in 2014 to elucidate the persistent low interest rates observed before the pandemic.

The secular stagnation hypothesis posits that factors such as those mentioned in previous sections of this chapter have collectively driven down equilibrium interest rates since 1980. These factors include demographic shifts leading to increased savings, such as longer life expectancy, as well as reduced desired investments due to factors such as sluggish economic growth, heightened corporate share buybacks, and the rise of technology that requires fewer capital investments.[2]

A critical aspect of this theory is its assertion that these factors have driven down the equilibrium real interest so much that even its nominal counterpart (equilibrium real interest rate plus inflation) has become negative.

---

[2] When future economic prospects appear bleak, businesses tend to hesitate in initiating new investments. Also, Summers (2014) argues that the advent of internet-based companies, for example, requires significantly lower initial capital compared to traditional manufacturing enterprises, thereby reducing demand for fixed investments. Finally, a notable trend in the United States has been the rising prevalence of share buybacks by corporations instead of reinvesting profits into new ventures.

This implies that actual nominal interest rates will be higher than the equilibrium rate due to the constraints faced by central banks, particularly the zero lower bound. As a result, central banks are unable to lower rates sufficiently to stimulate the economy effectively. Interest rates thus remain stuck at levels too high to achieve full employment, robust economic growth, and sufficient inflation. Furthermore, the theory posits that because prevailing interest rates are too high relative to the equilibrium rate, investments remain subdued, thereby dampening future economic growth.

Advocates of the secular stagnation hypothesis, including Summers (2014) and Furman and Summers (2020), argue that in circumstances where monetary policy is constrained by the zero lower bound, fiscal policy should adopt a highly expansionary stance. They contend that given the low-interest-rate environment that prevailed before the pandemic, governments need not fear adverse consequences from increased public debt. This argument will be revisited in Chapter 12.

## 9.8 Decomposing the Fall in Real Rates into Underlying Factors

This chapter has explored several factors contributing to the decline in real interest rates since 1980. While pinpointing the exact significance of each factor is challenging, statistical models offer insights into their relative importance. Rachel and Summers (2019) have undertaken such an analysis.

Rachel and Summers (2019) examined the relative importance of various factors that influenced the decline in real interest rates across advanced economies from 1970 to 2017. They assessed both public policies that tended to elevate equilibrium real interest rates and private sector dynamics that exerted downward pressure on them, and decomposed their relative contributions to the trajectory of equilibrium real interest rates. The summarized effects of these factors are presented in Table 9.1.

According to Rachel and Summers (2019), expansionary public policies contributed to raising equilibrium real interest rates. Specifically, they estimate that increases in public debt, social security expenditures, and old-age healthcare collectively raised real interest rates in advanced economies by 3.5 per cent over the 1970–2017 period. Public debt alone is attributed to a 1.2 per cent increase, while social security and old-age healthcare each contributed 1.2 per cent and 1.1 per cent, respectively.

**Table 9.1** Factors affecting the fall in real interest rates in advanced economies during 1970–2017

|  | 1970–2017 |
| --- | --- |
| **Public policies** |  |
| Government debt | 1.2 |
| Social security | 1.2 |
| Old-age healthcare | 1.1 |
| *Total impact of public policies* | *3.5* |
| **Private sector forces** |  |
| Productivity growth | −1.8 |
| Population growth | −0.6 |
| Longer retirement | −1.1 |
| Inequality | −0.7 |
| Interactions | −1.1 |
| *Total impact of private forces* | *−5.3* |
| Other | −0.1 |
| **Total net effect** | **−1.9** |

Percentage points.
*Source:* Rachel and Summers (2019).

Conversely, private sector forces exerted downward pressure on equilibrium real interest rates. Rachel and Summers identify declining productivity growth—that is, declining economic growth—as the primary factor, which they estimate reduced rates by 1.8 per cent over the period. Demographic shifts, such as lower population growth and longer retirement spans, also played significant roles, collectively lowering rates by 1.7 per cent (0.6 per cent due to population growth and 1.1 per cent due to longer retirements which result from longer life expectancy). Additionally, increased inequality is estimated to have lowered rates by 0.7 per cent. The interaction of these private sector effects further contributed to a reduction of 1.1 per cent in real interest rates.

Overall, private sector forces exerted a more substantial influence, lowering long-run real interest rates by 5.5 per cent. As mentioned, public policies tended to raise rates by 3.6 per cent. Therefore, their model attributes a net decrease in real interest rates of approximately 1.9 per cent over the 1970–2017 period.

Rachel and Summers (2019) find that while their model can explain a significant portion of the 3.2 per cent decline in equilibrium real interest rates they estimate during this period, a residual decrease of 1.3 per cent

**174** How Low Interest Rates Change the World

remains unaccounted for. They suggest that this discrepancy indicates a possible underestimation of the private sector forces that have driven interest rates lower, rather than an overestimation of the impact of public sector factors.

### 9.8.1 Evidence from the US

In 2022, the International Monetary Fund (IMF) published a comprehensive study investigating the reasons behind the decline of $r^*$ in the US in recent decades; $r^*$ was introduced in Box 9.2. The study—Platzer and Peruffo (2022)—analyses the relative significance of various factors contributing to the decline in $r^*$ between 1975 and 2015. The relative importance of the difference sources is illustrated in Figure 9.10.

The IMF's study reveals that the US $r^*$ decreased by 2.2 per cent between 1975 and 2015. The primary driver identified by the IMF was slower economic growth (specifically, productivity growth), which accounted for one percentage point of the total decline. Demographic shifts, characterized by increased life expectancy compared to 1975, also played a significant role. Additionally, rising inequality contributed to the decline in $r^*$. Moreover, higher government debt was identified as a factor that independently raised real interest rates.

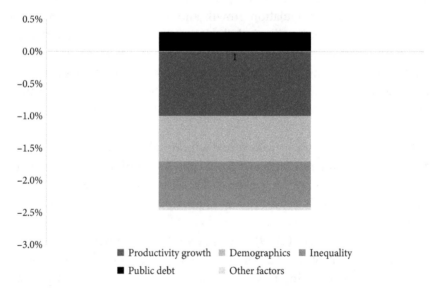

**Figure 9.10** Decomposition of fall in US $r^*$ between 1975 and 2015. IMF estimates.
*Source:* IMF.

In total, the factors outlined in the first sections of this chapter—lower economic growth, longer life expectancy, lower population growth, higher inequality, and so on—explain most of the decline in real interest rates after 1980 and up until the pandemic.

## 9.9 Checklist

This chapter has illustrated the following key points:

- Real interest rates are determined by the desired supply of savings and demand for investments. An increase in the desired supply of savings or a decrease in the desired demand for investments leads to lower real interest rates.
- In many economic models, real interest rates are positively linked to economic growth, population growth, and life expectancy.
- Economic growth rates have declined in recent decades, contributing to the decrease in real interest rates.
- Population growth rates have also declined, contributing to the decline in real interest rates.
- Increased life expectancies have led to a higher proportion of the population saving for retirement relative to those in retirement. This led to an increase in the global supply of savings, pushing down real interest rates.
- Wealth inequality has risen, and wealthier individuals tend to have higher savings rates. Concentration of wealth among the wealthy has increased the supply of savings, correlating with the decline in real interest rates.
- Firms have reduced their investments, possibly due to low economic growth and consequently lower returns on investments.
- The supply of safe assets has decreased, while central banks have heavily invested in safe assets since the 2008 financial crisis. The lower supply and the higher demand for safe assets such as government bonds have raised their prices and lowered their yields. This can help explain the low rates after the financial crisis of 2008 but not the decline in interest rates before that.
- The secular stagnation hypothesis posits that equilibrium interest rates have fallen significantly, with actual interest rates remaining higher than the equilibrium rate necessary for full employment.

- Empirical models estimate the relative importance of various factors influencing interest rate trends. In these models, factors such as lower economic and population growth rates, along with longer life expectancy, have reduced equilibrium real interest rates in advanced economies, whereas higher public debt has increased them. Overall, the former factors have outweighed the latter since the 1980s and up until the pandemic, thus pushing down real interest rates.

# 10

# What Caused the Rise in Inflation and Interest Rates after the Covid-19 Pandemic?

This book is set against the backdrop of a persistent and dramatic decline in interest rates from the early 1980s to 2020—a period spanning four decades. Earlier chapters have detailed this significant drop, exploring the reasons behind it and the societal impacts.

In early 2020, the world was struck by the Covid-19 pandemic, causing severe economic disruption. As the pandemic began to subside in 2021, something unusual happened: inflation surged rapidly and dramatically, reaching levels not seen since the early 1980s.

The significance of this shift in inflation dynamics cannot be overstated. For 40 years, inflation had been falling, and since the global financial crisis of 2008, it had remained subdued. Central banks exerted considerable effort to raise inflation, but it persistently stayed too low, frustrating policy-makers who could not meet their mandate of achieving modest, yet positive, inflation.

Then, quite suddenly, everything changed. Within a year, inflation soared to double-digit levels in many countries. In response, central banks raised their monetary policy interest rates, which in turn caused increases in other rates such as those on government bonds, mortgage bonds, and corporate bonds. This abrupt reversal ended a 40-year trend of declining inflation and interest rates.

The notable increase in nominal interest rates following the pandemic is significant, but it is at the same time important to highlight that inflation surged even more. As a result, real interest rates have not seen a corresponding rise. This observation—that real interest rates have remained largely unchanged post-pandemic—is important to remember when discussing the outlook for interest rates.

*How Low Interest Rates Change the World.* Jesper Rangvid, Oxford University Press. © Jesper Rangvid (2025).
DOI: 10.1093/9780198946410.003.0011

Why did this happen? What caused such a sudden and sharp rise in inflation, subsequently driving up nominal interest rates? What are the consequences? Will inflation and interest rates remain elevated compared to pre-pandemic levels, or will they revert to the lows experienced before the pandemic?

Understanding why inflation and nominal interest rates rose after the pandemic is crucial for making informed assessments of the future. This chapter focuses on the causes of the post-pandemic rise in inflation and nominal interest rates and analyses the reasons behind these changes, while subsequent chapters will address the outlook.

## 10.1 Putting the Post-Pandemic Rise in Inflation and Interest Rates into Perspective

The post-pandemic surge in inflation was striking. After being subdued for decades, inflation suddenly and dramatically increased as the world emerged from the pandemic in 2021, as shown in Figure 10.1.

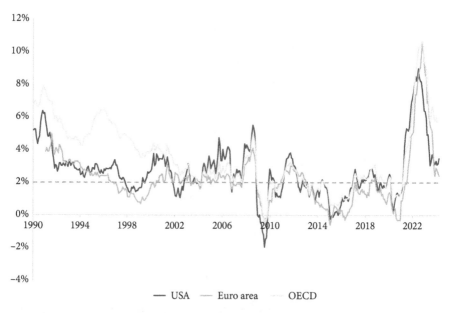

**Figure 10.1** Inflation in the euro area, the US, and across OECD countries. Two per cent inflation target indicated by dotted line. January 1990 to March 2024.
*Data source:* OECD.

Figure 10.1 illustrates how inflation in the euro area and the US had generally hovered around the Federal Reserve's (Fed's) and the European Central Bank's (ECB's) 2 per cent targets up until the financial crisis of 2008. However, following the financial crisis, inflation was persistently low, in particular in the euro area, averaging 1.4 per cent there and 1.8 per cent in the US from 2008 to 2020. In the rest of the Organisation for Economic Co-operation and Development (OECD) area, inflation remained relatively high during the 1990s but had fluctuated around 2 per cent since the turn of the millennium, though often undershooting the 2 per cent target since the financial crisis. To boost inflation after the financial crisis, central banks implemented aggressive monetary policies, such as quantitative easing, which was described in Section 9.6, and other expansionary policies.

Then, quite suddenly, inflation soared to levels unseen for three decades. The increase was remarkably swift: at the start of 2021, inflation was below 2 per cent across OECD countries, but just a year and a half later, it approached 10 per cent.

This surge was a major shock to central banks, governments, households, firms, and investors, all of whom had grown accustomed to low inflation.

While the overall inflation movements were similar across countries, a closer examination of the period when inflation rose reveals some important differences; see Figure 10.2. For instance, US inflation dynamics led those in other countries. By mid-2021, inflation in the US had reached around 6 per cent, while it remained at 2 per cent in the euro area. A few months later, inflation in Europe began to rise as well. Ultimately, inflation in Europe peaked higher than in the US, reaching nearly 11 per cent compared to 9 per cent in the US. Additionally, inflation in the US peaked in the spring/summer of 2022, whereas in the euro area and across other OECD countries, it peaked later in the autumn of 2022.

As a consequence of rising inflation, interest rates also increased, breaking a four-decade-long decline. Figure 10.3 illustrates the development in yields on long-term government bonds in selected advanced economies since 1990.

Figure 10.3 highlights the significant shift in interest rate dynamics following the pandemic. After several decades of persistent declines, with rates even entering negative territory in some countries before the pandemic, interest rates suddenly rose. By 2023, they had reached levels not seen in a decade.

Why did this happen?

**180** How Low Interest Rates Change the World

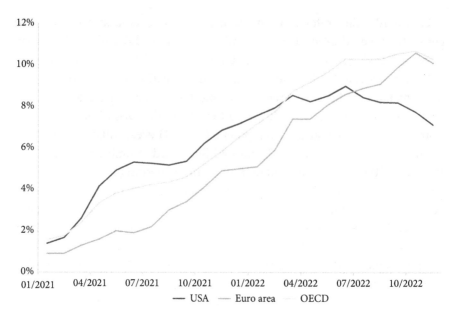

**Figure 10.2** Inflation in the euro area, the US, and across OECD countries, January 2021 to November 2022.
*Data source:* OECD.

**Figure 10.3** Nominal yields on 10-year government bonds in the US, Germany, France, and the UK, January 1990 to April 2024.
*Data source:* OECD.

## 10.2  Why Did Inflation Increase So Dramatically after the Pandemic?

Inflation occurs when firms raise prices on goods and services, typically due to high demand relative to supply.[1] While this explanation is correct, it is not comprehensive. We need to understand *why* demand exceeds supply or *why* supply falls short of demand.

In one paragraph, the main explanations behind the dramatic rise in inflation after the pandemic are as follows. The global recession resulting from the pandemic in early 2020 caused demand and inflation to plummet. In response, governments and central banks implemented massive relief packages and expansionary policies. This led to a rapid rebound in demand when the pandemic receded, which was further fuelled by a continuation of expansionary policies. Additionally, demand shifted from services to goods, while pandemic-related disruptions impaired supply chains. High demand and constrained supply created the ideal conditions for inflation, initially driving up prices of raw material, and later spreading to goods and service prices.

In summary, inflation rose post-pandemic due to:

- A surge in demand—fuelled by stimulative fiscal and monetary policies—as the pandemic waned.
- A shift in demand from services to goods in the initial phase of the pandemic, alongside supply-chain disruptions.
- Prices rose, beginning with commodity and goods prices, then extending to service prices.

While there are variations between countries, these factors were the primary drivers of the inflation flareup. The rest of this section will delve into each point in greater detail.[2]

## 10.2.1  The 2020 Recession and the Bounce-Back

To understand why demand soared after the pandemic, we must first grasp the severity of the brief recession it caused.

---

[1] In some countries, inflation also includes changes to owners' equivalent rent of residences, i.e. the cost of living in a home.

[2] Many researchers have investigated what caused the inflation flareup after the pandemic; see, for instance, Ha, Kose, and Ohnsorge (2021), Blanchard and Bernanke (2023), Arce et al. (2024), English, Forbes, and Ubide (2024), Giannone and Primiceri (2024), and Harr and Henderson (2024).

The pandemic led to a near-total pause in economic activity: schools closed, sending children home; factories and offices shut down, forcing workers to stay home; universities sent students away, and so on. Stringent lockdowns brought economic activity to a near standstill, causing economic output to plummet, unemployment to skyrocket, and stock prices to fall dramatically. This unprecedented and severe recession, though short-lived, had a profound impact. Figure 10.4 illustrates this, showing the weekly initial jobless claims in the US, which represent the number of people declaring unemployment each week.

Initial claims for unemployment insurance in the US have been published weekly since 1967. Historically, about 350,000 people become unemployed each week. Before the pandemic, the highest weekly unemployment claims were 700,000 in early October 1982. During the financial crisis of 2008–2009, the peak was 665,000 in late March 2009. These numbers are dwarfed by the pandemic's impact. In the first week of April 2020, over 6 million people filed for unemployment—a figure nearly 10 times greater than the previous record. Over four weeks, 22 million Americans lost their jobs, illustrating the unprecedented scale of the crisis.

Fortunately, the recession was short-lived. Figure 10.5 displays the quarterly percentage growth rate in US real GDP, highlighting the dramatic

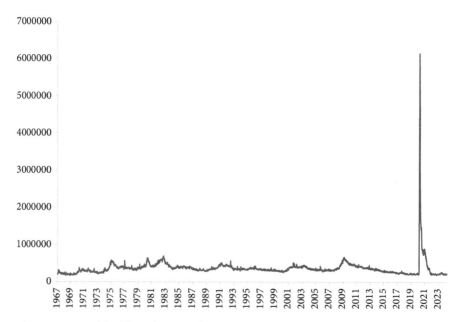

**Figure 10.4** Initial jobless claims in the US per week, January 1967 to April 2024.
*Data source:* St. Louis Fed Database.

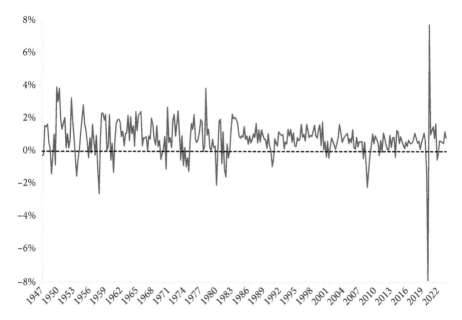

**Figure 10.5** Quarterly growth in US real GDP, 1947–2024.
*Data source:* St. Louis Fed Database.

economic contraction in the second quarter of 2020. Within that quarter, the US economy contracted by 7.9 per cent, the largest quarterly decline since records began in 1947. However, already in the next quarter, economic growth rebounded dramatically. In the third quarter of 2020, the US experienced the largest quarterly expansion in its economic history, making the early 2020 recession the shortest on record, lasting only two months.

#### 10.2.1.1 Demand Soared after the Pandemic

Why was the rebound so strong? The nature of the 2020 recession was unique. It was not a typical downturn; instead, economic activity was deliberately paused due to lockdowns aimed at protecting public health. As the pandemic receded, economic activity resumed, akin to pressing a play button after a pause. People returned to work, and the economy began to recover.

However, the recovery was not merely a mechanical reopening, and strong post-pandemic economic growth was not only a US phenomenon. Economic activity continued to expand throughout 2021, as illustrated in Figure 10.6, which shows annual growth in real GDP for the euro area and the US. In 2021, both regions experienced their fastest growth in several decades, with economic activity expanding by 6 per cent. The previous peak over the past two decades was 4 per cent in 2000.

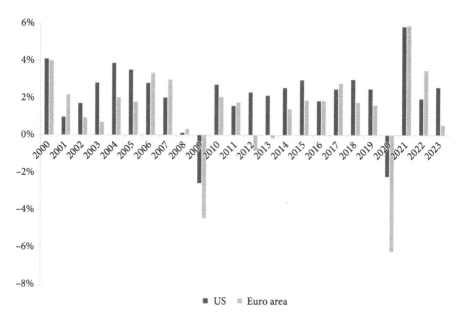

**Figure 10.6** Annual percentage growth in real GDP in the US and the euro area, 2000–2023.
*Data source:* St. Louis Fed Database and OECD.

One reason for the strong growth was the substantial savings accumulated by people during the initial phase of the pandemic, which they later used to finance increased consumption.

When households spend less than they earn, they save. Figure 10.7 depicts disposable personal income and personal outlays in the US since 2013. Personal outlays include personal consumption expenditure, interest payments, and transfer payments, with consumption expenditure making up over 96 per cent of total outlays. Savings are calculated as the difference between disposable income and outlays.

Before the pandemic, for instance in January 2020, US households collectively earned just over $1.38 trillion and had outlays of about $1.28 trillion. This resulted in savings of $100 billion for the month, equating to a savings rate of 7.2 per cent, a typical savings rate before the pandemic. However, at the onset of the pandemic, savings surged to nearly $500 billion in April 2020, remaining unusually high throughout 2020 and the first half of 2021. From March 2020 to December 2022, savings averaged over $200 billion per month, vastly exceeding average monthly savings of $80 billion between January 2016 and December 2019. Furthermore, throughout 2020 and 2021, the savings rate averaged 14 per cent, double the average rate observed in the previous decade (2010–2020).

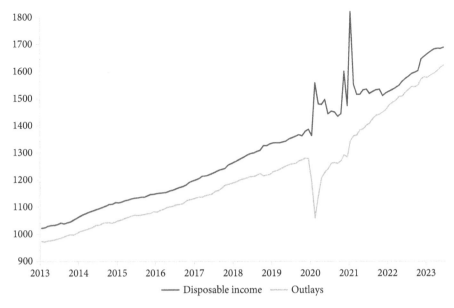

**Figure 10.7** Total personal disposable income and personal outlays in the US, monthly data, billions of USD.
*Data source:* FRED of St. Louis Fed.

As Figure 10.7 illustrates, savings increased not only because outlays fell. Incomes also rose. But why did incomes grow so much when employment and GDP fell so dramatically (Figures 10.4 and 10.5)? They did because substantial pandemic aid packages—such as the CARES Act, the Consolidated Appropriations Act, and the American Rescue Plan Act—significantly boosted household incomes starting in April 2020 and continuing through January 2021 and March 2021, respectively. Concurrently, consumption was curtailed due to restrictions on spending in services, as many providers like restaurants and sports facilities were closed during lockdowns. Consequently, spending sharply declined in April 2020 and remained subdued throughout the year. The boosts to incomes and reductions in spendings mathematically caused savings to rise.

This surge in savings was not limited to the US. Many countries experienced similar increases in household savings, as highlighted in Figure 10.8, based on data from Soyres, Moore, and Ortiz (2023).

Figure 10.8 shows 'excess savings', defined as the amount accumulated due to savings rates exceeding historical trends. It underscores how pandemic-related policies led to widespread savings accumulation across various economies globally.

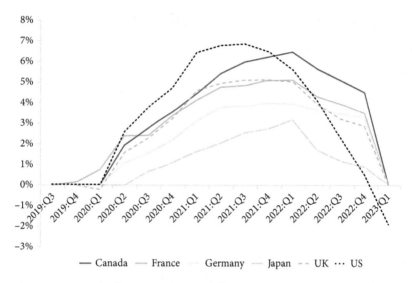

**Figure 10.8** Stock of excess savings in different countries, percentage of GDP.
*Data source:* Soyres, Moore, and Ortiz (2023).

Leaving the pandemic, people thus had money to spend, and they did so eagerly. As a result, economic activity surged. The combination of robust consumer spending, fuelled by substantial savings, significantly bolstered demand and contributed to inflationary pressures in the economy. Indeed, it turns out that the trends in excess savings closely mirrored the dynamics of inflation with a one-year lag, as depicted in Figure 10.9.

Figure 10.9 illustrates that US core inflation tracked the rise and fall of accumulated excess savings of US households by approximately one year. As excess savings began to increase in 2020, inflation followed suit one year later. The peak in excess savings occurred in autumn 2021, and inflation reached its peak one year thereafter. Subsequently, as excess savings have diminished, inflation has also decreased with a corresponding one-year lag.

While it may be tempting to attribute this inflationary episode solely to excess savings, which facilitated increased post-pandemic consumption and thereby fuelled inflation, this is only part of the explanation. Other factors also played significant roles, as detailed in the following section.

### 10.2.2 Expansionary Policies

During the pandemic, both fiscal and monetary policies were exceptionally expansionary, contributing further to inflationary pressures.

Interest Rates after the Covid-19 Pandemic? 187

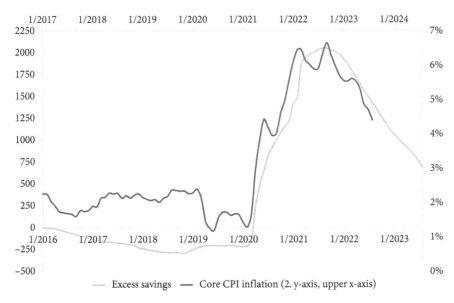

**Figure 10.9** Accumulated excess savings in the US (billions of USD, 1. y-axis, lower x-axis) and US core CPI inflation with a one-year lag (annual percentage change, 2. y-axis, upper x-axis) in the US. Monthly data.
*Data source:* FRED of St. Louis Fed.

Firstly, fiscal policies were notably expansive, particularly in the US, as already touched upon in the previous section. Historically, recessions typically entail hardship for households due to income reductions. Figure 10.10 illustrates this for the US, showing how real disposable income typically declines alongside real GDP during economic contractions. For instance, during the financial crisis of 2008–2009, both GDP and real income growth contracted, highlighting the economic challenges faced by individuals.

During the pandemic, the economic situation was markedly different. Despite a significant contraction in the economy, people's incomes rose. This was largely due to substantial government support measures that buoyed individuals through the crisis, as mentioned above.

The United States was not alone in implementing highly expansionary fiscal policies. Across OECD countries, public debt surged by 20 percentage points, climbing from 106 per cent of GDP in 2019 to 127 per cent by the end of 2021, according to World Bank data on central government debt as a percentage of GDP. By comparison, following the global financial crisis of 2008, OECD countries experienced a 12 per cent increase in indebtedness relative to GDP.

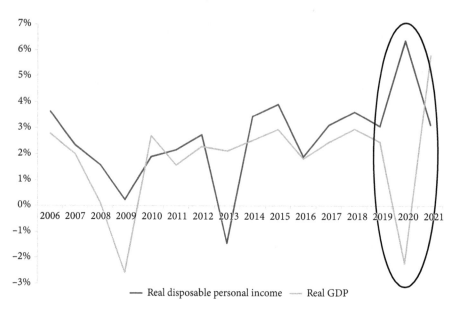

**Figure 10.10** Annual growth in real disposable income and real GDP in the US. The pandemic (2020) encircled, 2006–2021.
*Data source:* St. Louis Fed Database.

### 10.2.2.1 Monetary Policy

Monetary policy was also highly expansionary. In 2020, central banks aggressively reduced policy interest rates to their lowest feasible levels and engaged in substantial government bond purchases. Figure 10.11 illustrates this, showing the combined asset holdings of the ECB and the Fed measured in US dollars together with the S&P 500 stock market index.

In response to the Covid-19 crisis in March 2020, central banks embarked on massive asset purchases totalling trillions of USD to bolster economic activity. This swift action immediately boosted the stock market, as depicted in Figure 10.11. The surge in stock prices augmented people's wealth. Real estate values also rose. When individuals feel wealthier, they tend to spend more. Economists refer to this phenomenon as the marginal propensity to consume (MPC) out of wealth. Although there is some uncertainty about the exact size of the MPC, economists agree it is positive; see, for instance, Campbell and Cocco (2007) and Di Maggio, Kermani, and Majlesi (2020). Hence, rising stock and housing prices brought about by very expansionary monetary policies boosted aggregate demand, increasing inflationary pressures.

Criticism of the expansive policies during the early phase of the pandemic is unwarranted. As earlier sections of this chapter have demonstrated, the

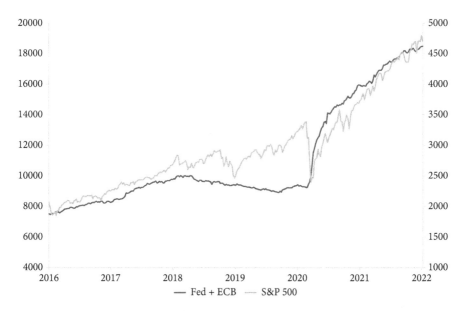

**Figure 10.11** Combined values of Fed and ECB balance sheets in billions of US dollars and the S&P 500 (right-hand scale). Weekly data, January 2016 to October 2022.
*Data source:* FRED of St. Louis Fed and Thomson Datastream via Refinitiv.

economic contraction was unprecedented, and uncertainties surrounding the pandemic's duration and impact were profound. Thus, providing support to households and businesses early on was prudent.

However, fiscal and monetary support persisted for an extended period. By autumn 2021, inflationary pressures were mounting, yet monetary policy rates remained exceedingly low (negative in Europe and near zero in the US), and both the Fed and the ECB continued their substantial asset-purchase programmes instead of raising rates and halting bond purchases. This lack of policy adjustment contributed to the escalation of inflation.

Expansionary monetary policies also expanded the money supply, as explained in Box 10.1.

## Box 10.1  Money supply growth and inflation during the post-pandemic inflation flareup

Chapter 8 concluded that according to the monetary theory of the price level, inflation correlates directly with the growth rate of the money supply, given exogenous velocity and economic growth. Economists generally dismiss this theory as a robust explanation for inflation, citing a lack of consistent correlation between money growth and inflation across business cycles. The relationship appears to emerge primarily during periods of exceptionally high inflation, where it is difficult to determine the direction of causality, Chapter 8 mentioned.

Ironically, however, the monetary theory appears to find validation during the post-pandemic inflation surge. In several countries, the aggregate money supply expanded significantly during the pandemic, followed by the subsequent inflationary spike.

Figure 10.12 illustrates the annual growth rate of the US aggregate money supply (M2) advanced by 15 months alongside US inflation trends. Immediately following the outbreak of the pandemic, the money supply expanded at its fastest rate since the Second World War. Subsequently, inflation surged, reaching levels not seen since the 1970s. As the growth rate of the money supply slowed down, inflation also decreased rapidly.

This phenomenon was not confined to the United States alone, although the situation there was particularly pronounced. An analysis by the Banque de France (2022) illustrates how the money supply in Europe also experienced rapid growth during this period, coinciding with significant inflationary pressures across the continent.

While there is a strong correlation between money growth and inflation during this recent flareup, the challenge for the monetary explanation lies in the theory's assertion that this relationship holds universally and always. Figure 10.13 extends the analysis back to the early 1960s, leveraging monthly data on money growth.

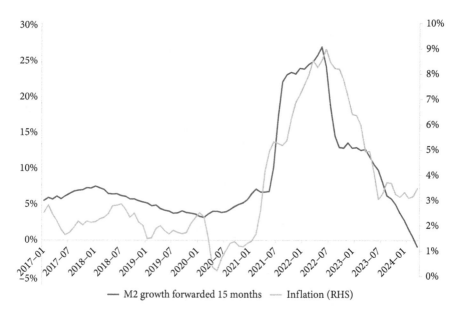

**Figure 10.12** Annual percentage growth in US aggregate money supply (M2) forwarded 15 months and US inflation, 2017–2024
*Data source:* FRED of St. Louis Fed.

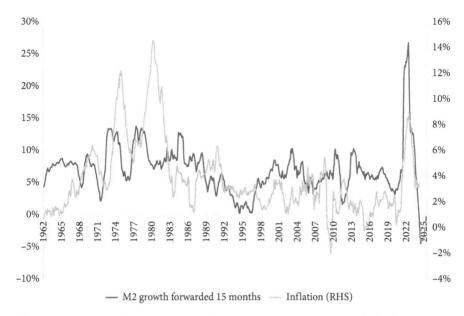

**Figure 10.13** Annual percentage growth in US aggregate money supply (M2) forwarded 15 months and US inflation, 1960–2024.
*Data source:* FRED of St. Louis Fed.

Until the onset of the pandemic, there was little correlation between money growth and inflation, consistent with the findings from Chapter 8. Therefore, while there appears to be a strong correlation for the period spanning 2020 to 2023, it remains weak over a longer timeframe. It is challenging to fully endorse a theory that only seems to apply under specific conditions.

But why did the money supply experience such rapid growth in 2020? The money supply measures the total amount of money circulating in the economy. Money primarily consists of readily accessible funds held by households and businesses, such as checking and savings deposits. To understand its surge in 2020, we must examine what happened to deposits.

As explained by Castro, Cavallo, and Zarutskie (2022), the sharp increase in deposits in 2020 was driven by two main factors: (i) precautionary savings by households and firms amid considerable uncertainty and (ii) exceptionally expansionary fiscal and monetary policies. These policies led to an unprecedented surge in deposits, thereby propelling the money supply to unprecedented levels.

As explained in previous sections of this chapter, as the pandemic subsided, expansionary policies and high precautionary savings bolstered demand, triggering a surge in inflation. While this also coincided with an increase in the money supply, the fundamental driver of inflation was more rooted in what caused the surge in the money supply (expansionary policies and precautionary savings) than the surge itself.

## 10.2.3 Goods/Services Demand Shifts and Supply-Chain Challenges

Demand surged immediately after the pandemic, largely driven by expansionary macroeconomic policies.

Furthermore, there was a notable shift in demand from services to goods. With restrictions in place during the pandemic, people were confined to their homes and unable to dine out, travel, or attend events like sports and concerts. Consequently, spending on services plummeted.

Simultaneously, the shift to remote work and home confinement prompted increased demand for goods such as office chairs, computer screens, new furniture, and entertainment devices like PlayStations and iPads. This shift is vividly illustrated in the data. Figure 10.14 depicts the ratio of personal consumption expenditures on goods in the US relative to total personal consumption expenditures, indicating the percentage spent on goods for every USD 100 of consumption.

The fraction of household consumption expenditures allocated to goods had been steadily declining for decades. In 1960, for example, out of every USD 100 spent on consumption, USD 53 went towards goods. By just before the pandemic, this ratio had dropped to USD 31.

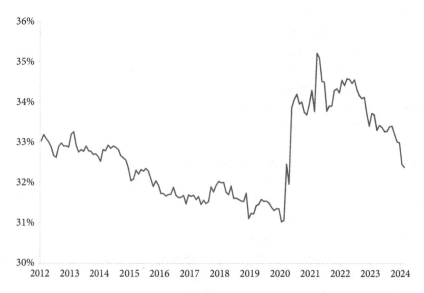

**Figure 10.14** Ratio of US personal consumption expenditures, goods, to US total consumption expenditures, 2012–2024.
*Data source:* St. Louis Fed Database.

However, the pandemic abruptly interrupted this long-term trend, as illustrated in Figure 10.14. With the onset of the pandemic in early 2020, the ratio of expenditures on goods relative to total consumption expenditures immediately surged.

Put another way, from June 2020 to June 2021, expenditures on services increased by 12 per cent, whereas expenditures on goods rose significantly more, by 17 per cent.

This reversal in consumption patterns—where goods consumption outpaced services—was a distinctive outcome of the post-pandemic period. Prior to the pandemic, the growth in services consumption had typically exceeded that of goods. In nominal terms, by 2020, goods consumption had increased 25-fold compared to 1960, while services consumption had risen 56-fold.

Businesses were caught off-guard by this sudden surge in goods demand. After years of declining relative demand for goods, the rapid shift in consumer behaviour towards goods drove up their prices.

Additionally, the production and transportation of goods were severely disrupted. Factories shut down due to pandemic-related restrictions, and supply chains were crippled as ships faced entry bans at ports. This dual impact—increased demand and reduced supply of goods—obviously led to price hikes.

The New York Fed has developed an index that tracks pressures on global supply chains, detailed in Figure 10.15.

Figure 10.15 illustrates the profound disruption of global supply chains following the onset of the pandemic in early 2020. The index surged abruptly from 0 (indicating no supply-chain disruptions) to 3. This global supply-chain index is designed to measure deviations from its historical average in standard deviations. Hence, immediately after the pandemic began, supply-chain disruptions were three standard deviations above the norm—a significant deviation.

As the pandemic's impact diminished, consumption patterns reverted to their pre-pandemic norms. People increased their spending on services while reducing the fraction of total consumption allocated to goods, Figure 10.14 reveals. Also, as of 2022, supply-chain disruptions eased, Figure 10.15 shows.

Ultimately, both increased demand and supply-chain disruptions contributed to the surge in inflation. To quantify these contributions, economists at the Federal Reserve Bank of San Francisco analysed the fractions of US inflation attributable to demand and supply factors. They categorized spending categories in the personal consumption expenditure basket into supply-driven, demand-driven, and ambiguous groups. This decomposition is depicted in Figure 10.16.

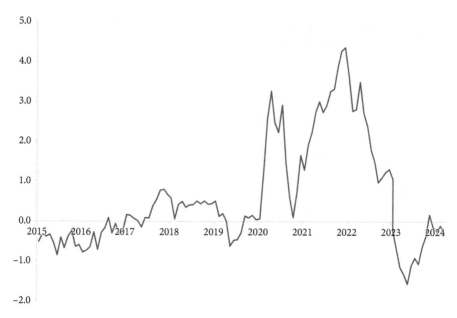

**Figure 10.15** Global supply-chain pressure index.
*Data source:* New York Fed.

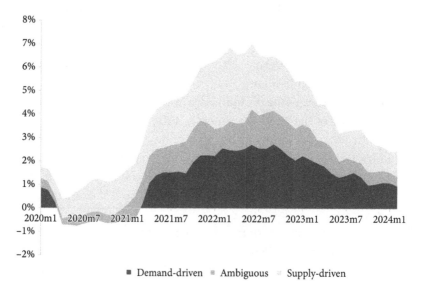

**Figure 10.16** Supply- and demand-driven inflation in the US, January 2020 to February 2024.
*Data source:* San Francisco Fed/Shapiro (2022).

Figure 10.16 illustrates that supply-chain disruptions predominantly drove inflation during the initial phase of the inflation surge. However, the significant acceleration in inflation occurred when the economy reopened and spending resumed in early 2021. By the peak of inflation in 2022, both demand and supply factors contributed equally to the inflationary pressures.

## 10.2.4 Rising Commodity Prices

Additionally, rising commodity prices played a role. The developments described above—heightened demand resulting from substantial savings releases and expansionary fiscal and monetary policies, alongside severe supply-chain disruptions—initially led to increases in commodity prices. Figure 10.17 depicts the 'All Commodity Price Index' developed by the International Monetary Fund (IMF), illustrating how prices across various commodities surged immediately after the pandemic outbreak, following a period of relative stability globally.

Many types of commodities experienced price increases, including oil, food, and agricultural products. While these price hikes were driven by factors similar to those affecting other goods, raw materials play a special role in economics in that they are used as inputs in the production of various goods and services. For instance, higher oil prices increase transportation costs,

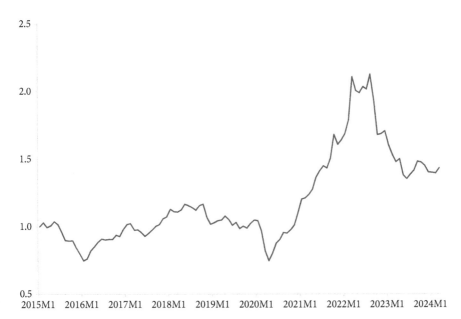

**Figure 10.17** Commodities for Index: All, excluding Gold, 2015=1.0, January 2015 to March 2024.

*Data source:* IMF.

leading to higher prices for transported goods. Similarly, increased wheat prices raise production costs for bakeries, reflecting in higher bread prices. Therefore, escalating commodity prices can trigger inflation, making them a significant factor behind the inflationary surge immediately following the pandemic.

## 10.3 Nominal Interest Rates Rose in Response to the Inflation Surge

In response to the significant surge in inflation, central banks implemented tighter monetary policies by raising their policy rates. However, they took these decisions belatedly. The Fed began increasing rates in March 2022, when US inflation had already reached 8 per cent, while the ECB followed suit in July 2022, when inflation in the euro area had reached 9 per cent.

The reasons behind these delayed policy reactions are perplexing. They likely stem from the prolonged period of low inflation prior to the pandemic, as discussed in Section 10.1, during which central banks were primarily concerned with inflation being too low rather than too high. Perhaps central banks initially believed that inflation would naturally subside on its own. This assumption proved erroneous, however. Instead, inflation became entrenched, necessitating a swift and robust monetary response.

As central banks eventually recognized that inflation persisted, they embarked on an accelerated tightening of monetary policy. This marked one of the fastest 'hiking cycles' in recent memory. Figure 10.18 illustrates for a few representative countries the movements in yields on short-term government bonds, which are strongly influenced by monetary policy rates, during this period.

Yields experienced a sudden and sharp increase after central banks began raising rates in early 2022 in the US and mid-2022 in the euro area. This rise was particularly striking in the euro area, where the ECB had maintained persistently negative monetary policy rates before the pandemic. Yields surged from negative levels to nearly 4 per cent by 2023.

This upward movement in yields extended across various sectors of the economy. Long-term government bond yields rose, mirroring similar trends in mortgage bonds, corporate bonds, and other interest rates.

It is important to note that while the rise in nominal rates was both significant and abrupt, they generally did not increase as much as inflation. Consequently, real interest rates did not rise. This point is illustrated in

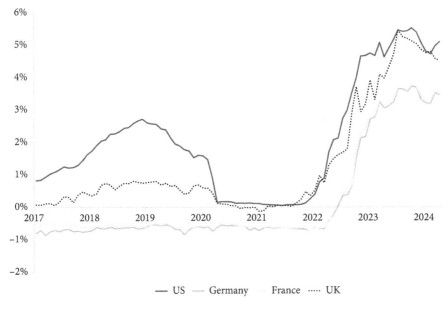

**Figure 10.18** One-year yields (government bonds) in the US, the UK, France, and Germany.
*Data source:* FRED of St. Louis Fed.

Figure 10.19, which shows real interest rates—calculated by subtracting current inflation from nominal yields on 10-year government bonds—for several selected countries.

As inflation surged to around 10 per cent in many countries (see Figure 10.1), nominal yields in most cases increased to just 5 per cent or less (see Figure 10.3). This disparity indicates that inflation outpaced the rise in yields, resulting in a significant drop in real yields, as illustrated in Figure 10.19. Therefore, the post-pandemic increase in yields is confined primarily to nominal yields.[3]

The abrupt increase in nominal yields halted a four-decade-long trend of declining rates. This prompts the question of whether it signifies the beginning of a new era where interest rates will remain higher than the pre-pandemic norms or if nominal rates will revert once inflation is brought under control. Subsequent chapters will deal with these questions.

---

[3] This conclusion remains valid when examining $r^*$, which represents estimates of underlying equilibrium real interest rates. BIS (2024) compares various estimates of $r^*$ across different countries following the pandemic and finds that, although there are some indications that $r^*$ may have risen slightly, this 'assessment is surrounded by a very high degree of uncertainty'. Consequently, it appears to be the case that real interest rates have not increased in tandem with nominal interest rates after the pandemic.

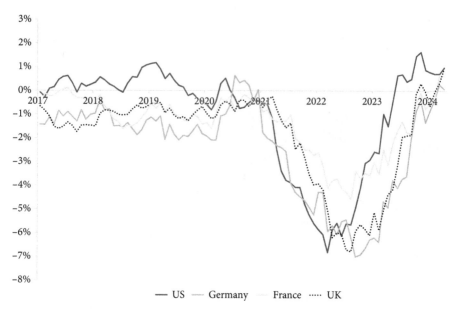

**Figure 10.19** Real interest rates in selected countries, calculated as the yield on 10-year government bonds minus the current inflation rates.
*Data source:* FRED of St. Louis Fed.

## 10.4 Checklist

This chapter has highlighted several key factors contributing to the inflation surge after Covid-19:

- The Covid-19 pandemic triggered global lockdowns, disrupting supply chains worldwide.
- To mitigate the pandemic's economic fallout, fiscal and monetary policies became highly expansionary. As a result, households' savings rose, facilitating a strong economic bounce-back as the pandemic receded.
- The combination of supply-chain disruptions and expansionary policies led to a surge in global inflation. By 2022, inflation had reached its highest levels in 40 years, peaking at around 10 per cent in most advanced economies.
- This book concludes that both demand and supply factors contributed to the inflation surge, but places particular emphasis on the importance of policies' contributions. Prolonged aggressive fiscal and monetary policies amplified demand relative to constrained supply, driving inflation higher.

- In essence, one could state that inflation rose because of the pandemic and the measures taken to mitigate its economic fallout. Stated differently, without the pandemic, there would not have been a spike in inflation.
- Central banks were slow to acknowledge that inflation was not transitory. Eventually, high inflation rates necessitated a sharp increase in nominal interest rates, though not in real rates.
- After four decades of decline, nominal interest rates suddenly surged alongside inflation. The critical question now is whether interest rates will stabilize at levels higher than pre-pandemic norms or revert to previous lows.

## PART IV

# WHAT DOES THE FUTURE HOLD?

# 11
# Trends That Could Keep Rates Low

Between 1980 and 2020, interest rates steadily declined. In 2021, this trend abruptly reversed because of the Covid-19 pandemic, as detailed in the preceding chapter. The pivotal question now is whether this shift in rate dynamics signified the onset of a new era, where inflation and interest rates will be higher than before the pandemic, or if it was merely a transient event, with rates eventually returning to previous lows.

Over the short term—spanning a few years—interest rates fluctuate with the business cycle. Economic slowdowns and booms significantly influence monetary policy, which in turn has a primary impact on interest rates. During periods of economic strength and mounting inflationary pressures, central banks tighten monetary policy by raising rates, causing other interest rates to follow suit. Conversely, in economic downturns, central banks lower rates, triggering the opposite effect. While crucial for understanding short-term rate movements and economic trends, this topic does not constitute the primary focus of this book.

This book explores long-term trends in interest rates—beyond the fluctuations induced by the business cycle. Will interest rates in the next decade or two replicate the trajectory of the past four decades, characterized by persistently low rates, or will they surpass the pre-pandemic levels? Nobody knows, and arguments exist for both scenarios.

The fact that uncertainty prevails does not mean that we cannot say anything, though. We can lay out the arguments for both scenarios, and then we can assess them. The subsequent chapters will do so.

This chapter reviews arguments advocating for low interest rates. There are several reasons to suspect that interest rates will remain low in the future. Most importantly, many of the trends discussed in Chapter 9 that have contributed to lowering rates over the past four decades are likely to persist. The chapter argues that four trends are likely to continue keeping interest rates low in the future. These are:

---

*How Low Interest Rates Change the World.* Jesper Rangvid, Oxford University Press. © Jesper Rangvid (2025).
DOI: 10.1093/9780198946410.003.0012

**Trend 1.** Rates have been falling for 700 years, so why should this trend stop?
**Trend 2.** Population growth rates are likely to keep declining.
**Trend 3.** Life expectancies are expected to continue rising.
**Trend 4.** Economic growth rates will probably remain relatively low.

This chapter will analyse these and other anticipated trends and their implications for future interest rates. Then, the next chapter will explore developments that might drive interest rates higher, and Chapter 13 weighs the arguments against each other to present this book's perspective.

## 11.1 Trend 1. Interest Rates Have Been on a Downward Trajectory for the Past 700 Years. Why Should This Change?

The first argument for expecting low interest rates in the coming years stems from the consistent empirical observation that global interest rates have steadily declined over the past seven centuries, as previously discussed in Chapter 1 and reiterated in Figure 11.1 for reference.

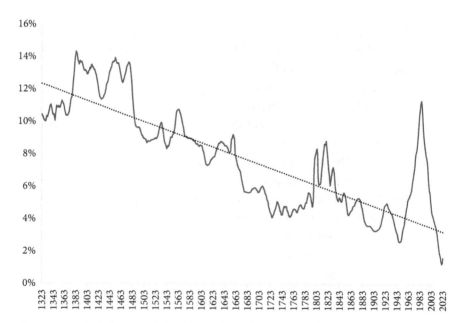

**Figure 11.1** Global nominal yield, 1310–2023. Seven-year rolling average.
*Data source:* Bank of England/Schmelzing (2020).

Figure 11.1 shows that while there have been fluctuations around the downward-sloping trend, global interest rates have exhibited a steady decline over the past 700 years. Given this, there is reason to expect that the trend will continue.

Some of the fluctuations are worth highlighting, not least the significant deviation from the trend during the 1960s and 1970s. Global nominal yields surged to levels unprecedented since 1480. While sporadic spikes in yields have occurred throughout history, the magnitude of the 1970s spike was unprecedented, marking a 10-percentage point increase from previous lows.

This surge in interest rates during the early 1970s was driven by inflation rather than real interest rates. Chapter 2 showed how inflation escalated during the 1960s and 1970s, while real interest rates remained relatively stable. Subsequently, real interest rates rose in the 1980s as inflation subsided, a point discussed in detail in Chapter 2.

Rogoff, Rossi, and Schmelzing (2024) explore the long-term decline in real interest rates, finding a consistent 'gentle but firm downward trend (averaging about 1.6% every 100 years)'. This trend carries profound implications: with interest rates having steadily fallen over the past seven centuries, the most reasonable forecast is for this trend to continue. While investment advisors caution that 'past returns are no guarantee of future results', the persistence of declining interest rates across nearly a millennium suggests a compelling case for continuity.

Of course, there are limits to how low nominal interest rates can go. At some point, they will reach the zero lower bound and face constraints on further decline. Yet, if the factors driving this decline persist, the most probable scenario is for rates to remain low.

Thus, the initial argument for anticipating low interest rates in the future rests simply on the historical precedent spanning 700 years. This argument draws not from economic theory but from the enduring empirical trend observed in interest rate movements over centuries.

## 11.2  Trend 2. Population Growth Falls

While the previous section relied on statistical evidence—a historical empirical fact that interest rates have declined over the past 700 years—the arguments presented next are grounded in economic theory. Box 9.1 in Chapter 9 outlined a foundational economic model often used by economists to understand interest rate determinants. It was concluded that real interest rates tend to be lower under certain conditions:

# 206　How Low Interest Rates Change the World

- When population growth rates are lower.
- When life expectancy increases.
- When economic growth rates are lower.

This subsection will delve into the first argument: what are the prospects for population growth rates and how will they contribute to interest rates? Subsequent sections will address life expectancy and economic growth.

Recall from Chapter 9 that a reduced rate of population growth implies a smaller workforce. Given a fixed capital stock in the economy, a smaller workforce increases the capital-to-labour ratio. When there are fewer workers relative to capital, investments in new capital—such as machinery—result in less significant increases in production compared to periods with abundant labour. In simpler terms, if a company invests in a new machine but lacks enough workers to operate it effectively, production will not expand as much. Thus, the marginal productivity of capital declines with lower population growth rates, and as the marginal productivity of capital determines the real interest rate, economic models predict that lower population growth will lead to lower real interest rates.

What can we anticipate regarding future population growth rates? It is a widely shared and robust forecast among international organizations, including the United Nations and others focused on demographic trends, that global population growth rates will decrease. Figure 11.2 illustrates these projections for the world and different continents.

Starting with the global population, as of 2024, approximately 8 billion people inhabit planet earth. Projections indicate a growth in the global population of slightly less than 1 per cent in 2025, equating to an increase of 80 million individuals. However, the key point is that this growth rate is expected to decline steadily. By 2040, the global population growth rate is forecasted to drop to 0.6 per cent, decreasing further to 0.45 per cent by 2050, and continuing this trajectory. According to current estimates, around 2085, global population growth is projected to turn negative, marking a decline in the global population.

This downward trend in population growth is anticipated across all continents: Africa, Asia, Europe, and the Americas. Notably, Europe presents a distinct pattern as its population growth is already negative and is projected to remain so for the next three decades. Afterward, there might be a slight increase, but the population growth in Europe is expected to remain negative in the long term. The trends illustrated in Figure 11.2 suggest that real interest rates are likely to remain low or even decline in the future.

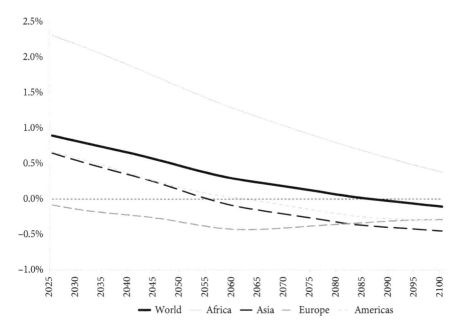

**Figure 11.2** Projected population growth rates in different regions of the world.
*Data source:* United Nations.

As mentioned, the reason lower population growth correlates with lower interest rates lies in its impact on the capital-to-labour ratio, which influences the marginal productivity of capital and thus interest rates. Some argue, with good reason, that the growth rate of the working-age population (ages 25–65) may be more pertinent than the total population growth rate. Interestingly, the growth rate of the global working-age population mirrors that of the total population shown in Figure 11.2. It is projected to decrease globally over time, with growth rates falling from approximately 1 per cent in 2025 to near zero by 2100 across all regions.

In summary, whether examining total population growth or the working-age population growth, the consensus suggests a declining trend, continuing to keep interest rates low in the foreseeable future.

Figure 11.2 indicates a global population growth turning negative by the end of the century. Jones (2022) models the potential macroeconomic implications of such trends using endogenous idea-driven growth models. According to Jones, a shrinking population results in fewer workers across all professions, including researchers, leading to a reduction in new ideas. In models of endogenous growth, new ideas are pivotal for economic advancement. Consequently, with fewer people and fewer innovative ideas, economic growth could stagnate, potentially resulting in what Jones (2022) terms 'the Empty Planet' scenario, where knowledge and living standards plateau or decline. In such a scenario, interest rates would likely be extremely low.

## 11.3 Trend 3. We Will Live Longer

Theory posits that the equilibrium interest rate decreases as life expectancy increases, for two interrelated reasons explained in Chapter 9. Firstly, extended life expectancy necessitates longer periods of saving. For instance, if one starts saving at 30 and expects to live until 75, savings must span 45 years before being utilized. If life expectancy extends to 85 years, the waiting period increases to 55 years. In economic models, this translates into greater patience: since savings are tied up for longer durations, there is less urgency to earn high interest rates to motivate saving, as detailed in Box 9.1.

Secondly, longer life expectancies mean longer retirement periods, prompting individuals to save more during their working years. This amplifies the overall supply of savings, pushing down the equilibrium interest rate, as outlined in Section 9.1's savings/investment argument. In summary, economic models consistently associate longer life expectancies with lower interest rates.

Demographic experts largely agree that global life expectancies will continue to rise in the foreseeable future. Figure 11.3, based on United Nations projections, illustrates the expected increase in the number of years a newborn globally can expect to live, spanning males, females, and their average.

In 2023, the average life expectancy for a newborn boy is projected to be 70.8 years, while for a newborn girl, it is expected to be 76.0 years. Combining these, the average life expectancy at birth is estimated at 73.4 years. Looking ahead, life expectancy is anticipated to increase steadily over the coming decades. By 2035, the average life expectancy for newborns is forecasted to reach 75 years, rising to 80 years by 2077, and further to 82.1 years by 2100 (with estimates of 79.9 years for boys and 84.3 years for girls born in that year). To put it another way, a newborn in 2100 is expected to live 8.7 years longer than one born in 2025, marking a 12 per cent increase in global life expectancy.

This remarkable—and positive—progress in life expectancy carries profound implications for global interest rates via two channels.

Firstly, as life expectancy increases, retirement savings need to last longer. This extended savings period requires greater patience from savers, which—according to the framework in Box 9.1—leads to lower interest rates.

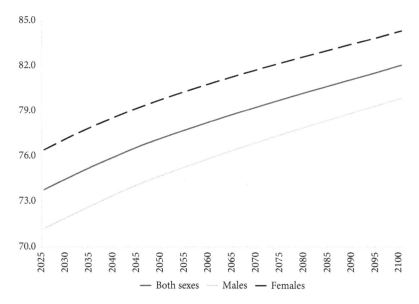

**Figure 11.3** Global life expectancy at birth.
*Data source*: United Nations.

Secondly, if retirement ages do not adjust accordingly—see below—the savings accumulated during working years must sustain an additional 8.7 years of retirement for individuals born in 2100 compared to those born in 2025. In practical terms, this necessitates a substantial increase in savings to fund extended longevity. Therefore, longer life expectancies exert considerable downward pressure on global interest rates.

Figure 11.3 illustrates global life expectancy, reflecting the average across all countries. Notably, life expectancy is strongly correlated with income levels. Generally, individuals and countries with higher incomes tend to enjoy longer life expectancies. It could be hypothesized that higher-income countries—where people already live longer—may not experience as significant an increase in life expectancy as lower-income counterparts. However, in absolute terms, life expectancy is projected to rise equally much across low- and high-income countries, as Figure 11.4 shows. The figure depicts expected trends in life expectancies for newborns (average across genders) in low-, middle-, and high-income countries.

Figure 11.4 illustrates that life expectancy is projected to increase by approximately the same amount—around nine years—across low-, middle-, and high-income countries from 2025 to 2100. Consequently, the nearly two-decade gap in life expectancy between newborns in low-income and high-income countries is expected to persist over the next 75 years.

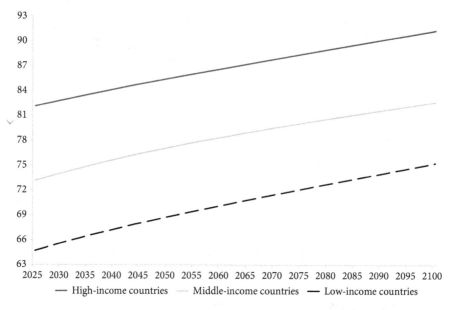

**Figure 11.4** Expected developments in life expectancy for a newborn in low-, middle-, and high-income countries.
Source: United Nations.

Global savings and wealth, which heavily influence global interest rates, are concentrated in high-income countries. If longevity were to increase predominantly in low-income nations, the impact of longer life expectancy on global interest rates might be less pronounced due to a smaller increase in global savings. However, as Figure 11.4 shows, longer life expectancies will affect all types of countries, thereby anticipating a rise in global savings in the years ahead.

Increased longevity necessitates greater savings during working years to ensure sufficient income during retirement, assuming retirement ages do not adjust accordingly. Conversely, if retirement ages increase alongside longevity, individuals may not need to enhance their savings during their working lives.

While retirement ages are anticipated to rise in many countries, the increase in life expectancy is expected to outpace these adjustments. For example, according to OECD (2021), retirement ages in Organisation for Economic Co-operation and Development (OECD) countries are projected to increase by approximately two years in the future, while life expectancy at age 65 is expected to rise by an average of around four years. Moreover, the OECD notes that the proportion of adult life spent in retirement is increasing for cohorts entering the labour market today compared to those retiring now.

When a larger proportion of adult life is spent in retirement, individuals must save more during their working years to finance these additional retirement years. Overall, the prolonged increase in life expectancy is anticipated to necessitate higher levels of global savings. This elevated savings level is likely to exert downward pressure on global interest rates moving forward.

## 11.4  Trend 4. Lower Economic Growth Rates Reduce Real Rates

Expected future economic growth influences equilibrium real interest rates. If economic activity and consumption are projected to increase, individuals can anticipate higher future income and spending. In such scenarios, the incentive to save today diminishes because tomorrow's consumption needs are already anticipated to be substantial. Therefore, when future economic growth is high, indicating robust consumption growth, the interest rate today must be higher to incentivize saving, as explained in Box 9.1.

Conversely, if future consumption growth is expected to decline, individuals anticipate lower future consumption levels. In this case, they are more willing to sacrifice some current consumption in favour of saving to maintain a stable consumption level over time. With lower expected future consumption growth (resulting from lower economic growth), the interest rate required to encourage saving does not need to be as high.

Empirically, there is consensus that global economic growth is projected to decrease in the coming years, as depicted in Figure 11.5, based on OECD estimates. Global real economic growth is forecasted to decrease from approximately 3 per cent annually in 2025 to around 1.5 per cent by 2060—a 50 per cent reduction in expected annual economic growth. All else being equal, this substantial decline in economic growth rates is likely to exert downward pressure on global real equilibrium interest rates in the future.

The decline in global economic growth is primarily driven by expectations of reduced growth in emerging markets. Meanwhile, in advanced economies such as the US and Europe, economic growth is forecasted to remain relatively stable in the coming years.

Let us take a moment to reflect. The preceding sections have collectively painted a future where several long-term trends converge: a decreasing global population growth rate, a slowdown in the growth rate of the global working-age population, increased life expectancy, a higher proportion of life spent in

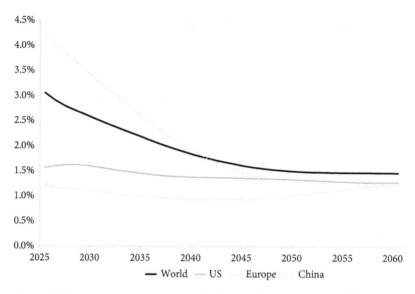

**Figure 11.5** Expected economic growth, 2025–2060, measured in USD at constant prices and purchasing power parities (PPPs) of 2010.
*Source*: OECD.

retirement, and either stagnant or declining economic growth rates. These persistent trends collectively exert downward pressure on global real interest rates.

This future scenario resembles the pre-pandemic world—a world characterized by prolonged periods of low interest rates. Furthermore, there are several newer developments that also point towards sustained low interest rates in the foreseeable future.

## 11.5 Uncertainty: Climate Risk and Geopolitical Risk

The model outlined in Box 9.1 provides a framework without incorporating uncertainty, yet the future is inherently uncertain. While Figures 11.1 to 11.5 offer informed predictions, the future might diverge from these projections due to unforeseen events.

Economists have developed models that account for uncertainty, integrating risk into the canonical interest rate model described in Box 9.1. In such models, interest rates are determined by:

$$r = \delta + \gamma \Delta c + n - (\gamma^2/2)\sigma^2$$

where—relative to the expression in Box 9.1—the term $\sigma^2$ has been added as a determinant of interest rates. This term measures the uncertainty (risk) of future consumption growth, and $\gamma$ represents risk aversion—indicating how averse individuals are to risk.

The model predicts an inverse relationship between uncertainty (or risk) and the interest rate. When people are risk-averse, they tend to save more in anticipation of uncertain future events, thereby pushing down the interest rate. In the equation, this is reflected by a negative coefficient before the measure of risk, $\sigma^2$. Higher uncertainty (larger $\sigma^2$) results in a lower interest rate.

Individuals' attitudes towards risk influence how changes in risk affect interest rates. High risk aversion (higher $\gamma$) implies that people significantly increase their savings in response to increased uncertainty. Consequently, the interest rate declines even more when uncertainty rises if individuals are more risk averse.

Looking ahead, new types of risk, such as climate risk, are expected to shape the future economic landscape significantly. Climate change introduces unique risks that are likely to be more prevalent than in previous decades. Bylund and Jonsson (2020) provide insight into these risks related to climate change and their potential impact on interest rates. The world faces physical risks—such as heightened occurrences and severity of natural disasters like droughts, floods, hurricanes, heatwaves, and rising sea levels. Moreover, the global transition towards a sustainable economy introduces transition risks, including the possibility of new taxes and regulations to alter consumption patterns, and challenges in extracting fossil-based resources. Bylund and Jonsson (2020) also argue that fundamental risks will emerge, where global warming could trigger self-sustaining patterns leading to disastrous consequences, such as accelerated ice melting contributing further to global warming.

These various risks tend to increase precautionary savings, thereby exerting downward pressure on interest rates. Additionally, the economic repercussions of climate change—such as the costly mitigation of natural disasters and the destruction of productive assets like homes and factories—could reduce overall economic activity. This potential decline in economic growth resulting from negative climate changes is another factor contributing to expectations of lower interest rates in the future. Mongelli, Pointner, and End (2022) review evidence on the effects of climate changes on $r^*$, and similarly conclude that the overall effect on interest rates is likely to be negative, and maybe even substantially so.

### 11.5.1 Higher Geopolitical Risk

At the time of writing in 2024, numerous geopolitical risks loom large: Russia's invasion of Ukraine and the ensuing conflict, tensions between China and the US, strained relations involving Russia and the US, ongoing conflicts in the Middle East and Israel, China's stance towards Taiwan, and other significant global tensions. These geopolitical risks introduce uncertainty, prompting individuals and businesses to increase precautionary savings, thereby exerting downward pressure on interest rates.

In 2022, researchers Caldara and Iacoviello developed an index to quantify global geopolitical risks. Their methodology involves tracking the frequency of articles in leading international newspapers that cover adverse geopolitical events. Geopolitical risks, as defined by Caldara and Iacoviello (2022, p. 1195), encompass 'the threat, realization, and escalation of adverse events associated with wars, terrorism, and any tensions among states and political actors that affect the peaceful course of international relations'.

Figure 11.6 illustrates the trajectory of this index since 2010, highlighting recent trends. The figure compares the average index values between 2010 and 2021 with those recorded from 2022 to 2024, following Russia's invasion of Ukraine.

Figure 11.6 depicts a notable escalation in geopolitical risks following Russia's invasion of Ukraine. Since the invasion, global geopolitical tensions have remained heightened. Persistent high geopolitical risks could prompt increased precautionary savings and subsequently lead to lower interest rates.

However, it is important to exercise caution regarding the magnitude of this effect. While geopolitical risks have indeed increased after 2022, they are not exceptionally high when viewed from a long-term historical perspective. Figure 11.7, which tracks the geopolitical risk index since 1900, provides context for this observation.

The index is normalized to 100 over the entire 1900–2024 period. When the index spikes to around 500, such as during the onset of the First and Second World Wars, the attack on Pearl Harbor (December 1941), and D-Day (June 1944), there are approximately five times more articles about geopolitical risks in newspapers compared to the average over the entire period. Other notable peaks occurred at the beginning of the Gulf War in early 1991, 11 September 2001 (9/11), and the subsequent Iraq War in March 2003.

Figure 11.7 illustrates that geopolitical risks are not persistent; they do not exhibit prolonged periods of consistent increase or decrease, unlike interest rates. Therefore, fluctuations in geopolitical risks cannot explain persistent

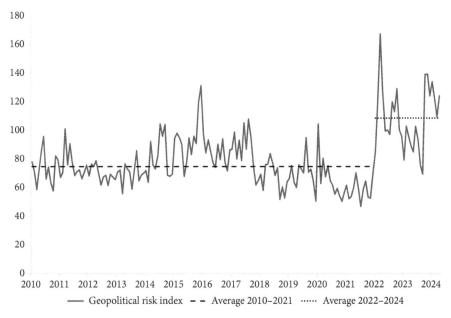

**Figure 11.6** Geopolitical risk index since 2010. Averages over 2010–2022 and the period following Rusia's invasion of Ukraine in 2022 are indicated by dotted lines. *Data source*: Caldara and Iacoviello (2022).

trends in interest rates, such as the sustained rise during the 1960s and 1970s, or the decline since 1980. Based on historical data, it appears challenging to argue that geopolitical risks drive enduring movements in interest rates.

## 11.6 Deglobalization

Perhaps the world is undergoing a retreat from globalization, influenced by Brexit, Make-America-Great-Again policies, escalating geopolitical tensions, and firms reshoring their supply chains post-pandemic to reduce reliance on foreign suppliers.

Globalization traditionally bolsters economic growth by facilitating efficient procurement of goods and services globally and fostering competition, in the end enhancing productivity and efficiency across borders.

Therefore, if globalization is indeed receding, this could pose adverse implications for economic growth. A deceleration in growth typically exerts downward pressure on interest rates.

But has globalization truly waned? One commonly used gauge of globalization is the openness of the global economy, measured by the combined value of exports and imports relative to GDP. This was shown in Figure 8.6.

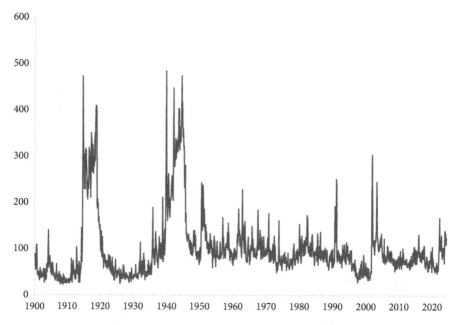

**Figure 11.7** Geopolitical risk index since 1900.
Source: Caldara and Iacoviello (2022).

That figure illustrated the steady rise in globalization from 1970 until the global financial crisis of 2008. During this period, countries increasingly opened, and international trade as a share of economic output expanded. However, since the global financial crisis, this trend has stalled, and there are indications it may have even begun to reverse. If this shift portends lower economic growth in the future, it could contribute to a reduction in equilibrium real interest rates.

Chapter 8, on the other hand, argued that globalization has played a role in keeping inflation low. If the world shifts towards deglobalization, this trend could reverse, potentially leading to higher inflation.

In conclusion, deglobalization—if it occurs—could result in lower real interest rates by dampening economic growth. At the same time, it could lead to higher inflation. As a result, the net impact on nominal interest rates remains uncertain.

## 11.7 Nominal versus Real Interest Rates

The arguments presented in previous sections of this chapter primarily build on models designed to explain movements in real interest rates. Collectively, they suggest that real interest rates will remain low in the future. But what about nominal interest rates?

Considering the negative consequences of inflation and the changes to monetary policy strategies described in Chapter 8, a reasonable hypothesis is that central banks will continue to prioritize maintaining low and stable inflation. This chapter predicts such a focus. This will mean that inflation is expected to be low going forward.

If inflation is expected to remain low and stable in the long run, the trends affecting real interest rates will similarly impact nominal interest rates.

## 11.8 Checklist

This chapter has underscored several factors likely to maintain low interest rates in the foreseeable future:

- **Trend 1**. Interest rates have been falling for centuries. It is not clear why this megatrend should suddenly come to a halt.
- **Trend 2**. Population growth is expected to continue declining.
- **Trend 3**. Life expectancy is projected to continue rising.
- **Trend 4**. Economic growth prospects are subdued.
- In addition to these persistent long-term trends, uncertainty stemming from climate risks may elevate precautionary savings, lowering interest rates.
- Similarly, heightened geopolitical risks could also increase precautionary savings, although historically, geopolitical risks have not correlated with long-term interest rate movements.
- When central banks are expected to keep inflation low and stable in the future, the above-mentioned tendencies calling for low future real interest rates will imply that future nominal interest rates will be low too.

# 12

# Trends That Could Elevate Rates

The previous chapter explored trends that may contribute to keeping interest rates low for the foreseeable future. However, there are also compelling reasons to anticipate higher interest rates going forward. This chapter will emphasize two main trends that could drive interest rates higher:

**Trend 5**. There will be fewer young people relative to elder people.
**Trend 6**. Public debt levels are on unsustainable paths in some countries.

The trends that may drive interest rates higher in the future are referred to as Trends 5 and 6. This numbering continues from the four trends discussed in Chapter 11, which could lead to lower interest rates.

Regarding Trend 5, the previous chapter discussed how longer life expectancies and declining population growth rates are likely to continue exerting downward pressure on real interest rates in the coming years. Nonetheless, another perspective on these demographic shifts suggests a different outcome. For instance, with projections indicating a decline in population growth and an increase in life expectancy, there will be a larger proportion of elderly individuals relative to the younger population. This demographic shift implies fewer savers compared to individuals in need of drawing down their savings, which typically leads to upward pressure on interest rates. Thus, while the previous chapter emphasized demographic reasons for expecting low interest rates, this chapter will explore how a different reading of these trends might indicate higher interest rates.

Furthermore, another trend likely to push interest rates upwards is the mounting levels of debt across many countries. As detailed in Chapter 3, four decades of low interest rates have spurred a significant increase in debt levels, which are projected to continue rising. Historically, interest rates have managed to decrease despite rising debt levels between 1980 and 2020. However, there comes a point where high levels of debt push up interest rates as investors demand greater compensation for assuming additional risk.

In addition to these two main trends, the chapter will discuss several additional factors that could contribute to higher interest rates, such as substantial

*How Low Interest Rates Change the World.* Jesper Rangvid, Oxford University Press. © Jesper Rangvid (2025).
DOI: 10.1093/9780198946410.003.0013

investments required for the transition to a sustainable economy, heightened defence spending due to increased geopolitical risks, and advancements in artificial intelligence (AI) that enhance productivity and could contribute to higher interest rates. Finally, certain factors that contributed to lower interest rates after the global financial crisis, such as extensive central bank asset purchases, are unlikely to be repeated.

In conclusion, several factors suggest that interest rates are poised to rise relative to the four-decade decline observed prior to the pandemic. Thus, we have good reasons to expect low future interest rates, laid out in the previous chapter, but we also have good arguments to expect higher interest rates, as explained here. The next chapter will delve into synthesizing these perspectives to offer this book's view.

## 12.1 Trend 5. More Retired People Relative to the Number of Working People

The previous chapter demonstrated that population growth is projected to decline while life expectancies are expected to rise. Higher life expectancy means greater patience of investors, and—if retirement ages do not rise correspondingly—higher savings, while lower population growth will lead to a lower capital-to-labour ratio, all of which will tend to reduce interest rates, as explained in Box 9.1.

However, the combination of these demographic shifts also implies a future where there will be a greater proportion of elderly individuals compared to younger ones. This shift has implications for total savings, which in turn influence interest rates.

Younger individuals typically save money in preparation for retirement, whereas older individuals draw upon their savings to support their consumption during retirement. Therefore, if there is a larger elderly population that tends to dissave (use savings) and a smaller younger population that saves, the total amount of savings in the economy is likely to decrease. This reduction in aggregate savings should, theoretically, lead to an increase in equilibrium interest rates. Goodhart and Pradhan (2020) have emphasized this argument.

To examine this argument further, Figure 12.1 illustrates the expected developments in the proportions of the global population aged 25–65, those above 65 years old, and the difference between these two groups for the 2025–2100 period. Figure 12.1 continues from Figure 9.7 that showed developments in these variables for the 1950–2022 period.

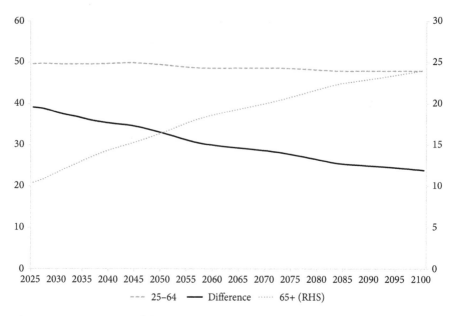

**Figure 12.1** Proportion of the global population aged 25–65, above 65 years old (right-hand scale), and the difference between the two groups.
*Data source:* United Nations.

Figure 9.7 showed that the fraction of the population saving (25–64 years old) rose faster than that of the population dissaving between 1980 and 2020, arguing that this caused an increase in global savings over the period pushing interest rates down. Going forward, this trend will reverse. The proportion of the global population aged 25–65, representing the working-age group, is anticipated to remain stable over the coming decades, comprising approximately 50 per cent of the global population, but the proportion of individuals aged 65 and older is expected to increase from approximately 10 per cent to around 25 per cent of the global population. This demographic shift implies a shrinking difference between the younger and older age groups, decreasing from a 40-percentage-point gap in 2025 to an estimated 25 per cent by 2100. In other words, there will be relatively fewer people that save and relatively more that dissave, driving a decline in global savings and pushing up interest rates.

Another way to visualize this trend is shown in Figure 12.2, depicting the projected ratio of the number of individuals aged 25–65 to those aged 65 and older globally. In 2025, there are five working-age individuals (25–64) for every one elderly person (65+). By 2100, this ratio is expected to decrease to approximately two working-age individuals for each elderly person.

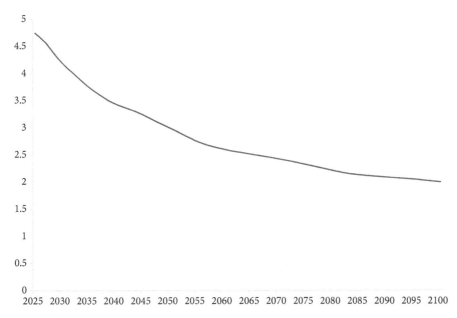

**Figure 12.2** Ratio of people in age group 25–65 to people in age group 65+, globally.
*Data source:* United Nations.

The implication of Figures 12.1 and 12.2 is that net aggregate savings are likely to decline because there will be relatively fewer in the working-age group with high savings rates.

In the previous chapter, we explored how declining population growth rates and increasing life expectancies are likely to exert downward pressure on interest rates. In contrast, this section discusses how shifts in population composition may act to push interest rates upward. The net effect hinges on the relative magnitudes of these opposing forces—specifically, the increased savings by those expecting longer lives versus the reduced savings by a higher number of retirees. Chapter 13 will revisit this discussion.

## 12.2  Trend 6. Rising Debt Levels

Public debt rises when government spending exceeds revenues, boosting aggregate demand and potentially driving up interest rates. Moreover, increased debt issuance raises the supply of bonds and other debt instruments, typically lowering their prices and thereby increasing interest rates. In essence, higher public debt should exert upward pressure on interest rates.

What can we expect regarding future increases in public debt levels? Chapter 3 explored the long-term historical trends in public deficits and debt levels in the UK and the US to provide specific examples of possible debt developments. Now, let us consider potential future scenarios for these two countries, discuss the implications for interest rates, and then discuss the broader global outlook across many countries.

### 12.2.1 Scenarios for UK Public Finances

The Office for Budget Responsibility (OBR) serves as the official watchdog for public finances in the UK. Figure 12.3 presents scenarios from its 2023 Fiscal Sustainability Report, projecting the expected evolution of the UK public sector deficit relative to UK GDP over the next five decades, until 2073. These scenarios represent the OBR's best estimates of how public deficits will develop under current policies.

The phrase 'under current policies' indicates that these projections do not assume any changes in policy measures aimed at addressing deficits or debt levels in the future. Based on projections of key economic variables

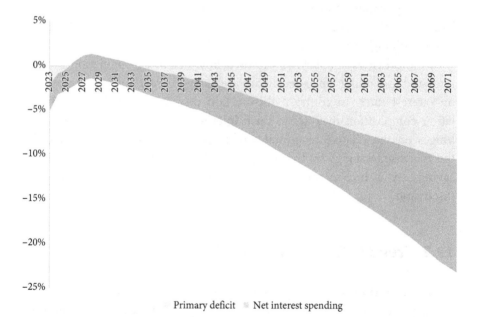

**Figure 12.3** Scenarios for UK public deficits relative to expected UK GDP, 2023–2073.
*Data source:* Office for Budget Responsibility.

such as GDP, interest rates, population trends, and inflation, Figure 12.3 illustrates the anticipated trajectories of public deficits based on policies in place.

The trajectory of public finances depends on both government expenditures and revenues, as well as interest payments on existing debt. The primary deficit measures the difference between government revenues (from taxes, etc.) and expenditures (including defence, education, retirement benefits, etc.), before accounting for interest payments. According to Figure 12.3, the UK is projected to achieve a surplus on its primary balance for the next decade, followed by a shift to deficits starting in the early 2030s. These deficits are anticipated to grow substantially over time, with the primary deficit expected to exceed 10 per cent of UK GDP by the end of the 50-year forecasting period.

Simultaneously, as debt levels rise (see below), the burden of interest rate payments will also increase. While the UK allocates approximately 3 per cent of its GDP towards servicing debt interest in 2023, this figure is projected to escalate to 13 per cent of GDP by the end of the 50-year period.

The combination of the primary deficit and interest payments constitutes the government's borrowing requirement. Based on current policies, Figure 12.3 indicates that the UK will need to accumulate additional debt equivalent to around 25 per cent of GDP year by year when we reach 2070.

Because of these substantial deficits and rising interest costs, public debt levels are expected to soar. Figure 12.4 shows projections that UK public debt will surpass three times its GDP by 2073.

It is important to note that the scenarios depicted in Figure 12.4 are projections based on current policies, rather than forecasts as such. In fact, the outcomes outlined in Figures 12.3 and 12.4 are not possible. As the OBR cautioned in 2021, 'no government could sustain these fiscal paths indefinitely without encountering financing challenges'; that is, much higher interest rates.

Thus, adjustments will inevitably be necessary. The crucial question is how these adjustments will be made: through increased taxes borne by taxpayers, reductions in public expenditures, or a combination of both. The magnitude of these required changes is significant; the OBR estimates that fiscal policy must improve by 3 per cent of GDP per decade to attain a debt-to-GDP ratio of 75 per cent by 2070.

In essence, the projections shown in Figures 12.3 and 12.4 point towards considerably higher interest rates going forward.

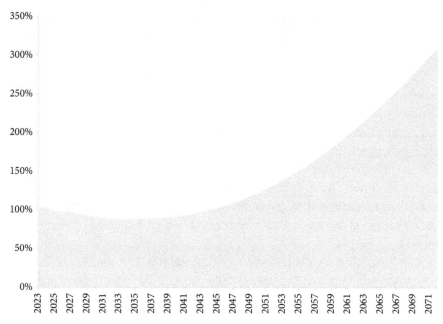

**Figure 12.4** Scenarios for UK public debt to expected UK GDP, 2023–2073.
*Data source:* Office for Budget Responsibility.

### 12.2.2 Scenarios for US Public Finances

The situation in the US mirrors that of the UK. The Congressional Budget Office (CBO) projects long-term budget scenarios under current policies. Figure 12.5 illustrates historical trends in US public debt since the early 20th century and provides scenarios for future developments spanning the 2021–2051 period.

Like the UK, public debt in the US is projected to increase significantly unless policies are revised. US public debt held by the public is expected to be nearly double the size of US GDP by 2053.[1] This represents a substantial increase compared to the previous peak in US public debt, which occurred during the Second World War.

According to the CBO, the annual deficit is anticipated to continue widening, potentially reaching close to 10 per cent of GDP by 2053. The primary driver behind this expanding deficit is the cost of interest payments. In 2053,

---

[1] This is similar to the UK situation. By 2053, the UK's debt-to-GDP ratio is projected to approach 200 per cent, as illustrated in Figure 12.3. Looking further ahead, Figure 12.3 extends its projections to 2070, foreseeing UK public debt climbing to 300 per cent of UK GDP by that year.

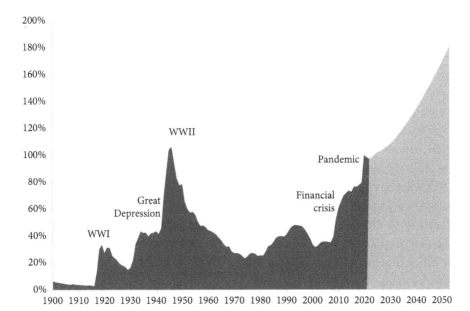

**Figure 12.5** Historical developments in US federal debt held by the public and scenarios, both relative to US GDP, 1900–2051.
*Data source*: Congressional Budget Office.

it is projected that seven percentage points of the 10 per cent deficit will be attributable to net interest expenses.

The escalation of fiscal deficits and debt levels is likely to exert upward pressure on interest rates. Rachel and Summers (2019) compile estimates from the academic literature on the relationship between public debt and interest rates, finding that the long-run neutral real interest rate increases by 3.5 basis points for each one-percentage-point rise in the government debt-to-GDP ratio. Given the baseline estimate that the US debt-to-GDP ratio could increase by 100 per cent under current policies, extrapolating this relationship suggests a potential increase of 350 basis points, or 3.5 percentage points, in the real interest rate. This represents a substantial effect, indicating that sustained large fiscal deficits have the capacity to significantly elevate interest rates.

If the estimate also holds for the UK, its 250 per cent increase in indebtedness implies a 10 per cent increase in interest rates, a massive rise.

## 12.2.3 Other Countries

The previous subsections provided outlooks for the UK and the US, two major economies, to illustrate potential future public debt dynamics.

While not all countries face challenges as severe as those confronting the UK and the US, many are in similar situations. For example, the International Monetary Fund (IMF) (2024) examined the long-term outlook for China, another large economy, and compared it to the US. The projections for China are even more concerning. According to the IMF, public debt in the US is expected to rise from about 100 per cent of US GDP in 2024 to nearly 170 per cent by 2054. In China, however, public debt is projected to double from approximately 120 per cent of Chinese GDP in 2024 to around 240 per cent by 2054, marking a significant expansion.

The European Commission regularly monitors and updates its analyses of long-term public budget projections, focusing on public debt over the next decade and beyond. Their reports include projections for public debt over the next 10 years, as well as the adjustments needed if primary deficits should stabilize or achieve a sustainable debt level (60 per cent of GDP) over a 50-year horizon.

According to the EU (2024), public debt across the 28 European Union (EU) member states is expected to increase by about 10 percentage points between 2023 and 2033, driven by the rising costs of an ageing population and higher interest expenditures.

For long-term projections, the EU classifies individual member states as 'high risk', 'medium risk', or 'low risk' based on the extent of the adjustments to primary fiscal deficits needed to stabilize debt as a percentage of GDP over the long term. EU (2024) concludes that 19 member states face high or medium risk, while only eight are considered low risk. In other words, the majority of EU member states risk encountering significant public debt burdens in the future unless decisive action is taken.

The takeaway is that rising public debt is likely to become a global persistent trend, potentially leading to higher global interest rates.

## 12.2.4 Public Debt Also Rose between 1980 and 2020

This section has argued that higher debt might increase interest rates going forward. The counterargument is that interest rates did not climb but rather fell during 1980–2020 despite the rise in public debt during the period. The reason why interest rates did not rise despite higher debt levels during that period was that other factors exerted stronger downward pressures on interest rates, counteracting the effect of debt accumulation.

The study by Rachel and Summers (2019), discussed in Chapter 9, found that from 1970 to 2017, higher public debt increased equilibrium real interest rates by 1.2 percentage points in advanced economies. This suggests that, even before the pandemic, rising public debt tended to push rates up. However, other factors, such as slower productivity growth and declining population growth, had an even greater impact, ultimately driving interest rates down. Whether these factors will continue to outweigh the upward pressure from increased public debt remains an open question, which Chapter 13 will revisit. The main point of this chapter is that public debt is expected to rise significantly, surpassing the increase seen during the 1980–2020 period, and thus exerting considerable upward pressure on interest rates.

The two trends highlighted above—fewer people of working age relative to retirees and higher public debt levels—are megatrends that are likely to persist and have a significant effect on global interest rates. In addition to these trends, a number of other factors might contribute to raising interest rates.

## 12.3 Transition to a More Sustainable Economy

Section 11.5 explored how uncertainty surrounding climate risks might increase precautionary savings, potentially lowering interest rates. Concurrently, in the coming decades, substantial investments—both private and public—will be essential to facilitate the transition towards a sustainable economy. For example, the IMF (2021) estimates that global investments must rise by up to 1 per cent of global GDP to achieve climate neutrality by 2050. These investments could exert upward pressure on equilibrium interest rates, as outlined in the investment–savings model introduced in Chapter 9.

The impact of investments in transitioning to a sustainable economy on interest rates is a subject of ongoing study. According to the survey by Mongelli et al. (2022), climate-induced effects on equilibrium interest rates can be significant if these investments are substantial. However, the overall conclusion in Mongelli et al. (2022) is that, in many scenarios, the negative effect on interest rates from climate-related uncertainties and precautionary savings mentioned in Chapter 11 dominates the positive effect from larger climate investments.

## 12.4 Investments in Defence

Following Russia's invasion of Ukraine in February 2022, many countries, particularly in Europe, have reevaluated their defence spending commitments. NATO member states are committed to allocating 2 per cent of their GDP to defence spending, a target that numerous European NATO members had not met prior to 2022. In fact, since the end of the Cold War in the late 1980s and early 1990s, many European nations reduced defence expenditures and reaped what became known as the 'peace dividend'. For instance, Dorn et al. (2024) estimate this dividend amounted to 1.8 trillion euros, nearly matching the 2 per cent NATO target.

Since 2022, countries are now compelled to increase their defence budgets. This raises the question of whether such increases will impact interest rates. This depends on several circumstances.

Firstly, will heightened defence spending lift overall government expenditures? If additional defence outlays are added to general government spending, public deficits will rise (or surpluses will decrease), thereby boosting aggregate demand in the economy. In this scenario, an increase in interest rates seems likely. However, many governments may need to adjust elsewhere. Some countries simply cannot afford much higher deficits due to already high levels of public debt and taxation rates, as noted in the previous section and by Dorn et al. (2024). Consequently, in many countries, cutting other government expenditures may be necessary to finance increased defence spending. In such cases, it is uncertain whether defence spending will yield a net positive effect on aggregate demand and, consequently, on interest rates.

Secondly, even if there is a net increase in government spending, the impact on economic growth is not straightforward. It depends on various factors, including the types of spending, the productivity of investments, and their effects on other sectors of the economy. A substantial body of literature has explored the relationship between defence spending and economic growth. Cepparulo and Pasimeni (2024) review this literature. Their main finding is that there is little consensus on the existence, direction of causality, or nature of the relationship between defence spending and economic growth. The authors conclude that many studies find a negative relationship between defence spending and economic growth, many find no effect, and many find a positive effect. The conclusion is that it remains uncertain whether increased defence spending will positively impact economic growth and interest rates.

## 12.5 Central Bank Asset Purchases

As discussed in Chapter 9, many central banks started to buy government and mortgage bonds following the 2008 financial crisis due to persistently low inflation and near-zero or negative central bank interest rates. The chapter also illustrated how the balance sheets of the Federal Reserve (Fed) and the European Central Bank (ECB) expanded roughly 10-fold over a decade as a result of these asset purchases. Such extensive asset buying should exert a positive influence on bond prices and have a negative effect on yields. Chapter 9 also examined empirical evidence on the impact of these asset purchase programmes. The consensus is that quantitative easing (QE) initially lowered yields, but later rounds of QE have been less successful.

With inflation surging post-pandemic, central banks have ceased and even reversed these programmes. This reversal should have the opposite effect of QE, leading to lower bond prices and higher yields. Furthermore, given the experience with QE, central banks will probably be hesitant to reintroduce QE in the future. The absence of QE may not elevate interest rates but could make a return to pre-pandemic lows less probable. Consequently, the potential absence of QE is expected to exert upward pressure on interest rates relative to their levels between the financial crisis of 2008 and the pandemic of 2020, the period QE programmes were in effect.

## 12.6 AI, Productivity, and Interest Rates

AI (artificial intelligence) has the potential to significantly enhance productivity and spur economic growth, which could in turn lead to higher interest rates.

AI enables tasks to be completed faster, more efficiently, and with reduced manpower requirements, thereby boosting the productivity of workers. The extent of this productivity gain depends on the number of jobs affected by AI and the resulting cost savings. However, estimating these effects is complex and uncertain.

Some forecasts suggest a substantial impact. Goldman Sachs (2023) predicts a 1.5 per cent increase in annual US productivity growth over the next decade due to AI. McKinsey (2023) also anticipates notable positive effects, forecasting a 1.5–3.5 per cent annual GDP growth increase in advanced economies.

However, there is dissent regarding AI's impact on productivity. Acemoglu (2024), drawing from recent economic growth literature, suggests a more modest effect compared to the optimistic forecasts by Goldman Sachs and McKinsey. Acemoglu's analysis indicates that AI exposure affects 19.9 per cent of US labour force tasks, of which 23 per cent can be profitably automated. When these tasks are automated, it results in a cost reduction of 15.4 per cent for them, Acemoglu argues. These figures imply a modest productivity increase of 0.7 per cent over a decade, or 0.07 per cent annually—a marginal impact on productivity growth and, consequently, on interest rates.

In summary, AI holds potential to elevate productivity growth and thereby interest rates. However, given the current divergence of opinions and the early stage of AI implementation, reaching a definitive conclusion on its precise impact on interest rates remains challenging.

## 12.7 Weak Link between Economic Growth/Population Growth and Interest Rates over the Very Long Run

The final point discussed here challenges the premise that lower rates of economic and population growth inevitably lead to lower equilibrium real interest rates, as argued in Chapters 9 and 11.

As detailed in Chapter 9, most economic models suggest that lower rates of economic and population growth should theoretically result in lower equilibrium real interest rates. Moreover, Chapter 11 presented evidence that global economic growth is anticipated to decelerate significantly in the coming decades: the OECD projects that global real economic growth will decline from approximately 3 per cent annually in the 2020s to just above 1.5 per cent by 2060. Similarly, Chapter 11 showed that global population growth is expected to diminish from about 1 per cent annually in the 2020s to potentially zero or slightly negative rates by 2100. These trends provide a rationale for anticipating lower real interest rates in the future.

While economic theory supports a negative relationship between economic growth and interest rates, empirical evidence over long periods has been more challenging to establish. Rogoff, Rossi, and Schmelzing (2024) demonstrate that economic growth rates and population growth rates have not followed a similar downward trajectory as nominal and real yields over the past 700 years. In fact, economic growth remained relatively stable until the 19th century, after which it began to increase. This suggests, if anything, a negative—rather than a positive—relationship between real economic growth and real interest rates. Rogoff, Rossi, and Schmelzing (2024) argue that a similar pattern characterizes the relationship between real interest rates and population growth. Over the past seven centuries, interest rates have shown a consistent decline, while the rate of population growth has remained relatively constant, with a slight tendency towards a small increase, if any.

Seven centuries is a long period, encompassing significant changes in economic structures and societies. Today, data quality is notably superior compared to centuries ago. Thus, it might be argued that 700 years is simply too long a timeframe to discern systematic relationships, given the extensive transformations in economic structures that have occurred over time. However, even when examining data from more recent decades, establishing a robust relationship between economic growth and real interest rates remains challenging. For instance, Hamilton et al. (2016)—which was also mentioned in Chapter 9—extensively analysed the correlation between economic growth and interest rates in the US and other OECD countries since the 1970s. Their findings cast doubt on the strength of this relationship, stating that interest rates' 'relationship with trend GDP growth is much more tenuous than widely believed' and expressing scepticism towards analyses placing economic growth at the core of real interest rate determination.

The implication of such findings is that even if economic and population growth rates decline in the future, it may not necessarily result in lower interest rates. This does not necessarily mean that future interest rates will be higher. However, it suggests that some arguments presented in Chapter 11 for future low interest rates may be less robust than they initially appear.

## 12.8 Checklist

This chapter has highlighted several factors that could potentially drive interest rates higher in the future:

- **Trend 5**. The ratio of working-age individuals to retirees will most likely decline. As retirees draw down savings while workers save for retirement, and there will be more of the former and fewer of the latter, overall net saving is likely to decrease, exerting upward pressure on interest rates.
- **Trend 6**. High levels of debt are expected to persist and increase further. Elevated debt levels typically lead investors to demand higher risk premiums, resulting in increased interest rates.
- In addition to these global trends, central banks played a significant role as bond buyers between the global financial crisis and the pandemic, which suppressed yields during that period. However, it is unlikely

that central banks will continue such aggressive purchasing, potentially leading to higher interest rates.

- Increased investments are necessary for financing the transition to a more sustainable economy, alongside heightened defence spending in a more uncertain global environment. While these investments might intuitively boost economic growth and interest rates, the chapter has shown that the evidence regarding their impact on interest rates is less robust.
- Overall, the preceding chapter argued for expectations of low interest rates in the future, while this chapter has discussed reasons to anticipate higher rates. The next chapter will present what this book believes are the more likely net effects.

# 13

# Putting It All Together

## What Is the Outlook for Rates?

Chapter 11 outlined four major trends, along with several additional developments, that are likely to exert downward pressure on interest rates in the future, mirroring patterns observed over the four decades preceding the pandemic. Conversely, Chapter 12 identified two major trends, along with other contributing factors, that could signal potential structural shifts in economic dynamics, potentially leading to upward pressure on interest rates going forward.

The lingering question is: which factors wield the greatest influence and what implications do they hold for future long-term interest rate trends? This chapter examines this question.

Researchers employ two primary methodologies to derive expectations for future interest rates. First, economic theory guides projections based on anticipated movements in variables that theoretically impact interest rates. This approach provides a model-driven perspective. Second, data from financial markets can be used to extract market-implied expectations, revealing what investors expect about interest rates and inflation. This method offers a theory-agnostic outlook.

Overall, regardless of the method used, the consensus suggests that interest rates are expected to remain relatively low in the future. While not as extraordinarily low as seen immediately before the pandemic, they are projected to be lower than the historical norm.

A caveat is warranted before proceeding: forecasting interest rates is inherently challenging due to the unpredictable nature of global developments and their impact on rates. Despite our best efforts and informed judgements, uncertainty pervades the projections presented here. It should thus be acknowledged that the world may, and probably will, evolve differently than anticipated over the coming decades. Bering this in mind, let us proceed to examine the net outlook for interest rates.

*How Low Interest Rates Change the World*. Jesper Rangvid, Oxford University Press. © Jesper Rangvid (2025).
DOI: 10.1093/9780198946410.003.0014

## 13.1 Summarizing the Main Channels Affecting Future Interest Rates

Chapters 11 and 12 explore influential factors shaping future interest rates. Table 13.1 provides a summary of these factors and their impact on future interest rates. The table categorizes them into two main groups: first, six major trends that are likely to influence interest rates going forward and, second, other emerging factors discussed in Chapters 11 and 12.

The first four major trends listed in Table 13.1 are trends that drove interest rates lower from 1980 to 2020 and that are expected to continue, thereby likely contributing to keeping future interest rates low. These major trends include sluggish economic growth, declining population growth rates, and extended life expectancies.

For instance, transitioning from a current global population growth rate of 1 per cent to an anticipated 0 per cent in the future (Chapter 11) is poised to exert a significant downward pressure on future interest rates. Similarly, the prospect of an almost nine-year increase in life expectancy from 2025 to 2100 implies a more patient perspective on savings, dampening interest rates.

Moreover, a projected drop in global economic growth rates—from approximately 2.5 per cent in 2030 to around 1.5 per cent by 2050 (Chapter 11)—suggests a substantial reduction in long-term interest rates. According to our canonical economic model (Box 9.1), which links economic

**Table 13.1** The main effect (positive or negative) on future interest rates of factors affecting interest rates

|  | Mainly negative effect | Mainly positive effect |
| --- | --- | --- |
| **Six major trends that affect interest rates** | | |
| 1. Rates have been falling for centuries, and this continues | √ | |
| 2. Lower population growth | √ | |
| 3. Lower life expectancy | √ | |
| 4. Lower economic growth | √ | |
| 5. Fewer people working/more people in retirement | | √ |
| 6. More public debt | | √ |
| **Newer challenges** | | |
| More uncertain world/climate risk | √ | |
| Investment in climate change | | √ |
| Central bank bond purchases will stop | | √ |
| Deglobalization | | √ |
| Artificial intelligence | | √ |

growth linearly to interest rates ($r = \delta + \gamma\Delta c + n$), all else being equal and assuming an intertemporal rate of substitution of one ($\gamma = 1$), this shift could lead to a full percentage-point decline in long-run real interest rates. Many models indicate a higher intertemporal rate of substitution (see, for instance, the classic 2002 Vissing-Jørgensen study), amplifying this effect further.

Overall, the cumulative effect of these continuing megatrends is expected to exert a pronounced negative impact on future interest rates.

Simultaneously, there are other megatrends that are likely to push interest rates higher in the future. These are listed as Trends 5 and 6 in Table 13.1. Notably, escalating levels of debt anticipated in many major economies could potentially elevate interest rates significantly. Based on estimates in the literature on the effect of public debt on interest rates, and considering projected debt developments, Chapter 12 mentioned that this could potentially lift interest rates by several percentage points over the coming decades. Moreover, as longevity increases, there will eventually be more people dissaving during retirement, which tends to elevate interest rates.

In addition to the six persistent trends discussed in Chapters 11 and 12, and mentioned in Table 13.1, the chapters also discussed a number of other developments that could influence future interest rates, such as a more uncertain world, the integration of artificial intelligence (AI) into production processes, and so on. These factors are also listed in Table 13.1. Interestingly, most of these point towards higher interest rates going forward. At the same time, as Chapters 11 and 12 discussed, the importance of these factors is subject to discussion, which is why they are not highlighted as major trends in the book but included for completeness.

In summary, while the trends favouring lower interest rates may appear dominant, a comprehensive assessment using formal economic models is necessary to aggregate these individual effects and provide perspectives on their net effects.

## 13.2 Evidence from Statistical Analyses in the Literature on Future Real Interest Rates

To assess the overall impact of various factors influencing interest rates, models incorporating these factors and providing specific numerical predictions are essential. This section discusses findings from such models.

Chapter 9 discussed the reasons behind the evolution of real interest rates over the past decades. It mentioned that Rachel and Summers (2019) found that public policies, such as increased public debt and expansions in social security and old-age healthcare, had elevated real interest rates in advanced economies by 3.6 per cent from 1970 to 2017, while private sector dynamics—lower productivity growth, reduced population growth, longer retirement periods, and increased inequality—exerted downward pressure, collectively lowering real interest rates by 5.5 per cent over the same period. As these private sector forces outweighed public policy impacts, equilibrium real rates in advanced economies exhibited a persistent decline over recent decades.

Rachel and Summers also projected the implications of likely developments in both public policies and private sector dynamics on equilibrium real rates from 2017 to 2070. Their findings are summarized in Table 13.2.

Their analysis anticipates that higher public debt levels will increase real interest rates by 1.9 per cent over the entire 1970–2070 period that they study—0.7 per cent higher than the impact observed from 1970 to 2017. This is the effect of Trend 6 of Table 13.1. Additionally, expanded social security and old-age pensions are forecasted to elevate real interest rates by 0.5 per cent during the 2017–2070 timeframe. In total, public policies are expected to lift real interest rates by 1.2 per cent until 2070.

Conversely, private sector factors are expected to counteract these upward pressures. Projected stagnation in productivity growth over the 2017–2070 period, as explained in Chapter 11, suggests minimal change in economic growth for advanced economies. This is Trend 4 in Table 13.1. Demographic

**Table 13.2** Effects on equilibrium real interest rates from selected public policies and private sector forces

|  | 1970–2017 | 1970–2070 | 2017–2070 |
|---|---|---|---|
| **Public policies** | | | |
| Government debt | 1.2 | 1.9 | 0.7 |
| Social security | 1.2 | 1.5 | 0.3 |
| Old-age healthcare | 1.1 | 1.3 | 0.2 |
| *Total impact of public policies* | *3.5* | *4.7* | *1.2* |
| **Private sector forces** | | | |
| Productivity growth | −1.8 | −1.5 | 0.3 |
| Population growth | −0.6 | −1.3 | −0.7 |
| Longer retirement | −1.1 | −1.2 | −0.1 |
| Inequality | −0.7 | −0.9 | −0.2 |
| Interactions | −1.1 | −1.6 | −0.5 |
| *Total impact of private sector forces* | *−5.3* | *−6.5* | *−1.2* |
| Other | −0.1 | −0.2 | −0.1 |
| **Total net effect** | **−1.9** | **−2** | **−0.1** |

Estimates from Rachel and Summers (2019). The table shows percentage-point changes in real interest rates in advanced economies due to different developments over the 1970–2017, 1970–2070, and 2017–2070 periods.

shifts, including declining population growth (Trend 2) and longer retirement (Trend 3), are projected to reduce real rates by 0.8 per cent over the next five decades. Furthermore, increasing inequality is anticipated to lower real rates by 0.2 per cent. Interactions among these private sector forces are expected to further reduce real rates by an additional 0.5 per cent. Overall, private sector influences are expected to decrease real interest rates by slightly more than 1 per cent over the next five decades.

Thus, the competing forces of public and private sector dynamics are projected to largely offset each other. Rachel and Summers therefore predict no significant change in real interest rates over the coming decades, suggesting that real interest rates will remain low until 2070, reflecting their low starting point—around 0 per cent—at the time of their analysis.

Other studies corroborate the forecast that interest rates are likely to remain relatively low in the future. Christensen and Pedersen (2023) examine the impacts of declining fertility rates (Trend 2 of Table 13.1), increasing life expectancy (Trend 3), and sluggish productivity growth (Trend 4) on real interest rates. Their model forecasts a significant decrease in global real interest rates, represented by US rates, of nearly two percentage points from 1950 to the present day, with a further decline of approximately 0.25 per cent expected by 2050 starting from the mid-2020s.

Kopecky and Taylor (2020) construct a model focusing on how demographic shifts influence not only the equilibrium interest rate but also the risk premium and stock returns. Their simulations indicate that demographic trends responsible for lowering interest rates over the past decades will continue exerting negative pressure, reducing rates by around two percentage points from 2017 to 2050.

In the euro area, Papetti (2021) attributes a significant portion of the decline in interest rates over recent decades to ageing demographics. Projecting forward, Papetti finds that interest rates are likely to remain low compared to levels seen in the 1980s, with a potential slight increase of approximately 0.5 percentage points expected from 2040 to 2060. Despite this increase, rates are anticipated to remain considerably lower than those observed in the early 1980s.

Several other academic analyses also support the conclusion that factors driving down future interest rates outweigh those pushing rates higher. Studies by Carvalho et al. (2016), Kara and von Thadden (2016), Bielecki et al. (2020), Eggertson et al. (2019), and Obstfeld (2023) collectively underscore the empirical strength of these downward pressures on interest rates.

Overall, studies that use economic models to forecast real interest rates typically suggest a continued environment of low interest rates. Largely, these effects are driven by Trends 1–4 in Table 13.1 (demographic developments and subdued economic growth), which are expected to outweigh Trends 5 and 6 (higher future debt burdens and other private policies).

## 13.3 The Future of $r^*$

Chapter 9, Box 9.2, introduced the concept of $r^*$ (or r-star), which denotes the real interest rate prevailing when the economy is in equilibrium—where production equals its potential and inflation remains stable. Several studies exist that project future developments in $r^*$.

### 13.3.1 Evidence from the US

The New York Federal Reserve's (Fed's) renowned $r^*$ estimates, also discussed in Chapter 9, link the evolution of $r^*$ to trend output growth. Consequently, projecting future paths for $r^*$ involves forecasting real economic growth. Figure 13.1 illustrates $r^*$ alongside trend growth, as estimated by the New York Fed since the early 1960s, supplemented by projections of real potential output in the US sourced from the Congressional Budget Office. These projections extend over the next three decades.

As trend growth has declined from approximately 6 per cent in the early 1960s to about 2 per cent today, $r^*$ has followed suit with a similar decrease. Looking ahead, expected underlying economic growth in the US is projected to hover around 2 per cent annually, gradually tapering off over time. If $r^*$ continues to align closely with underlying trend growth, it suggests that $r^*$ will remain low in the foreseeable future.

It is noteworthy that $r^*$ experienced a sharper decline than trend growth following the financial crisis, and this gap has persisted, with $r^*$ consistently lagging trend growth by approximately 0.5–1 percentage points. There is a possibility that this gap may narrow, potentially restoring the historically close relationship between $r^*$ and trend growth. In such a scenario, $r^*$ could rise from its current level of around 1 per cent to approximately 1.5 per cent, which is still relatively low in a historical context. Assuming inflation remains near the central bank's target of 2 per cent, this implies that the nominal equilibrium US interest rate could settle around 3.5 per cent in the future.

Chapter 9 referenced the International Monetary Fund (IMF) study by Platzer and Peruffo (2022) of $r^*$ in the US, detailing factors contributing to its decline from 1975 to 2015. Moreover, the study projects $r^*$ up to the year 2150. It finds that $r^*$ will bottom out at 0.38 per cent by 2030 and gradually increase to approximately 1 per cent thereafter.

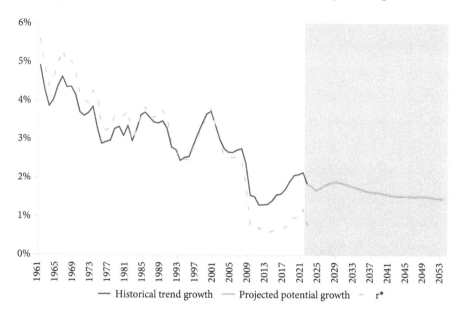

**Figure 13.1** Historic trend growth and $r^*$, as estimated by the New York Fed, and potential real economic growth, as projected by the Congressional Budget Office. Projection period (2023–2053) shaded.

*Data source:* New York Fed and Congressional Budget Office.

According to the Platzer and Peruffo (2022) study, two primary factors will contribute to slightly higher interest rates after 2030. Firstly, the retirement of the large baby boomer generation around 2030 will lead to a drawdown of their savings, resulting in lower aggregate savings and consequently higher interest rates (that is, Trend 5 in Table 13.1). Secondly, there is expected to be a significant increase in US government debt (which is Trend 6). Still, the key takeaway from the IMF study is that despite expectations of a modest rise in real interest rates after 2030, they are anticipated to stabilize around 1 per cent in the future, thus remaining significantly lower than the historical norm.

### 13.3.2 Global Evidence

While much of the research on $r^*$ has focused on the US, global $r^*$ outlooks have been provided by the IMF (2023). IMF researchers have estimated $r^*$ for 16 advanced economies spanning the last 150 years and analysed future trends. Figure 13.2 presents IMF (2023) forecasts for $r^*$ across several major economies.

The IMF anticipates that $r^*$ will continue to be low across advanced economies like Germany, the UK, and the US. Conversely, in emerging

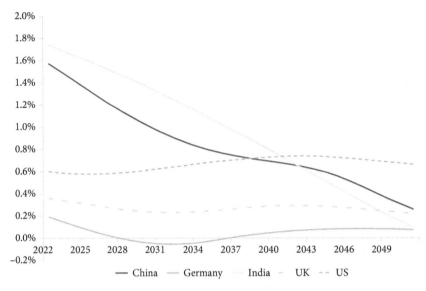

**Figure 13.2** Projections of $r^*$ in large economies, 2022–2050.
*Data source:* IMF (2023).

economies, real interest rates are expected to decline significantly. The IMF's central message underscores that equilibrium interest rates will stay subdued: 'Our analysis indicates that the recent upticks in real interest rates are likely transitory.'

## 13.4 Market Expectations

Financial asset prices can be used to extrapolate interest rate expectations of market participants. By observing the prices investors are willing to pay for financial assets of different maturities, we can infer the implicit future interest rates investors anticipate. These are known as market-implied forward interest rates.

Market-implied forward interest rates differ from equilibrium interest rates discussed in the previous sections of this chapter. Equilibrium rates are grounded in robust theoretical frameworks and assess the influence of various factors on future rates based on consistent structural economic relationships. In contrast, forward interest rates reflect investor expectations without assuming a specific economic model.

The calculation of market-implied forward interest rates involves current interest rates across different maturities. For instance, if today's one-year interest rate is 4 per cent and the two-year rate is 5 per cent, the implied one-year forward interest rate (the one-year interest rate expected one year from now) can be calculated as follows:

$$F_{1,1} = \left( \frac{(1 + 5\%)^2}{(1 + 4\%)^1} \right)^{\frac{1}{2-1}} = 6\%$$

The so-called 'expectations theory of interest rates' argues that such calculated rates (like 6 per cent in this example) represent the market's best estimate of future interest rates. This stems from the principle that the return on a two-year bond should equal the return expected from purchasing a one-year bond today and another one-year bond next year. Thus, from the one-year and the two-year interest rates we can observe today, we can infer what investors expect the one-year interest rate to be in one year.

This calculation can be extended to bonds with various maturities. For instance, by using today's yields on a 10-year bond and a 20-year bond, we can determine the market's implied expectation for the 10-year interest rate in 10 years' time—the implied 10-year forward interest rate in 10 years:

$$F_{10,10} = \left( \frac{(1 + i_{0,20})^{20}}{(1 + i_{0,10})^{10}} \right)^{\frac{1}{20-10}}$$

Figure 13.3 illustrates the historical trends of the yield on 10-year US Treasuries (denoted as 10y), the market-implied 10-year forward rate in 10 years (10y10y), and the market-implied 10-year forward rate in 20 years (20y10y), since data on yields of these maturities is available; that is, since the early 1950s.[1]

Figure 13.3 yields two main observations. Firstly, market-implied forward interest rates track the movements of current interest rates: when current 10-year rates decline, 10-year forward rates in both 10 and 20 years also decline, and vice versa. Secondly, while forward rates generally align with current rates, they typically exhibit a slight premium over them.

At the time of writing in 2024, 10y, 10y10y, and 20y10y rates are nearly identical (with 10y10y slightly surpassing 10y). This suggests that investors expect that interest rates will remain relatively unchanged from current levels. Specifically, with 10-year interest rates standing at 4.5 per cent in the summer of 2024, markets expect that the 10-year interest rate in both 2034 and in 2044 (i.e. in 10 and 20 years, respectively) will be more or less the same. At the same time, Figure 13.3 shows that while expected interest rates in 2024 are higher than they were right before the pandemic in 2020, expected

---

[1] US interest rates are the focus of this study due to the availability of robust data on real interest rates, as detailed in the next section. This contrasts with other countries where such detailed data may not be available.

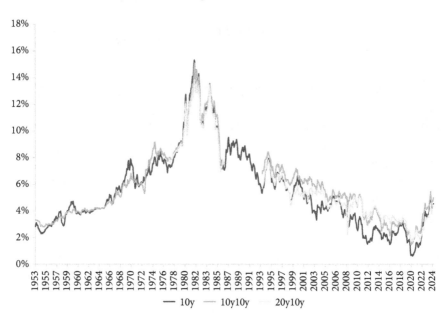

**Figure 13.3** Yield on 10-year Treasuries, 10-year forward rates in 10 years (10y10y) and 10-year forward rates in 20 years (20y10y), 1953–2024.
*Data source:* FRED of St. Louis Fed.

interest rates are still relatively low in a historical context. For instance, the last time expected interest rates were as low as they are in 2024—excluding the period between the financial crisis and the pandemic—was in the 1960s. These expectations, thus, do not indicate high interest rates going forward.

### 13.4.1 Expected Real Rates

Applying a comparable methodology to inflation-indexed bonds allows us to calculate expected real interest rates. Figure 13.4 illustrates the outcomes of such computations for the US since 2005, the period for which we have data on inflation-indexed bonds such that we can calculate implied forward real interest rates.

Figure 13.4 illustrates the historical trends of current 10-year US real interest rates, expected 10-year real interest rates in 10 years (10y10y), and expected 10-year real interest rates in 20 years (20y10y). Like the nominal interest rates discussed above, investors expect future real interest rates to remain relatively stable compared to current levels. As of summer 2024, the 10-year real interest rate is approximately 2 per cent. This rate is projected to remain stable over the next decades and expected to hover around 2 per cent in both 2034 and 2044.

**Figure 13.4** Yield on 10-year inflation-indexed Treasuries, 10-year forward real interest rates in 10 years (10y10y), and 10-year forward real interest rates in 20 years (20y10y), 2005–2024, though 20y10y for 2010–2024.
*Data source:* FRED of St. Louis Fed.

Real interest rates are not always expected to be constant. For instance, during and immediately after the pandemic, the 10-year real interest rate plummeted to −1 per cent, as depicted in Figure 13.4. This meant that purchasing a 10-year inflation-indexed bond in 2020 would result in a negative real return of −1 per cent annually over the subsequent decade.

Investors did not foresee such negative real interest rates enduring. During the pandemic in 2020, the 10y10y rate hovered near 0 per cent, while the 10-year rate was at −1 per cent. This indicated expectations of a negative annual return of −1 per cent from 2020 to 2030, followed by a 0 per cent return in the decade spanning 2030 to 2040.

Since 2021, alongside the uptick in nominal interest rates and inflation, real rates and expected future real rates have also climbed. As of summer 2024, as mentioned, an inflation-indexed bond is expected to yield slightly above a 2 per cent annual real return over the next decade, the next decade a decade from now as well as in two decades.

## 13.4.2 Expected Inflation

First, we computed expected nominal interest rates. Then, in Section 13.4.1, we calculated expected real interest rates. By subtracting the latter from the

**Figure 13.5** Expected inflation over the next 10 years (10y), expected inflation over the next 10 years, 10 years from now (10y10y), and expected inflation over the next 10 years, 20 years from now (20y10y), 2005–2024, though 20y10y for 2010–2024.
*Data source:* FRED of St. Louis Fed.

former, we can derive expected inflation rates (excluding the effects of risk premiums).

Figure 13.5 depicts the outcomes of this computation, presenting the developments in anticipated annual inflation rates for the next 10 years (10y), expected annual inflation over the following decade a decade from now (10y10y), and in two decades (20y10y).

Figure 13.5 reveals intriguing insights into expected inflation trends following the surge observed in 2021. Prior to the pandemic, inflation and anticipated future inflation closely mirrored each other. However, following the pandemic-induced inflation spike, expected inflation rates for the next 10 and 20 years have diverged noticeably. Investors now anticipate inflation slightly above the Fed's 2 per cent target over the 2024–2034 decade, averaging 2.3 per cent annually. For the subsequent decade (2034–2044), expectations rise further to 2.7 per cent per year.

Interestingly, long-term (20y10y) inflation expectations have remained relatively stable around 2 per cent before, during, and after the recent inflation surge. This implies investor confidence that the Fed will eventually regain control of inflation, although they anticipate it will take considerable time.

Another notable observation from Figure 13.5 is the significant downward revision of inflation expectations during economic crises. During the global financial crisis of 2008, investors expected minimal inflation, barely exceeding 0 per cent over the subsequent decade (2008–2018). A similar pattern emerged during the pandemic, with expectations of 1 per cent inflation from 2020–2030. Despite these short-term adjustments, long-term inflation expectations (20y10y) remained anchored around the 2 per cent target, reflecting investor confidence in the Fed's ability to achieve stability over the long haul.

### 13.4.3 Are Market-Based Measures of Expectations Good Measures of Future Outcomes?

The observation that market-implied forward rates track current interest rates suggests caution in using them as precise predictors of future realized interest rates. When a temporary shock causes current interest rates to rise, market-based expectations tend to adjust accordingly. However, if the shock is indeed temporary, future interest rates should not necessarily be impacted.

Refer again to Figure 13.3 that showed implied forward interest rates since the early 1950s. This period encompasses both periods of rising interest rates, such as the 1960s and 1970s, and periods of declining rates over the past four decades.

One main conclusion from Figure 13.3 was a tight correlation between current interest rates and market-implied forward rates. This tight correlation implies that when interest rates soared to 15 per cent in the early 1980s, market-implied forward rates also peaked. If forward interest rates accurately predicted future rates, this would imply that in 1982—when rates were at their highest—investors expected rates to remain unchanged 10 years later in 1992. Specifically, they should anticipate a 10-year interest rate of 15 per cent in 1992. However, actual rates in 1992 had dropped significantly by about eight percentage points to 7 per cent.

A similar pattern emerged during periods of rising interest rates. In the early 1970s, when rates were at 6 per cent, investors projected that rates would still be 6 per cent a decade later, in the early 1980s. Instead, rates in the early 1980s surged by nearly 10 percentage points from their early 1970s level. These instances illustrate that market-based expectations can often be inaccurate.

As mentioned, the concept that forward interest rates reflect expected future short-term rates aligns with the 'expectations theory of interest rates', extensively explored in academic literature. It turns out that the theory is frequently challenged in empirical work, as demonstrated in seminal studies by Fama (1984), Campbell and Shiller (1991), and Bekaert and Hodrick (2001). Nonetheless, examining investor expectations through market-implied forward interest rates remains informative.

## 13.5 Concluding on the Outlook for Interest Rates

After declining for four decades, interest rates began to rise following the pandemic. The question arises whether the world is headed towards a future with permanently higher interest rates than those experienced before the pandemic, or if rates will revert to the lows seen in earlier periods. While the definitive answer remains elusive, we can draw some tentative suggestions.

Most academic studies examining the future trajectory of interest rates suggest that the factors responsible for driving rates down prior to the pandemic persist. These analyses generally conclude that underlying equilibrium interest rates are likely to remain low in the foreseeable future. Although not expected to be as exceptionally low as immediately before the pandemic, they are anticipated to remain lower than they were a decade or more ago. This perspective aligns with the viewpoint presented in this book.

Chapter 2 highlighted that 'real yields tend to fluctuate around an average of approximately 2 per cent over the long term'. Before the pandemic, real interest rates were below this historical average, often hovering around 0 per cent or even dipping into negative territory. This means that if real interest rates are expected to be higher than pre-pandemic levels but lower than the historical long-run average, future real interest rates could settle somewhere between 0 and 2 per cent on average.

Furthermore, if expecting that central banks follow their mandates of keeping inflation close to 2 per cent, this means nominal interest rates could be higher than 2 per cent but lower than 4 per cent in the long run.

It is important to note that actual interest rates will likely experience fluctuations—sometimes exceeding the long-term average and sometimes falling below it.

The primary risk to this outlook, this book believes, is the trajectory of public debt. Should public debt continue to rise significantly, interest rates could increase substantially in response.

## 13.6 Checklist

Interest rates are influenced by numerous factors; some suggest sustained low rates in the future, while others point to potential increases. Assessing the overall impact requires careful estimation.

- This book believes that the factors keeping interest rates low outweigh those pushing them higher. As a result, interest rates are expected to stay relatively low in the future. The primary risk to this forecast is the evolution of public debt.

This chapter will not introduce further items to the checklist.

# 14

# Debt, Inequality, and House and Stock Prices Considering Interest Rate Scenarios

This final chapter concludes the book. Building on preceding chapters that outlined future interest rate scenarios, the chapter briefly discusses their implications. As in the previous chapters, the discussion relates to the long-run outlook for interest rates and their impacts.

## 14.1  What Happens If Interest Rates Fall?

What should we expect will happen if interest rates over coming decades were to return to the pre-pandemic era of falling and exceptionally low interest rates, potentially even dipping slightly into negative territory?

Supporting this scenario are structural economic megatrends, such as sustained lower economic growth rates, declining population growth, the centuries-long trend of declining interest rates, and increasing life expectancies, as explained in Chapter 11.

Based on the evidence and theories presented in this book, it is reasonable to expect that further declines in interest rates would perpetuate trends caused by falling interest rates over the past four decades; that is, higher levels of indebtedness, asset prices, and inequality.

But how much can interest rates fall? While there is no lower bound on real interest rates, because there is no upper bound on inflation, nominal interest rates cannot decline indefinitely. Although the lower bound on nominal interest rates is not fixed, it nevertheless implies that there is a limit to how far nominal interest rates can feasibly fall. The consequence of such a lower bound is that potential future reductions in nominal interest rates will be less pronounced than the substantial declines witnessed over the past four decades. For instance, during the early 1980s, many countries had interest rates exceeding 10 per cent, which subsequently dropped to near-zero levels

*How Low Interest Rates Change the World.* Jesper Rangvid, Oxford University Press. © Jesper Rangvid (2025).
DOI: 10.1093/9780198946410.003.0015

before the pandemic—a decrease of over 10 percentage points. Presently, with interest rates generally below 5 per cent in advanced economies, the scope for another 10-percentage-point decrease is improbable.

At the same time, although there is no upper limit on inflation—historical episodes of hyperinflation, discussed in Box 2.2 of Chapter 2, illustrate this—it seems unlikely that hyperinflation will reoccur. As noted in Chapter 13, this book believes that the negative experiences with high inflation in the 1970s, reinforced by the recent post-pandemic inflation shock, have made central banks vigilant in controlling inflation. If inflation stabilizes around central banks' inflation target in the long run, it will also place a limit on how far long-term real interest rates can decline.

A scenario of declining interest rates implies that, although this could lead to further increases in inequality, asset prices, indebtedness, and financial risk-taking, the resulting changes may not reach the dramatic levels seen between 1980 and 2020.

## 14.2  What Happens If Interest Rates Rise?

What would happen in the converse scenario where interest rates rise—potentially even significantly so—relative to pre-pandemic levels? In such a scenario, many macroeconomic trends observed over the past four decades may reverse.

Higher interest rates increase the cost of servicing debt, thereby reducing the attractiveness of borrowing. This should lead to lower levels of indebtedness. It should also lead to lower house prices, as people cannot afford as large a mortgage when interest rates are higher, dampening the demand for housing and house prices. Additionally, the present value of future cash flows declines when interest rates rise, which tends to decrease the value of financial assets like stocks and bonds. Lower asset prices would affect affluent people more, reducing inequality.

The magnitude of these effects and the overall trajectory of a world with consistently higher interest rates will hinge on how such a scenario plays out. Will interest rates rise suddenly or gradually? Will they rise a lot or only little?

Consider a scenario where interest rates rise sharply over a relatively short period. In this scenario, the effects will materialize swiftly. This means that abrupt increases in interest rates could lead to sharp immediate declines in asset prices and levels of indebtedness.

The year 2022 serves as an example of such a situation: due to rapidly rising interest rates, both stock and bond markets saw declines of around 20 per cent. Inequality fell as a consequence, and ratios of debt to GDP fell, because nominal GDP rose with inflation. However, as discussed in Chapter 10, only nominal interest rates rose; real interest rates fell. Furthermore, while nominal interest rates rose, they did so for a relatively short period. If interest rates—both nominal and real—had risen more drastically and persistently, the impacts would likely have been more severe.

The magnitude of a rate rise also matters. Chapter 1 explained that interest rates rose persistently during the 1960s and 1970s. Although this book does not consider such a development to be likely, it cannot be entirely ruled out that a similar situation could arise again.

A scenario with considerably higher interest rates is undesirable, especially during the transition to such a new regime. As asset values decline rapidly, people's savings diminish, prompting reduced consumption. Moreover, many borrowers may struggle to meet higher interest expenses in a rapid rate increase scenario. Some borrowers may default on their obligations, causing lenders to incur losses and potentially triggering financial instability reminiscent of the events preceding the 2008 financial crisis.

Higher interest rates tend to mitigate inequality, as asset prices decline and wealth disparities narrow. While reducing inequality may be seen as a positive goal, achieving it through economic crises imposes a substantial human cost, disproportionately impacting those with fewer financial resources.

The reason why interest rates rise is also important. If interest rates rise because investors are concerned about persistent increases in debt levels, and thus require a higher risk compensation, there is little that is good to be said about higher interest rates. On the other hand, if interest rates rise because economic prosperity blossoms, then there is reason to view higher interest rates in a more favourable light.

In the end, a scenario where interest rates rise significantly and remain persistently high remains concerning given already high global debt levels and asset prices, and thus could lead to adverse economic conditions.

## 14.3 What Happens If Interest Rates Stay Where They Are?

The final scenario envisions future interest rates fluctuating around current levels, with no clear long-term trend towards either an increase or decrease. Given nominal global interest rates of around 3 per cent at the time of writing—see Chapter 1—this is a scenario where interest rates are higher than the lows seen before the pandemic but are not notably high from a historical perspective. This book argues that this scenario is the most probable, as discussed in the preceding chapter.

In a scenario where interest rates are higher than before the pandemic, but not much higher, many borrowers can manage their interest payments. Individuals and nations would need to allocate more resources towards servicing their debt than before the pandemic, but not much more, so the adjustments to other expenditures should be manageable. While defaults on a larger scale are avoided in this scenario, overall levels of indebtedness are unlikely to decrease substantially. Put simply, debt levels are expected to remain elevated, albeit without significant increases driven by falling rates.

At the same time, a world with slightly higher interest rates than before the pandemic would likely encourage investors to be more cautious when borrowing for investments in financial assets or real estate, thereby tempering rapid rises in asset prices and fostering less financial risk-taking. In essence, a world where borrowing comes at a cost is more desirable than one where debt is essentially free, as before the pandemic with interest rates at zero, or even being negative. While asset prices could still rise from current levels, they would do so for other reasons than the interest rate. Additionally, stable interest rates are unlikely to contribute significantly to reducing inequality.

In summary, while a scenario where future interest rates remain around current levels is probably both the best and also the most likely scenario, it does not address the underlying challenges of high indebtedness, asset prices, and inequality driven by four decades of falling interest rates.

## 14.4 Checklist

Table 14.1 summarizes the effects discussed in this chapter.

**Table 14.1** Different interest rate scenarios and their effects

| Change in interest rate: | Falls | Rises | | No change |
|---|---|---|---|---|
| | | Slowly | Fast | |
| Effect on: | | | | |
| Indebtedness | ↑ | ↓ | ↓↓ | ↔ |
| Asset prices | ↑ | ↓ | ↓↓ | ↔ |
| Inequality | ↑ | ↓ | ↓↓ | ↔ |
| Financial risk-taking | ↑ | ↔ | ↓ | ↔ |

- If interest rates decrease in the future, the trends outlined in Chapters 3–7 are likely to persist: debt levels, asset prices, inequality, and financial risk-taking may continue to rise, albeit probably not to the same extent as observed before the pandemic, simply because nominal interest rates cannot fall as much as they did over the 1980–2020 period due to the lower bound on nominal interest rates.
- Conversely, if interest rates increase, the opposite effects are expected: debt levels, asset prices, and inequality are likely to decline. The speed and way interest rates rise—whether abruptly or gradually, and by how much and why—will determine whether the adjustments are disruptive, potentially leading to financial and economic crises, or more manageable, allowing economies to adapt without major challenges.
- If interest rates remain at current levels—that is, higher than during the years before the pandemic but not much higher—they are unlikely to cause significant changes in indebtedness, asset prices, inequality, and financial risk-taking.
- As discussed in the previous chapter, this book argues that the more likely long-term scenario is the latter one of relatively low interest rates, albeit higher than the levels seen just before the pandemic.

# References

Acemoglu, D. (2002). Technical change, inequality, and the labor market. *Journal of Economic Literature* 40, 7–72.

Acemoglu, D. (2024). The simple macroeconomics of AI. NBER Working Paper no. 32487.

Alesina, A. and L.H. Summers (1993). Central bank independence and macroeconomic performance: Some comparative evidence. *Journal of Money, Credit and Banking* 25, 151–162.

Ampudia, M., D. Georgarakos, J. Slacalek, O. Tristani, P. Vermeulen, and G.L. Violante (2018). Monetary policy and household inequality. ECB Working Paper no. 2170.

Andersen, A.L., N. Johannesen, M. Jørgensen, and J.-L. Peydró (2023). Monetary policy and inequality. *Journal of Finance* 78, 2945–2989.

Andonov, A., R.M.M.J. Bauer, and K.J.M. Cremers (2017). Pension fund asset allocation and liability discount rates. *Review of Financial Studies* 30, 2555–2595.

Arce, O., M. Ciccarelli, A. Kornprobst, and C. Montes-Galdon (2024). What caused the Euro Area post-pandemic inflation? ECB Occasional Paper no. 2024/343.

Auerbach, A.J. and Y. Gorodnichenko (2011). Fiscal multipliers in recession and expansion. NBER Working Paper no. 17447.

Auerbach, A.J. and Y. Gorodnichenko (2012). Measuring the output responses to fiscal policy. *American Economic Journal: Economic Policy* 4, 1–27.

Auten, G. and D. Splinter (2024). Income inequality in the United States: Using tax data to measure long-term trends. *Journal of Political Economy* 132, 2179–2227.

Bank of England (2022). Bank of England announces gilt market operation. News release from the Bank of England, 28 September.

Banque de France (2022). The increase in the money supply during the Covid crisis: Analysis and implications. *Bulletin de la Banque de France* 239/2.

Barro, R.J. and D.B. Gordon (1983). Rules, discretion and reputation in a model of monetary policy. *Journal of Monetary Economics* 12, 101–121.

BBC Bitesize (n.d.). The Weimar Republic 1918–1929. www.bbc.co.uk/bitesize/guides/z9y64j6/revision/5.

Bean, C.A., C. Broda, T. Ito, and R. Kroszner (2015). Low for long? Causes and consequences of persistently low interest rates. Geneva Report on the World Economy 17.

Bekaert, G. and E. Engstrom (2010). Inflation and the stock market: Understanding the Fed model. *Journal of Monetary Economics* 57, 278–294.

Bekaert, G. and R.J. Hodrick (2001). Expectations hypotheses tests. *Journal of Finance* 56, 1357–1394.

Berisha, E., J. Meszaros, and E. Olson (2018). Income inequality, equities, household debt, and interest rates: Evidence from a century of data. *Journal of International Money and Finance* 80, 1–14.

Bernanke, B.S. (2005). The global saving glut and the U.S. current account deficit. Remarks at the Sandridge Lecture, Virginia Association of Economists.

Bernanke, B.S. (2015). Monetary policy and inequality. Commentary, Brooking Institution.

Bielecki, M., M. Brzoza-Brzezina, and M. Kolasa (2020). Demographics and the natural interest rate in the Euro area. *European Economic Review* 129, 103535.

## References 253

BIS (2024). Quo vadis, r*? The natural rate of interest after the pandemic. *BIS Quarterly Review*, March, 17–30.

Blanchard, O.J. and B.S. Bernanke (2023). What caused the US pandemic-era inflation? NBER Working Paper no. 31417.

BMO (2017). Liability driven investment explained. BMO Global Asset Management note.

Bordo, M.D. and J. Landon-Lane (2013). What explains house price booms? History and empirical evidence. NBER Working Paper no. 19584.

Brand, C., M. Bielecki, and A. Penalver (2018). The natural rate of interest: Estimates, drivers, and challenges to monetary policy. ECB Occasional Paper Series no. 217.

Brunnermeier, M.K. and C. Julliard (2008). Money illusion and housing frenzies. *Review of Financial Studies* 21, 135–180.

Bylund, E. and Jonsson, M. (2020). How does climate change affect the long-run real interest rate? *Sveriges Riksbank Economic Commentaries* 11, 1–12.

Caballero, R.J., E. Farhi, and P.O. Gourinchas (2017). The safe assets shortage conundrum. *Journal of Economic Perspectives* 31, 29–46.

Caldara, D. and M. Iacoviello (2022). Measuring geopolitical risk. *American Economic Review* 112, 1194–1225.

Campbell, J.Y. (2006). Household finance. Presidential Address to the American Finance Association. *Journal of Finance* 61, 1553–1604.

Campbell, J.Y. and J.H. Cochrane (1999). By force of habit: A consumption-based explanation of aggregate stock market behavior. *Journal of Political Economy* 107, 205–251.

Campbell, J.Y. and J.F. Cocco (2007). How do house prices affect consumption? Evidence from micro data. *Journal of Monetary Economics* 54, 591–621.

Campbell, J.Y. and R.J. Shiller (1988a). The dividend-price ratio and expectations of future dividends and discount factors. *Review of Financial Studies* 1, 195–228.

Campbell, J.Y. and R.J. Shiller (1988b). Stock prices, earnings, and expected dividends. *Journal of Finance* 43, 661–676.

Campbell, J.Y. and R.J. Shiller (1991). Yield spreads and interest rate movements: A bird's eye view. *Review of Economic Studies* 58, 495–514.

Campbell, J.Y., A.W. Lo, and A.C. MacKinlay (1996). *The econometrics of financial markets*. Princeton University Press.

Carroll, C.D. (1998). Why do the rich save so much? NBER Working Paper no. 6549.

Carvalho, C., A. Ferrero, and F. Nechio (2016). Demographics and real interest rates: Inspecting the mechanism. *European Economic Review* 88, 208–226.

Castro, A., M. Cavallo, and R. Zarutskie (2022). Understanding bank deposit growth during the COVID-19 pandemic. FEDS note, 3 June.

Cecchetti, S.G., M.S. Mohanty, and F. Zampolli (2011). The real effects of debt. BIS Working Paper no. 352.

Cepparulo, A. and P. Pasimeni (2024). Defence spending in the European Union. European Economy Discussion Paper 199.

Choi, J. and M. Kronlund (2018). Reaching for yield in corporate bond mutual funds. *Review of Financial Studies* 31, 1930–1965.

Christensen, F. and J. Pedersen (2023). Drivers of real interest rates in a two-country, general-equilibrium, OLG model. Working Paper no. 193, Danmarks Nationalbank.

Chudik, A., K. Mohaddes, M.H. Pesaran, and M. Raissi (2017). Is there a debt-threshold effect on output growth? *Review of Economics and Statistics* 99, 135–150.

Cochrane, J.H. (2020). Wealth and taxes. Tax and Budget Bulletin no. 86, Cato Institute.

Coibion, O., Y. Gorodnichenko, L. Kueng, and J. Silvia (2017). Innocent bystanders? Monetary policy and inequality. *Journal of Monetary Economics* 88, 70–89.

## 254 References

Daniel, K., L. Garlappi, and K. Xiao (2021). Monetary policy and reaching for income. *Journal of Finance* 76, 1145–1193.

Darmouni, O.M. and A. Rodnyansky (2017). The effects of quantitative easing on bank lending behavior. *Review of Financial Studies* 30, 3858–3887.

De Long, J.B. (1997). America's peacetime inflation: The 1970s. In *Reducing inflation: Motivation and strategy, edited by* Christina Romer and David Romer, 247–280. University of Chicago Press.

Di Maggio, M., A. Kermani, and K. Majlesi (2020). Stock market returns and consumption. *Journal of Finance* 75, 3175–3219.

Dorn, F., N. Potrafke, and M. Schlepper (2024). European defence spending in 2024 and beyond: How to provide security in an economically challenging environment. Ifo Institute Economic Policy Report 45.

Dow, C.H. (1920). *Scientific stock speculation*. The Magazine of Wall Street, New York.

Duesenberry, J. S. (1949). *Income, saving, and the theory of consumer behavior.* Harvard University Press.

Dynan, K., E.J. Skinner, and S.P. Zeldes (2004). Do the rich save more? *Journal of Political Economy* 112, 397–444.

Eggertsson, G.B, N.R. Mehrotra, and J.A. Robbins (2019). A model of secular stagnation: Theory and quantitative evaluation. *American Economic Journal: Macroeconomics* 11, 1–48.

English, B., K. Forbes, and A. Ubide (2024). Monetary policy responses to the post-pandemic inflation. Centre for Economic Policy Research report.

European Union (2024). Debt sustainability monitor. EU Commission Institutional Paper 271.

Fabo, B., M. Jancokova, E. Kempf, and L. Pastor (2021). Fifty shades of QE: Comparing findings of central bankers and academics. *Journal of Monetary Economics* 120, 1–20.

Fama, E.F. (1981). Stock returns, real activity, inflation, and money. *American Economic Review* 71, 545–565.

Fama, E.F. (1984). The information in the term structure. *Journal of Financial Economics* 13, 509–528.

Fama, E.F. and K.R. French (1988). Dividend yields and expected stock returns. *Journal of Financial Economics* 22, 3–25.

Farah-Yacoub, J.P., C.M. Graf von Luckner, and C.M. Reinhart (2024). The social costs of sovereign default. NBER Working Paper no. 32600.

Fisher, I. (1930). *The theory of interest, as determined by impatience to spend income and opportunity to invest it.* Macmillan.

Forbes, K. (2019). Has globalization changed the inflation process? BIS Working Paper no. 791.

Friedman, M. (1957). *A theory of the consumption function.* Princeton University Press.

Friedman, M. and A.J. Schwartz (1963). *A monetary history of the United States, 1867–1960.* Princeton University Press.

Furman, J. and L. Summers (2020). A reconsideration of fiscal policy in the era of low interest rates. Manuscript.

Giannone, D. and G.E. Primiceri (2024). The drivers of post-pandemic inflation. Paper presented at the ECB Forum on central banking: Monetary Policy in an Era of Transformation.

Goldman Sachs (2023). *Generative AI could raise global GDP by 7 percent.* Goldman Sachs Insights.

Goodhart, C. and M. Pradhan (2020). *The great demographic reversal: Ageing societies, waning inequality, and an inflation revival.* Palgrave Macmillan.

Greenwald, D.L., M. Leombroni, H. Lustig, and S.V. Nieuwerburgh (2023). Financial and total wealth inequality with declining interest rates. https://ssrn.com/abstract=3789220.

## References    255

Guiso, L. and P. Sodini (2013). Household finance: An emerging field. In *The Handbook of the Economics of Finance*, edited by George M. Constantinides, Milton Harris, and Rene M. Stulz, 1397–1532. Elsevier.

Ha, J., M.A. Kose, and F. Ohnsorge (2021). Inflation during the pandemic: What happened? What is next? CEPR Discussion Paper no. DP16328.

Haldane, A.G. (2015). Stuck. Speech given by Bank of England Chief Economist A.G. Haldane.

Hamilton, J.D., E. Harris, J. Hatzius, and K. West (2016). The equilibrium real funds rate: Past, present and future. *IMF Economic Review* 64, 660–707.

Harr, T. and C. Henderson (2024). *The great inflation resurgence: Why inflation returned in the 2020s and what to expect next*. Palgrave Macmillan.

Heider, F., F. Saidi, and G. Schepens (2019). Life below zero: Bank lending under negative policy rates. *Review of Financial Studies* 32, 3728–3761.

Hicks, J. R. (1950). *A contribution to the theory of the trade cycle*. Oxford University Press.

IMF (2019). Global Financial Stability Report, October.

IMF (2021). COVID-19, crypto, and climate: Navigating challenging transitions. Global Financial Stability Report, October.

IMF (2023). The natural rate of interest: Drivers and implications for policy. World Economic Outlook, April.

IMF (2024). Fiscal monitor, April.

Ioannidou, V., R. Pinto, and Z. Wang (2022). Corporate pension risk-taking and funding pressure. Manuscript.

Jiménez, G., S. Ongena, J.-L. Peydró, and J. Saurina (2014). Hazardous times for monetary policy: What do twenty-three million bank loans say about the effects of monetary policy on credit risk-taking? *Econometrica* 82, 463–505.

Jones, C.I. (2022). The end of economic growth? Unintended consequences of a declining population. *American Economic Review* 112, 3489–3527.

Jordà, O. and A.M. Taylor (2019). Riders on the storm. NBER Working Paper no. 26262.

Jordà, O., M. Schularick, and A.M. Taylor (2015). Betting the house. *Journal of International Economics* 96, S2–S18.

Jordà, O., M. Schularick, and A.M. Taylor (2016). The great mortgaging: Housing finance, crises and business cycles. *Economic Policy* 31, 107–152.

Kacperczyk, M.T. and M. di Maggio (2017). The unintended consequences of the zero lower bound policy. *Journal of Financial Economics* 123, 59–80.

Kara, E. and L. von Thadden (2016). Interest rate effects of demographic changes in a New-Keynesian life-cycle framework. *Macroeconomic Dynamics* 20, 120–164.

Keynes, J.M. (1936). *The general theory of employment, interest and money*. Harcourt, Brace.

Knoll, K., M. Schularick, and T. Steger (2017). No price like home: Global house prices, 1870–2012. *American Economic Review* 107, 331–353.

Kopecky, J. and A.M. Taylor (2020). The murder-suicide of the rentier: Population aging and the risk premium. NBER Working Paper no. 26943.

Krishnamurthy, A. and A. Vissing-Jørgensen (2011). The effects of quantitative easing on long-term interest rates. *Brookings Papers on Economic Activity* 21, 215–287.

Krishnamurthy, A. and A. Vissing-Jørgensen (2013). The ins and outs of LSAP. Kansas City Federal Reserve's Jackson Hole Symposium.

Krishnamurthy, A., S. Nagel, and A. Vissing-Jørgensen (2015). ECB policies involving government bond purchases: Impacts and channels. *Review of Finance* 22, 1–44.

Kuttner, K.N. (2014). Low interest rates and housing bubbles: Still no smoking gun. *In The role of central banks in financial stability: Has it changed?*, edited by D.D. Evanoff, C. Holthausen, G.G. Kaufman, and M. Kremer, 159–185. World Scientific.

## 256 References

Kydland, F.E. and E.C. Prescott (1977). Rules rather than discretion: The inconsistency of optimal plans. *Journal of Political Economy* 85, 473–492.

Larsen, L.S., C. Munk, R.S. Nielsen, and J. Rangvid (2024). How do interest-only mortgages affect consumption and saving over the life cycle? *Management Science* 70, 1970–1991.

Levin, A.T., B.L. Lu, and W.R. Nelson (2022). Quantifying the costs and benefits of quantitative easing. NBER Working Paper no. 30749.

Lian, C., Y. Ma, and C. Wang (2019). Low interest rates and risk-taking: Evidence from individual investment decisions. *Review of Financial Studies* 32, 2107–2148.

Lucas, R.E. (1980). Two illustrations of the quantity theory of money. *American Economic Review* 70, 1005–1014.

Luck, S. and T. Zimmermann (2019). Ten years later: Did QE work? Federal Reserve Bank of New York Liberty Street Economics (blog).

Luck, S. and T. Zimmermann (2020). Employment effects of unconventional monetary policy: Evidence from QE. *Journal of Financial Economics* 135, 678–703.

Maddaloni, A. and J.-L. Peydró (2011). Bank risk-taking, securitization, supervision, and low interest rates: Evidence from the Euro-area and the U.S. lending standards. *Review of Financial Studies* 24, 2121–2165.

McCallum, B.T. and E. Nelson (2011). Money and inflation: Some critical issues. In *Handbook of Monetary Economics, edited by* B. Friedman and M. Woodford, 97–154. North-Holland.

McKinsey (2023). The economic potential of generative AI: The next productivity frontier. Report.

Mian, A.R., L. Straub, and A. Sufi (2021a). What explains the decline in r*? Rising income inequality versus demographic shift. Paper presented at the 2021 Jackson Hole Economic Symposium hosted by the Federal Reserve Bank of Kansas City.

Mian, A.R., L. Straub, and A. Sufi (2021b). The saving glut of the rich. Technical report, NBER.

Mongelli, F.P., W. Pointner, and J.W. van den End (2022). The effects of climate change on the natural rate of interest: A critical survey. ECB Working Paper no. 2744.

Mumtaz, H. and A. Theophilopoulou (2017). The impact of monetary policy on inequality in the UK: An empirical analysis. *European Economic Review* 98, 410–423.

Obstfeld, M. (2023). Natural and neutral real interest rates: Past and future. Manuscript.

OECD (2021). *Pensions at a glance 2021: OECD and G20 indicators*. OECD Publishing.

Owyang, M.T. and H.G. Shell (2016). Taking stock: Income inequality and the stock market. *Economic Synopses, Federal Reserve Bank of St. Louis*, no. 7.

Papetti, A. (2021). Demographics and the natural real interest rate: Historical and projected paths for the Euro area. *Journal of Economic Dynamics and Control* 132, 104209.

Patillo, C., H. Poirson, and L. Ricci (2002). External debt and growth. IMF Working Paper 02/69.

Philippon, T. (2019). *The great reversal: How America gave up on free markets*. Harvard University Press.

Phillips, A.W. (1958). The relation between unemployment and the rate of change of money wage rates in the United Kingdom, 1861–1957. *Economica* 25, 283–299.

Pigou, A.C. (1951). Professor Duesenberry on income and savings. *Economic Journal* 61, 883–885.

Piketty, T., E. Saez, and G. Zucman (2018). Distributional national accounts: Methods and estimates for the United States. *Quarterly Journal of Economics* 133, 553–609.

Piketty, T., E. Saez, and G. Zucman (2024). Income inequality in the United States: A comment. Manuscript.

Platzer, J. and M. Peruffo (2022). Secular drivers of the natural rate of interest in the United States: A quantitative evaluation. IMF Working Paper no. 2022/030.

Rachel, L. and L. Summers (2019). On secular stagnation in the industrialized world. Brookings Papers on Economic Activity, Spring.

Rangvid, J. (2006). Output and expected returns. *Journal of Financial Economics* 81, 595–624.

Rangvid, J. (2021). *From Main Street to Wall Street.* Oxford University Press.

Rangvid, J. (2022). Where is the liquidity? (blog).

Reinhart, C.M. and K.S. Rogoff (2011). *A decade of debt.* Peterson Institute for International Economics.

Rogoff, K.S., B. Rossi, and P. Schmelzing (2024). Long-run trends in long-maturity real rates, 1311–2022. *American Economic Review* 114, 2271–2307.

Saez, E. and G. Zucman (2016). Wealth inequality in the United States since 1913: Evidence from capitalized income tax data. *Quarterly Journal of Economics* 131, 519–578.

Saez, E. and G. Zucman (2020). Trends in US income and wealth inequality: Revising after the revisionists. NBER Working Paper no. 27921.

Saez, E. and G. Zucman (2022). Comments on Smith, Zidar and Zwick (2021). Manuscript.

Schmelzing, P. (2020). Eight centuries of global real interest rates, R-G, and the 'suprasecular' decline, 1311–2018. Bank of England Staff Working Paper no. 845.

Schnabel, I. (2021). Monetary policy and inequality. Speech at a virtual conference on 'Diversity and Inclusion in Economics, Finance, and Central Banking'.

Shapiro, A.H. (2022). How much do supply and demand drive inflation? *FRBSF Economic Letter* 2022–15.

Shiller, R.J. (1981). Do stock prices move too much to be justified by subsequent changes in dividends? *American Economic Review* 71, 421–436.

Siegel, J.J. (2016). The Shiller CAPE ratio: A new look. *Financial Analysts Journal* 72, 41–50.

Smith, M., O. Zidar, and E. Zwick (2023). Top wealth in America: New estimates under heterogeneous returns. *Quarterly Journal of Economics* 138, 515–573.

Smolyansky, M. (2023). End of an era: The coming long-run slowdown in corporate profit growth and stock returns. Finance and Economics Discussion Series 2023-041.

Soyres, F., D. Moore, and J. Ortiz (2023). Accumulated savings during the pandemic: An international comparison with historical perspective. FEDS notes 23 June.

Stansbury, A. and L.H. Summers (2020). The declining worker power hypothesis: An explanation for the recent evolution of the American economy. Brookings Papers on Economic Activity, Spring, 1–77.

Summers, L.H. (2014). *US economic prospects: Secular stagnation, hysteresis, and the zero lower bound.* Speech, National Association of Business Economics.

Sutton, G., D. Mihaljek, and A. Subelyte (2017). Interest rates and house prices in the United States and around the world. BIS Working Paper no. 665.

Taylor, J.B. (1993). Discretion versus policy rules in practice. *Carnegie-Rochester Conference Series on Public Policy* 39, 195–214.

Teles, P., H. Uhlig, and J.V. Azevedo (2016). Is quantity theory still alive? *Economic Journal* 126, 442–464.

United Nations (2020). *World social report 2020: Inequality in a rapidly changing world.* New York.

Vissing-Jørgensen, A. (2002). Limited asset market participation and the elasticity of intertemporal substitution. *Journal of Political Economy* 110, 825–853.

Wanniski, J. (1978). Taxes, revenues, and the 'Laffer curve'. *The Public Interest*, Winter.

Weiss, K. (2019). *Central banks contribute to inequality.* American Institute for Economic Research.

Wolff, E.N. (2021). Household wealth trends in the United States, 1962 to 2019: Median wealth rebounds... but not enough. NBER Working Paper no. 28383.

World Bank (2024). How do current oil market conditions differ from those during the price shocks of the 1970s? World Bank blog, January.

# Index

*For the benefit of digital users, indexed terms that span two pages (e.g., 52–53) may, on occasion, appear on only one of those pages.*

1929 Wall Street Crash, 69, 127–129
9/11, 214

AAA rating
  AAA-rated countries, 55
  AAA-rated firms, 21–22
Accounting rules, impact on stock
  valuations, 87
Adjustable-rate mortgages, 132
Aggregate demand, 82, 139, 141, 146, 188,
  221, 228
Alternative assets, 122–123
American Association of Individual
  Investors, 121
American Civil War, 49
American Rescue Plan Act, 185
Artificial intelligence (AI), 6, 218–219, 229,
  235
Asset prices
  Bubbles, 117–119, 126, 129
  Discounted cash-flows, 85
  Economic growth, 87
  Future interest rates, 8, 247–250
  Inequality, 4, 96–97, 106–107
  Monetary policy, 107–108
  Risk-taking, 118
Austerity, 55–56, 58

BAA rated-corporate bonds, 21–22
Baby boomer generation, 239
Backward induction, 127
Balance sheet, central bank, 169
Bank account, 121
Bank of England, 20–22, 22 n.7, 23 n.8, 25,
  38, 124, 133–134
Banking crises, 120
Bankruptcy, 58, 114–115
Banks
  General, 77, 114–115, 132
  Lending spread/profitability, 124–125
  Risk-taking, 117, 120, 125–126, 134

Shadow, 131
Behavioural finance, 127
Berlin Wall, fall of, 153, 164–165
Beta, 81 n.2
Bills, 123–124
Bonds
  Bond price, 93
  Bond returns, 79, 92–95
Borrowers
  Interest rates, 2, 13, 27–28, 36, 249–250
  Real interest rates, 45, 55, 65
  Risk taking, 120, 125–126, 132, 134
Borrowing
  Debt, 45, 47, 51, 54–55, 60, 63–65
  House prices, 67, 71, 74
  Inequality, 114–115
  Inflation, 141
  Interest rates, 2
  Nominal interest rates, 15–16, 21–22
  Real interest rates, 155–156, 159, 169
  Rising interest rates, 223, 248, 250
  Risk taking, 119, 132, 134
  Stock prices, 81, 88–89
Brexit, 215
Bubbles, 117–119, 126, 129, 132, 134
Budget deficits, 45, 132
Budget surplus, 49
Buffet Indicator, 87
Business cycle, 108, 189–190, 203
Buybacks, share, 80, 171, 171 n.2

Capital Asset Pricing Model (CAPM), 81 n.2
Capital requirements, 131
Capital-labour ratio, 160, 206–207, 219
CARES Act, 185
Cash flows
  Bubbles, 117–119, 126–127
  Value of house, 71–72
  Value of stocks, 3–4, 80 n.1, 80–82, 85,
    88–89, 95, 248
Causality, 4, 67, 77–78, 189–190, 228

## Index 259

Causation, 143, 153
Central bank independence, 148, 153
Climate change/risk, 212–215, 217, 227, 234t
Cold War, 228
Collateral, 67, 77, 133
Commissions, 125–126 n.1
Commodity prices, 195–196
Competition, 112, 151, 215
Consolidated Appropriations Act, 185
Consumer price index (CPI), 27, 29, 68 n.1
Consumption opportunities, 97
Consumption smoothing, 159, 165
Core inflation, 186
Corporate bonds, yields on, 21–22
Corporate debt, 45, 63
Corporate loans, 5, 21, 124
Corporate pension funds, 123, 132
Cost of borrowing, 2, 15–16, 22, 60, 67, 155–156
Cost of debt, 2, 80
Cost-push inflation, 141, 145–153
Coupon payments/rate, 92–93, 95
Covid-19 pandemic, 1, 5, 7, 8t, 30, 45, 49–50, 52–54, 63, 165, 177, 188, 198, 203
Crash, 69, 86–87, 127–129
Credit
  Credit risk, 122–123
  Creditworthiness, 115
Crowding out, 60
Cyclical Adjusted Price Earnings Ratio (CAPE), 85–86

Debt crisis
  European, 18, 169–170
  Greek, 18 n. 4, 56, 56b
  Historical, 18–19
Debt, total, 3, 45, 64–65
Debt-to-GDP ratio, 47, 50–52, 51b, 60–61, 223, 224 n.1, 225
Default
  Corporate, 21
  Greek, 58
  Household, 132, 134
  Sovereign, 18–19, 56, 56 n.1, 65
Defence spending, 223, 228, 231
Defined-benefit pension funds, 121–122, 132
Deflation, 32, 38–40, 149–150
Demand

Demand for housing, 60, 67, 71, 76, 78, 130–131, 248
Demand for investments, 2, 155–157, 159, 175
Demand-pull inflation, 141, 145–153
Demographic changes, 67, 110, 155, 166–168
Deposit-funded banks, 126
Deposits
  Investments in, 107
  Interest rate on, 21, 124, 155
  Money supply, 191
  Risk-taking in banks, 120
Derivatives, 133
Discount rate
  Asset prices, 85
  Constant discount factor, 127
  Consumer's, 159–160
  Discounting firms' cash flows, 3–4, 79–80, 80 n.1, 81 n.2, 85, 95, 126–127
  Interest rate and discount rate, 81–82, 88–89, 118
  Pension funds, 123
  Value of house, 71–72
Dissaving, 165–166, 220, 235
Diversification, 131
Dividends, 3–4, 80, 85, 87, 127
Dot-com bubble, 85–87, 117, 127–128
Downpayment, 2
Duration, 93–94, 188–189

Earnings
  Cyclical Adjusted Price Earnings Ratio (CAPE), 85–87
  Cash-flows, 3–4
  Earnings per share, 85–86
  Earnings yield, 89–90, 92, 95, 168
  Interest rate and earnings, 3–4, 80–81, 89
  Mispricing, 126–127
  Price-earnings ratio, 85–87, 90, 95
  Value of stocks, 80, 85
Economic shocks, 49–50, 52–54, 162
Education, 2, 54–55, 96, 98t, 115, 223
Emerging markets/countries, 14 n.1, 60, 164–165, 168, 211
Employment
  General, 54, 107–108, 170
  Full, 148 n.2, 163, 171–172, 175
Empty planet scenario, 207–208
Endogenous growth, 207–208

## 260 Index

Energy finance, 122–123
Equal society, 97, 113
Equilibrium
    Economic, 29, 67, 157, 160, 163, 238
    Interest rate, 155, 163–164, 171, 175, 208, 211, 219, 227, 237, 239–240, 246
European Central Bank (ECB), 58, 169–170, 179, 188–189, 196, 229
European Union, 226
Eurozone, 56, 58, 169–170
Ex ante real interest rate, 35, 35 n.2
Ex post real interest rate, 35, 35 n.2
Excess savings, 185–186
Expansion, economic, 54–55, 61, 85, 182–183
Expansionary
    Fiscal policy, 172, 181, 186–187, 191–192, 195, 198
    Monetary policy, 96–97, 108, 186, 188, 189, 191, 195, 198
Expectations theory of interest rates, 241, 245
Expected returns, 90, 92, 95, 117, 119, 123, 168

Face value, 15–16, 28, 132–133
Falling prices, 32, 38–40
Fed Funds rate
Federal Reserve Bank of San Francisco, 193
Fees, 126 n.1
Fertility rates, 6, 237
Financial innovation, 131, 134
Financial shocks, 118
Financial stability, 121–122, 133
First World War, 26, 32–33, 36–37, 39, 49, 52, 68–69, 75–76, 82–83, 102, 167–168
Fiscal discipline, 47, 50–51, 132
Fiscal multiplier, 54–55
Fiscal policy, 49–50, 172, 223
Fiscal prudence, 47
Fixed-income mutual funds, 121–122
Flow concept, 115
Frictions, 114–115
Fundamental/intrinsic value, 118–119, 126–128
Funding costs, 95, 125

GDP (total economic activity)
GDP growth, 60, 229, 231
Geopolitical risk, 212–215, 217–219

German marks, 34–35
German Reichsbank, 35
Gilts, UK, 133–134
Global financial crisis, 16–17, 49–50, 52–54, 56, 68, 85, 117–118, 129–132, 134, 163, 177, 187, 216, 218–219, 231, 244–245
Global Financial Stability Report, 121–122
Global savings, 164–166, 210–211, 220
Global Savings Glut, 164–165, 168
Global trends, 1, 3, 5, 7, 85, 231
Global warming, 213
Globalization, 139, 149–151, 153, 215–216
Goods
    Demand for, 54, 63, 81, 141, 181, 192–196
    General, 28, 192, 215
    Prices of, 29, 32, 181, 195–196
    Supply of, 141, 181, 193
Government expenditures, 2, 35, 55–56, 223, 228
Government spending, 55, 60, 221, 228
Great Depression, 38, 49, 85, 117, 127, 129, 171
Greek debt crisis, 18–19 n.4, 56, 56$b$
Guaranteed return, 121–122
Gulf War, 214

Healthcare, 2, 55, 172, 173$t$, 235–236, 236$t$
Hedge, 132–133
High-income earners, 108
House price index, 68 n.1
House prices, 3, 5, 7, 67, 83–85, 130–132, 134, 248
Household debt, 45
Hyperinflation, 17–18 n.3, 29–30 n.2, 34$b$, 34–35, 149, 248

Illiquid assets, 117, 123
Illiquidity premium, 123
Illiquidity risk, 122–123
Income distribution, 99–101, 111
Indebtedness, 3, 5, 7–8, 45–49, 51–52, 63–65, 187, 225, 247–248, 250
Inequality, 4–5, 6–7, 79, 92, 96, 171, 173–175, 236–237, 247–250
Inflation
    Inflation expectations, 34, 92, 141–142, 145, 148, 153, 244–245
    Anticipated/expected inflation, 27, 29–31, 35, 92, 243–245
    Inflation risk, 29

Inflation risk premium, 29
Inflation targeting, 145
Inflation-indexed bonds, 242–243
Infrastructure, 2, 54, 122–123
Institutional investors, 117, 121–124, 126
Interest expenses, 3–4, 47, 49, 51, 80, 88–89, 224–225, 249
International Monetary Fund (IMF), 48, 121–122, 174, 195, 225–226, 238
Intertemporal rate of substitution, 159, 234–235
Iranian Revolution, 152
Iraq War, 214

Jobless claims, 182

Laffer curve, 55–56
Lenders, 2, 13, 15, 22, 27–28, 30–31, 36, 64–65, 118, 249
Lending spread, 124–125
Leverage, 117–118, 132, 153
Liabilities, 122–123, 132–133
Liability-driven investments (LDI), 118, 132–134
Life expectancy, 7, 159–160, 164–167, 171, 173, 174–175, 205–206, 208–212, 217–219, 234, 237
Life insurers, 121–122
Loans, 2, 5, 13, 21, 55–56, 58, 71, 76, 78, 114, 117, 120, 124, 130–132, 134
Lockdowns, 182–183, 185, 198
Long-term interest rates, 22–23, 25, 90, 105, 111, 123, 234–235
Longevity, 110, 209–210, 235
Long-term commitments, 122–123
Long-term government bonds, 14–16, 19, 179
Low-income earners, 107–108

M2, 190
Macroeconomics, 159
Make-America-Great-Again policies, 215
Margin calls, 133
Marginal productivity of capital, 160, 206–207
Marginal propensity to consume (MPC) out of wealth, 188
Marginal propensity to save, 109–110
Market concentration, 112, 115
Market risk premium, 82

Market-funded banks, 126
Market-implied expectations, 233
Market-implied forward rates, 245
Mini-budget, 132–133
Monetarism, 140
Monetary policy interest rates, 5, 22, 22 n.7, 108, 123–125, 130, 145–146, 147–148, 148 n.2, 162, 189, 196
Monetary Theory of inflation, 139
Money illusion, 74
Money market funds, 123–124
Money supply
    Inflation, 142–145, 153, 189, 189$b$
    Hyperinflation, 35
    Monetary theory of inflation, 139–141
Mortgage
    Mortgage debt, 76–77
    Mortgage loans, 21, 71
    Mortgage rate, 58, 60
Mutual fund, 82, 121–122, 123–124, 134

Napoleonic Wars, 52
NATO, 228
Natural disasters, 55, 213
Negative interest rates, 15, 120, 126
New York Fed, 163–164, 193, 238
Newborn, 164, 208–209
Nominal stock prices, 82–83

Office for Budget Responsibility (OBR), 222–223
Oil
    Crisis, 36–37
    Intensity, 152
    Prices, 151–152, 195–196
    Price shock, 76, 84, 141, 153
Old-age healthcare, 172, 235–236
Openness, 150, 215
Overvaluation, 119, 127–129

Panic, investor panic, 119
Paper gains, 114–115
Peace dividend, 228
Peacetime, 45, 49, 52–54, 65
Pearl Harbor
Pension funds, 117, 121–123, 126, 132–133
Pension Obligations, 122, 133
Personal income, 184
Personal outlays, 184
Phillips curve, 146–148

**262** Index

Pooling loans, 131

Population growth, 5, 7, 140, 155, 159–160, 164, 167–168, 173, 175, 203, 205–208, 211–212, 217–219, 221, 227, 230–231, 234–237, 247

Population size, 158–159

Portfolio allocation, 119, 121

Precautionary savings, 191, 213–214, 217, 227

Predictor, 90, 245

Present value (of future cash-flows), 3–4, 71–72, 79–81, 88–89, 95, 118, 122, 123, 248

Price level, 27, 32, 68, 140

Price-earnings ratio, 87, 89–90

Price-output ratio, 87–88

Primary budget
Balance, 49, 51–52
Deficit, 223, 226

Private debt
Amount of, 61–64
Pros and cons, 63–64

Private Equity, 122–123

Productivity, 140, 173–174, 215, 218–219, 227–228, 229–230, 235–237

Profitability, 79–80, 87, 89, 120, 124–126

Profits, 79–80, 81–82, 88–89, 112, 125–126 n.1, 171 n.2

Public investment, 2, 54, 60

Public pension funds, 123

Public debt, 6, 8, 45, 47, 48–49, 51–52, 54–61, 63, 65, 172, 175, 187, 218, 222, 225–228, 235–236, 246
UK, 52–54
US, 48–52

Purchasing power, 13, 28, 104

Quantitative Easing (QE), 169–171, 179, 229

Quantity theory, 140

r*, r-star, 162*b*, 197 n.3, 238–240

Ramsey-Samuelson-Solow growth model, 158–160

Rate of time preferences, 158–159

Rational expectations, 148

Rationality, 127

Reaching for yield, 4, 132

Real
House prices, 68–70, 72–74, 76, 84, 130
Return, 28–29, 30–31, 90, 92, 243

Stock prices, 82–84

Recession, 54–55, 61, 63, 82, 85–86, 96–97, 101, 130, 132, 147, 181–187

Redistribution, 100, 115

Regulated banks, 131

Regulation, 77, 87, 117, 168, 213

Retail investors, 121, 126, 134

Retirement, 2, 6, 160, 164–167, 173, 175, 208–209, 210–212, 219, 223, 231, 235–237, 239

Retirement age, 209–210, 219

Return
Bond, 14–16, 28, 79, 92–95, 114, 155, 241
Stock, 79, 81 n.2, 87, 90–92, 95, 107, 118, 237
General, 2, 54, 60, 80, 97, 106–107, 115, 119–120, 124–126, 205
Housing, 71–72, 107
On investments, 2, 156, 160, 175
Pension funds, 121–123
Real, 28–29, 30–31, 243
Safe assets, 4, 117, 121, 125, 168

Richmond Fed, 163

Riksbanken, 22 n.7

Risk
Aversion, 92, 158–160, 213
Exposure, 120, 123, 126
Premium, 19—20, 27 n.1, 29, 81–82, 231, 237, 243–244
Tolerance, 82

Risky assets, 107, 110, 115, 117, 119, 121, 123, 126, 168

Risk-free
Asset, 121
Interest rate, 81–82, 121

Robert J. Shiller data, 85

Rolling average, 37, 161

Rules *versus* discretion in monetary policy, 148

S&P 500, 85–86, 127, 188

Safe asset, 55, 64, 110, 119, 121, 122–123, 168–171, 175

Safe-haven countries, 55, 168

San Francisco Fed, 193

Savings rate, 4, 110, 171, 175, 184–185, 221

Search for yields, 117, 134

Second World War, 16–17, 22, 24–26, 32–33, 36–40, 46–47, 48–49, 51–54, 68–69,

75–76, 78, 102–103, 127, 142–143, 149–150, 167–168, 190, 214
Secular stagnation, 155, 171–172, 175
Securitization, 131
Services
  Demand for, 28–29, 32, 54, 63, 79, 81, 141, 181, 185, 192–196, 215
  Housing, 71–72
  Welfare, 49–50
Seven Years' War, 52
Shadow banks, 131
Share buybacks, 80, 171, 171 n.2
Short-term
  Assets, 123–125
  Government bonds, 19, 196
  Interest rates/yields, 19–20, 25, 26, 126, 163, 245
Skilled workers, 111–112, 115
Slope of yield curve, 20
Smooth consumption, 5, 159, 165
Social
  Benefits, 100
  Security, 172, 235–236
Societal impact, 1, 9, 64, 177
Sovereign
  Bonds, 5, 132
  Debt, 61
  Debt crisis, 56, 56$b$, 65, 169–170
  Default, 56 n.1, 58, 65
Spanish Inquisition War, 52
Standard deviation, 193
Stock concept, 115
Stock market valuations, 3–4, 79, 86–87, 95
Stock prices
  Fundamental, 127–128
  General, 5–7, 79, 80–81, 82–85, 95, 106, 118, 182, 188
  US, 85–89
Structured credit obligations, 131
Supply chains, 181, 193, 198, 215
Supply of safe assets, 168, 175
Supply of
  Bonds, 221
  Credit, 67
  Goods and services, 141, 193
  Housing, 71
  Money, 140
  Savings, 2, 155–157, 160, 164, 175, 208
Sustainable economy, 6, 54, 213, 218–219, 227, 231

Systematic risk, 82
Systemic risks, 117, 126

Target, inflation, 145, 148 n.2, 179, 238, 244–245, 248
Tax rates
Taxes
  Corporate, 88–89, 213, 223, 228
  General, 55–56, 64, 100, 115
  Tax cuts, 132
Taylor rule, 148, 148 n.2
Technological progress, 111–112
Terminal value, stock prices, 127
Top (high-income) earners, 101–103, 108
Trend growth
  General, 161–162
  r*, r-star, 163, 238
Troika, 58

UK GDP, 52, 222–223, 224 n.1
Uncertainty, 81, 92, 127, 159, 191, 212–215, 217, 227
Undervalued, 127
Unemployment
  General, 50, 56, 58, 96–97, 107–108, 134, 141, 145, 146–148, 182
  Benefits, 49–50, 54
Union membership, 112
Urbanization, 71
US Congressional Budget Office (CBO), 104, 224–225, 238
US corporate equity, 87–88
US Federal Reserve, the Fed, 7P55, 131, 145–147, 169, 179, 188, 189, 196, 229, 244–245
US GDP, 3–4, 48–49, 85–88, 224
US government, 49–51, 52–54, 58
US stock market, 3–4, 85–89, 127, 129
Utility, 159

Valuations, 3–4, 79, 86–87, 90, 95
Velocity of money, 140–141
Volatility
  Bond returns, 94
  Earnings, 85–86
  Inflation, 33–34, 36–38
  Money supply, 143–144
  Oil prices, 152
  Stock market, 119, 127

Wage-price spiral, 148

**264** Index

Wartime, 45, 52, 65, 168

Wealth distribution, 96–97, 103, 106, 115, 155, 171

Welfare state, 76

Working-age population, 153, 207

Yield to maturity, 93

Yom Kippur War, 151

Young people, 6, 8, 218

Zero lower bound, 171–172, 205

Zero-coupon bond, 93

The manufacturer's authorised representative in the EU for product safety is
Oxford University Press España S.A. of el Parque Empresarial San Fernando de
Henares, Avenida de Castilla, 2 – 28830 Madrid (www.oup.es/en or product.
safety@oup.com). OUP España S.A. also acts as importer into Spain of products
made by the manufacturer.

www.ingramcontent.com/pod-product-compliance
Lightning Source LLC
Chambersburg PA
CBHW071040090825
30821CB00013B/36/J